Learning from Asian Philosphy

Learning from Asian Philosophy

Joel J. Kupperman

New York   Oxford
Oxford University Press
1999

Oxford University Press

Oxford   New York
Athens   Auckland   Bangkok   Bogotá   Buenos Aires   Calcutta
Cape Town   Chennai   Dar es Salaam   Delhi   Florence   Hong Kong   Istanbul
Karachi   Kuala Lumpur   Madrid   Melbourne   Mexico City   Mumbai
Nairobi   Paris   São Paulo   Singapore   Taipei   Tokyo   Toronto   Warsaw

and associated companies in
Berlin   Ibadan

Copyright © 1999 by Joel J. Kupperman

Published by Oxford University Press, Inc.
198 Madison Avenue, New York, New York 10016

Oxford is a registered trademark of Oxford University Press

Library of Congress Cataloging-in-Publication Data
Kupperman, Joel.
Learning from Asian philosophy / Joel J. Kupperman.
p.   cm.
Includes bibliographical references and index.
ISBN 0-19-512831-1 (cloth); ISBN 0-19-512832-X (pbk.)
1. Philosophy, Oriental.   2. Philosophy, Comparative.   I. Title.
B121   .K86   1999
181—dc21   98-32349

1 3 5 7 9 8 6 4 2
Printed in the United States of America
on acid-free paper

PREFACE

This book represents a long-standing commitment to the importance of classic Asian texts, not merely in their own right but
also as openings to live philosophical problems. There is a great temptation
to attempt to reduce differences between philosophers to differences in answers to what are essentially the same questions. In the case of the contrast
between classic Asian philosophy and contemporary Western philosophy, I
want to argue that the questions by and large are different, and that many
Western philosophers miss a great deal that they would begin to see if they
asked the questions of classic Asian texts.

Nine previously published articles are included in this book. The two earliest, "Confucius and the Problem of Naturalness" and "Confucius and the
Nature of Religious Ethics," were submitted to *Philosophy East and West*, and
appeared in 1968 and 1971, respectively. All of the others were invited. I wish
to thank *Philosophy East and West* for permission to use the two essays just
mentioned along with "Not in So Many Words: Chuang-tzu's Techniques of
Communication" (1989). I also wish to thank the *Journal of Religious Ethics*
for permission to reprint "The Supra-Moral in Religious Ethics: The Case of
Buddhism," which was invited for the inaugural issue in 1973. The University
Press of Hawaii kindly has given permission to reprint "Tradition and Moral
Progress," which first appeared in *Culture and Modernity*, ed. Eliot Deutsch
(1991). The State University of New York Press is to be thanked for permission
to reprint "The Emotions of Altruism, East and West," which first appeared
in *Emotions in Asian Thought*, ed. Joel Marks and Roger Ames (1995); "Falsity,
Psychic Indefiniteness, and Self-Knowledge," from *Self and Deception*, ed. Roger
Ames and Wimal Dissanayake (1996), and "Spontaneity and Education of the
Emotions in the *Zhuangzi*," from *Scepticism, Relativism, and Ethics in the
Zhuangzi*, ed. P. J. Ivanhoe and Paul Kjellberg (1996). E. J. Brill kindly gave

permission to use "Confucius, Mencius, Hume, and Kant on Reason and Choice," which first appeared in *Rationality in Question*, ed. S. Biderman and B. A. Scharfstein (1989). Those to be thanked for comments that were helpful in the writing of one or more of the essays include (in rough chronological order) T. S. Mou, Wong Yuk, Loren Lomasky, Diana Meyers, Donald Baxter, John Troyer, Joel Marks, Roger Ames, Chenyang Li, P. J. Ivanhoe, Paul Kjellberg, and Kwong-loi Shun. Bryan Van Norden recently provided some very useful comments on the earliest article, "Confucius and the Problem of Naturalness." Two anonymous reviewers for the press, and also Roger Ames, made suggestions that were extremely useful in editing the essays (none of which was left entirely untouched) and in providing the explanations and probes included in surrounding material. I wish to thank the University of Connecticut for a Chancellor's Research Award, which freed me in the spring semester of 1998 to finish this work.

There are two major debts that need to be acknowledged. One is to the great Confucian scholar Herrlee Glassner Creel, into whose seminar on Chinese philosophy I wandered as an undergraduate at the University of Chicago. Creel was a wonderful teacher, and the fact that there were only two other students in the seminar probably heightened the impact of what I learned. The other is to Karen Ordahl Kupperman, my main source of good sense during the last few decades. It was she who suggested that I put together this book.

CONTENTS

Learning from Asian Philosphy

INTRODUCTION

A normal scholarly book on Asian philosophy would attempt a balanced and comprehensive survey of major traditions, taking each on its own terms and being careful not to impose Western templates on Asian texts. This is not a normal scholarly book. It will observe caution in assimilating Asian thought to Western models, or for that matter any one Asian tradition to other Asian traditions. In other respects the project will deviate from scholarship. The goal will be to gain contributions to philosophical enterprises that are, in the end, primarily Western rather than Chinese or Indian. There will be, therefore, little attempt at balance or comprehensiveness. This is not to say that there will be willful distortions of Chinese and Indian texts, all of which will be treated with great respect. But they will be used in the way that most teachers of philosophy in Britain and America use, say, Descartes or John Locke: as reminders of problems or lines of thought that we might have forgotten about or ignored, and as suggestive philosophical activity that we can continue, revise, or debate in our own philosophical work.

A running theme of this book is that much of importance has been forgotten about or ignored in recent Western philosophy, especially ethical philosophy; and that great Asian philosophy, apart from its intrinsic interest, can be very useful in refocusing current philosophical enterprises. Here briefly are six topics that look different from the perspective of some Asian traditions than they do within the context of contemporary Western philosophy.

1. The formation of self is considered as an ethical problem. In many Asian traditions, how it is that one becomes the kind of person who leads a good life is regarded as the central problem of ethics. Contemporary Western philosophy gives it comparatively little attention.

2. Related to this is the fluidity of self, and the problem of how it can be consistent with a stable persona. There are suggestive lines of thought in the

early philosophy of Sartre and in postmodernism. But there is nothing in Western philosophy comparable to the sophisticated, and itself fluid, treatment in the great texts of Daoism.

3. The scope of ethics is itself a problem. Is it concerned only with our choices, or are there things that are not matters of choice that also should be important to ethics? Confucius in particular has been read as discounting the phenomenon of choice as an ethical topic. What is it to have a genuine choice? Are there matters not of genuine choice for which an agent nevertheless can be assigned ethical merit (or lack of merit)?

4. Is the scope of ethics broad enough to include all or almost all of life? Is it concerned with quality of life at moments at which we are not making major choices? If so, are all parts of life governed in some uniform or integrated way? Or are different parts subject to ethical review in different ways? As a familiar alternative: is ethics primarily concerned only with certain especially important or problematic moments in life?

5. There is also the question of whether the demands of ethics fall on all (at least, all who are mature and of sound mind, etc.) alike, or whether there can be sliding scales of ethical requirements. In many cultures religious vocation is held to create higher standards. But in some Asian traditions there is a sense that, even if we put to the side any considerations that we would normally think of as religious, ethics imposes higher standards on some people than on others.

6. Finally, there is the function of philosophy itself. Is it a search for truth? And if so, what kind of truth? Occasionally Asian philosophy is dismissed as "wisdom literature" rather than genuine philosophy. It is natural to ask what connection, if any, philosophy can have with wisdom. Related to this is the question of how philosophy communicates (when it does), and what counts as really effective communication.

Each of these six topics (or families of topics) will have its own part in this book. In every case, the part will begin with general reflections on the issues and on relevant philosophical context. There will follow then an essay or essays on Asian or comparative philosophy that is (or are) far more specific and text-based, illustrating lessons that can be learned from Asian philosophy. The section then will conclude with discussion of possible implications for philosophical practice.

There will be no suggestion, in relation to any topic, that Western philosophy is entirely uniform, or that it is on that topic consistently blind or misguided. What many or most contemporary philosophers miss a few may see. And on virtually every one of these topics there will be at least one major Western philosopher (often Plato, Aristotle, Hume, or Nietzsche) of the past who could supply some (although, I will argue, not all) of what can be gained from Asian philosophy.

Bearing these disclaimers in mind, we can construct a simple model of what are, from the point of view of this book, the most limiting tendencies of contemporary Western philosophical common sense. Call it CWPCS. This model holds that ethics is concerned first and foremost with choices of an especially significant nature. In one version of CWPCS especially significant choices are those of principle in which one of the available alternatives could not be willed to be a universal law or violates the requirement of respect for persons. In another version the especially significant choices are such that, if they are made badly, an urge to punish (see Mill, *Utilitarianism*, chapter 5, para. 14) is a legitimate response. Choices of which dessert to order, which film to see, or even such major life decisions as what career to pursue or whom to marry are, in the general run of cases, not in the core area of ethical concern. Instead they can be governed by hypothetical imperatives; or they may be viewed as being in the realm of liberty, and in a way no one's business other than that of the person who makes them.

Second, much as the natural sciences, in studying such phenomena as the descent of objects dropped from the Leaning Tower of Pisa, can discount such factors as the colors of the objects, smells in the air, the history of Pisa, and for that matter the life history and personality of the person who is releasing the objects, ethical philosophy can adequately study a choice merely in terms of the nature of what may be done and of what the alternatives are, and perhaps also what the consequences of the deed and of its alternatives would be or could be expected to be. It can rival physics in ruthless abstraction. The life history and personality of whoever is making the choice can be discounted. Both the scientist and the ethical philosopher thus can take as their subject matter a narrowly viewed process (the datum or the decision) with a precise starting point in time.

Third, the choice that is central to ethical philosophy requires that, at its starting point, there must be two or more possibilities (in some sense of "possibilities"). The practice of ethical judgment requires choice among genuine possibilities. ("Ought" implies "can.") This element of CWPCS has led to well-known difficulties in combining the practice of ethical philosophy with the hypothesis of determinism. Even if we put these to the side, there are subtle difficulties connected with the role of people's characters in determining the choices they make. By and large, by the time someone will be able to consider what kind of character she or he would prefer to have, she or he will already have one; and arguably characters are difficult in the long run, and perhaps impossible in the short one, to change through efforts of will. Hence, to the extent that our choices flow from our character, they may be less under our control than we would like to think.

Because of all of this, it should be no surprise that CWPCS allows so little room for ethical consideration of character formation. It is much easier to present choices as unambiguously under the control of the agent if they are wrenched out of the context of the agent's character and history. Thus it becomes congenial to CWPCS to abstract from character much as one abstracts from the colors and smells at Pisa, and to focus narrowly on what is the optimal solution to the ethical problem at hand.

In one version of CWPCS, this subject matter is viewed in relation to reasons and arguments that might justify a particular decision. This is related to a view of philosophy (much more common in Anglo-American than in "continental" CWPCS) that regards it as having arguments and reasoning as its peculiar concern. The strong appeal of this view can best be appreciated in the larger context of the modern problem of just what philosophy's function and distinctive contributions are supposed to be. To see this problem is to get a better idea of what the difference is supposed to be between "wisdom literature" and philosophy.

It is well known that the discipline of philosophy used to include forms of knowledge or speculation that, as they advanced, became separate disciplines: for example, the natural sciences, psychology, and linguistics. What is the distinctive mandate of philosophy? In the light of its history, it is tempting to answer in terms of forms of knowledge or speculation that are not advanced (or that perhaps cannot advance?). A kinder answer would be to see philosophy as concerned with matters of logic and structure that either underlie the sciences, or run parallel to their research, or perhaps govern the prescientific experience that remains a large part of life. The kinder answer has a double advantage. Not only does it preserve the sense that philosophy has a distinctive mission, one that cannot entirely be taken away (no matter how much our knowledge advances); but also it underwrites the image of philosophers as specially skilled intellectual workers, whose technical skills require special training.

The variety of ways in which philosophy could be claimed to study logic, or the structure of our concepts, or the structure of our experience provides an interesting subject, but one that would take us too far afield. To admire more than one kind of attempt is, in effect, to concede that the subject has no essence: that it is not the case that all of the accomplishments of philosophy are of the same sort. Indeed, why cannot some philosophy make clear to us what the established conceptual structures are at the foundations of our thought, while some philosophy (including perhaps some of the same philosophy) helps us to understand the structures of everyday experience? Then perhaps some philosophy has yet other accomplishments. A natural question is why ethical philosophy cannot offer something above and beyond conceptual analysis: something about values in life that can be supported by experience (even if not all testimony will agree)?

One putative accomplishment of some philosophy should be mentioned especially, both because it is inherently controversial and because it can be attributed to a good deal of Asian philosophy. This is the development of a moral psychology that provides understanding of the ways in which people's lives and purposes are organized. This moral psychology is a large element especially in Confucian philosophy. It also looms large in the work of three great Western philosophers already mentioned: Aristotle, Hume, and Nietzsche. What each of these says about ethics and about social attitudes can be viewed as a blend of philosophy and psychology, the elements of which cannot readily be disentangled.

What makes this blending controversial is that psychology is now an independent discipline that pursues scientific methods. This makes it tempting to view the psychological elements in Confucius, Mencius, Aristotle, Hume, and Nietzsche as prescientific and hence as of marginal value. On the other hand, some intelligent readers find some of these insights compelling. At stake are some fundamental issues, including that of what counts as evidence in psychology.

Here is an outline of one response, which I have argued at length elsewhere (see my *Character*, appendix 1, "Moral Psychology"). One element is to distinguish discovery from justification. A lay person, even a philosopher, can make useful psychological observations, which may be largely correct or even brilliant; but these will not meet one of the standards of scientific knowledge, namely that of impersonal, able-to-be-replicated testing. This does not mean, though, that the lay observations should be dismissed or that they necessarily cannot have important value. What it does mean is that, lacking one element of scientific knowledge, they will need to be treated as in this respect tentative. By and large they will lack the relatively uncontroversial character that much scientific knowledge has. At the least one will want to test them against one's own experience and judgment, although this, too, is hardly scientific validation.

Occasionally scientific psychology will parallel philosophical moral psychology. A good example is Stanley Milgram's experiments (see Milgram 1974), in which a subject who thinks she or he has volunteered for an experiment on the effects of punishment on learning is asked to administer electrical shocks of increasing severity to someone (ostensibly another subject, but actually an actor) who gives wrong answers. Roughly two-thirds of the subjects (the great majority of whom could be presumed to be ordinarily decent people) continued to give shocks up to the dangerous level of 450 volts; this confirms suggestions in Plato's *Republic* that the great majority of people who ordinarily behave in a virtuous manner could not be counted upon to make virtuous choices in difficult or disorienting circumstances (and hence cannot count as truly virtuous).

This congruence of psychological research with philosophical moral psychology is, however, unusual. One reason is that the data that will be decisive typically concern how people actually behave, especially in difficult or disorienting circumstances; often it will be especially useful to know about behavior over a period of time). Psychological researchers cannot obtain such data except by spying on people, perhaps both tracking and spying on subjects for a long period of time. Practical difficulties and the growing strength of ethical constraints thus combine to make such data usually largely unavailable (although in some cases subjects' spouses, lovers, children, and friends could tell researchers a thing or two). What people say about their ethical attitudes is a very poor substitute for these hard-to-get data, because there is no guarantee that it represents how they would actually behave in difficult or disorienting circumstances.

A further complication is that there is no scientifically acceptable experimental design to test some psychological claims in which there are normative elements. If what is at stake is a claim about people who genuinely have a certain level of virtue, how does a scientific psychologist make the initial determination of this group's membership? Thus it appears that some psychological claims that are crucial to ethics cannot be tested at all (unless certain ethical claims are accepted as part of the experimental design), and others are extremely difficult and impractical to test. Because of all of these difficulties, philosophers' accounts of the factors that contribute to someone's developing into a person who has a good life not only can be insightful in important ways but also can be in practice irreplaceable by anything more scientific.

Let us return to the thought (persistent in the Anglo-American versions of CWPCS) that arguments and reasons are crucial to philosophy, so that an activity cannot be philosophy if they do not have a major role, and the value of a philosophy will have a great deal to do with the worth of the argumentation that constitutes its spine. It may be tempting to regard this assumption as a product of recent "analytic" philosophy, more especially because analytic philosophers frequently will criticize a good deal of French, German, and Asian philosophy on the basis of an alleged shortage of argument. But the idea that argument is central to philosophy surely goes back to Plato, even if some of Plato's own arguments can seem less good than the philosophy in which they are embedded.

We can gain perspective on the issues by considering a few commonsense observations about arguments and reasons. One is that they often are ex post facto. That is, while arguments and reasons sometimes get people to conclusions, often it is the case that they arrive at the conclusions first and then come up with reasons to justify them. This practice is especially common in aesthetics. It would seem almost odd for someone to decide whether a painting or a poem was good on the basis of a chain of argument. Typically people arrive at a sense of the value of a work, and then look for reasons that will function both as explanations (of what went right or wrong) and as justifications. Something like this often happens in ethics: something just seems wrong or disgusting, and then one struggles to articulate just what it is that makes it wrong. (In both aesthetics and ethics, it should be added, the process of coming up with reasons can recoil: someone who can come up with no good reasons may then reconsider the original judgment.) Even in philosophy, it is by no means the case that every position is arrived at as a result of a chain of argument. Sometimes a philosopher's intuitions draw her or him to a position, and then the search for reasons becomes serious.

Second, reasons often do not convince everyone equally. Many would take its extreme repetitiveness as a good reason for thinking Ravel's *Bolero* a bad piece of music, but those who find it appealing will hardly be argued out of their favorable judgments. This may be no more than one expects in aesthetics, but there are many cases in philosophy in which what are widely agreed to be good reasons do not cause people to give up the positions that they tell against. There are few recorded conversions on the basis of reasons in the long-standing arguments between Kantians and consequentialists, or between realists and anti-realists. Philosophers sometimes do change their minds as a result of what they grant to be good reasons for the other side, but a response that seems at least as frequent is to modify (perhaps rather subtly) one's position so that the opposing reasons no longer seem quite so telling. Sometimes a position will not be modified even slightly although a philosopher concedes that some of the reasons on the other side are pretty good.

Related to this pattern is the fact that reasons often are regarded, even by people who take them as having great weight, as not the whole story of what counts for or against a position or a judgment. Sometimes it may be possible to articulate what the other elements are that count for or against a position or a judgment (thus formulating reasons that capture these elements), and to the extent to which this is successful it may seem that the weight of reasons approaches the entirety of what counts for or against. Often, though, it is not so easy to articulate (even in philosophy) all that seems relevant. A philosophical position can seem to make sense of the world and of everyday experience in ways that other positions cannot match. Thus someone who is drawn to, say, Spinoza's philosophy will hardly be able to explain its appeal merely in terms of the validity of Spinoza's deductions.

There is much to be said for the attempt to formulate reasons (as it were, a second round of reasons) to capture relevant factors that are not captured by the reasons one first gives. This is most obviously true in aesthetics. Indeed Arnold Isenberg, in a classic essay, suggested that the major function of critics' reasons was to guide our experience of the works of art to which they referred, the meaning of the reasons being filled out in that experience. Anyone who has observed critics at work knows how extraordinarily difficult it is to articulate many of the value-related elements that may seem to emerge in further seeing, reading, or listening, and how unusual it is to encounter anything that looks like complete success.

Let me suggest that something like this is true of ethics, especially of that portion (assuming that there is one) that is concerned with quality-of-life issues rather than with the moral propriety of choices that are viewed within a (temporally and personally) narrow context. When Aristotle talks about what counts toward *eudaemonia*, or when Confucius comments on the life experience of someone who is a sage (or is on the way to becoming one), the hearer or reader is meant to relate the claims to what may be part of his or her life experience or may have been witnessed in the lives of others. The argument, to the extent that there is one on the page, is, in other words, not self-contained. It points beyond itself to what can be seen or felt. (This is the most charitable way to read Aristotle—e.g., just how strong is the argument against hedonism that the people who accept it are the ones who prefer to live like cattle?—and it is the only way to read Confucius.) These other factors (the ones we are encouraged to see or feel, or to remember having seen or felt) can be talked about. But that is not to say that everything that is important in them can be clearly articulated.

This observation carries us to a third obvious point about reasons, which is that they are heterogeneous. It is tempting to hold up reasons that refer to deductive implications, or conversely to inconsistencies that can be demonstrated deductively, as paradigmatic. Admirers of Plato or of Descartes are especially likely to do this. (Those, like me, who think that Plato's philosophy is a lot better than his arguments will tend to hold back.) A survey, though, of what are advanced as reasons in various philosophical works undermines any tendency to regard the deductive as paradigmatic. This is true even if the survey is restricted to contemporary Anglo-American philosophy. It would be nice in a way to think that philosophical reasons are deductive, in that this would anchor the pretensions of philosophy to what is clearly a respectable subject (namely deductive logic). But what is agreeable is not necessarily the case.

An examination of the varieties of what can count as reasons in philosophy would carry us beyond the boundaries of this work. But three points should be made here. One is that part of the reasonable support for a philosophical position may lie outside of the reasons contained in the philosophy (even a philosophy that is highly argued). An example is the way in which subsequent advances in mathematical physics give support to Plato's claim that true knowledge is only of what is timeless and unchanging (although very few nowadays would advance such a position without major qualifications). A second point is that a coherence that cannot be explicated in terms of deductive reasoning can count heavily in favor of a philosophy. If this is so, then the fact that an element of the philosophy coheres well with other elements can be an implicit reason that supports it (even if no reasons actually are given). If one puts the two points together, also, an element can be implicitly supported by the consideration that it functions well as part of an orientation that is fruitful in making sense of the world. A third point is that if a philosopher refers to phenomena or to aspects of the world that lend support to the philosophy (perhaps because they support the moral psychology interwoven with the philosophy, or because the philosophy offers a frame of reference that is perspicacious in relation to them), this reference counts as a reason in favor of the philosophy. If one puts the last two points together, it appears that there are more reasons and arguments in philosophy than those that are clearly presented on the page as such.

This character of reasons and arguments has implications for the ways in which a philosophy communicates to a reader. The more closely a philosophy approaches logic, the more likely it is to be self-contained. The reader's mind is asked to make a circuit that begins, remains, and ends on the pages of the work. Philosophy that is intended to be perspicacious about the world, or especially about human lives, will not be self-contained. The reader's mind must leave the page and make appropriate connections between the work and the real world. There then will be two variables in the philosophy's mode of communication. One is in the degree of definiteness of the intended connections between the work and the world. It is arguable (and one of the chapters in this book argues this of the Daoist *Zhuangzi*, also known as *Chuang Tzu*) that in Daoist philosophy both the connections with the world and what will count as an appropriate response admit of considerable latitude, so that it is much more plausible to assign a range of meanings than a single meaning to the philosophy. A second variable is in the amount of guidance, in making connections with the world, that the philosopher gives the reader. Contemporary readers tend to want a lot of help. But it is arguable that people understand things better if they do much of the work themselves. Confucius especially is on record as holding that this (rather than "spoon feeding") is crucial to good teaching. He prefers a student (and presumably would prefer a reader) who, presented with one corner of a subject, comes back with the other three (see *Analects* VII.8, also V. 8). Hence, to the extent that the reasons that support his philosophy concern connections with human life experience, he indicates this in a general way and does not spell it out.

Given the broader view of philosophical reasons that I have been outlining, we can agree that reasons and arguments are of crucial importance to philosophy. A philosophy that provides little indication of what there is to be said for it is surely not worthy of being advanced. This agreement must be conjoined with two disclaimers. One is that (as has been noted) the reasons that give a philosophy strong support can be implicit rather than explicit. Perhaps it is always better that they be made explicit. But this is more easily accomplished in the case of some sorts of reasons than it would be for others, and (especially when we bear this in mind) we should be reluctant to dismiss philosophies just because the structure of argumentation is largely implicit. The second disclaimer is that we need not assimilate what counts as a reason to structures in formal logic, or indeed to anything like them. Philosophical reasons of some strength can concern connections of the philosophy with life experience, or can appeal both to its coherence and its heuristic role in our understanding of aspects of reality.

Life experience can include both a heightened sense of some relations of psychological causality and the awareness of possibilities in life that may be difficult to describe adequately or to anticipate. As I have argued at length (*Value . . . and What Follows*), it also can include the element of emotional awareness of value, so that a role of experience can be to put one in a position to make claims about value that (although not incorrigible) will have more warrant than they otherwise would have had. This argument is connected with an argument for a realism about value: some lives really do go better than others, and some things are more to be sought than others. Experience and reflection on experience can pave the way to more extensive knowledge of this.

Both the experience and the awareness of value are closely connected to what people normally mean by wisdom. Clearly wisdom is not the same as intellectual power, although it requires some degree of intellectual ability. Bertrand Russell comes to mind as an example of someone of great intellectual power who would not normally be referred to as "wise." To have wisdom paradigmatically requires some comprehensive vision of what good lives are, which will include both psychological insight born of experience and a reasonable set of values. (Someone who supported the Nazi party or the policies of Stalin could not be said to be wise.) Aristotle was wise, and so was Confucius; and both the *Nicomachean Ethics* and the *Analects* of Confucius can be argued to impart wisdom.

This view leads us to the question of whether a work like the *Analects* of Confucius, in which arguments are not conspicuous as such, can be regarded (unlike the *Nicomachean Ethics*) as "wisdom literature" rather than philosophy. We need here to be careful with our terms. Words like *wisdom* and *knowledge* have a range of meanings, rather than a single precise meaning. Someone who is able confidently to answer difficult questions in a subject because of great reasoning powers and a thorough familiarity with relevant data can be said to have knowledge. We also sometimes say that someone who guesses an answer correctly "knew it all along," especially if he or she had at some point seen the relevant information. Wisdom can range from the comprehensive (and rare) understanding of a sage to what is termed "conventional wisdom," which on some subjects should not be slighted.

One variable is what might be termed "depth." At the upper end of the range, wisdom manifests the working, over some period of time, of an unusually reflective intelligence that strives to relate diverse areas of experience and is sensitive to meanings and nuances. The more conventional wisdom of, say, a Benjamin Franklin—while definitely worth having—lacks this depth.

Books on how to live that function on this level, whether they are Asian or Western, might be termed "wisdom literature" (at least if they are worth anything) and certainly should not be considered philosophy. My suggestion is that books like the *Analects* or the Buddhist *Dhammapada*, while they could be termed "wisdom literature," should be considered philosophy because of their depth and the intricate implicit structure of argument.

In each case the reader must devote more work to understanding the intricate structure of argument than is usual in Western philosophy. One factor in this difficulty is that both the *Analects* and the *Dhammapada* are collections of fragments, and often the meaning of any given fragment cannot be appreciated at all well until it is related to the rest of the text. Something like this is sometimes true in Western philosophy, especially in much of Nietzsche. But the problem is made worse for the *Analects* and the *Dhammapada* because they are both less subversive of most of conventional morality than Nietzsche is; hence, any given fragment is likely (with most of its meaning not readily apparent) to present an initial appearance of blandness. The great danger then is that the reader's eye skates down the page, whereas for Nietzsche the risk is that it is entangled and comes to a halt. Intelligent reading and understanding of these Asian texts (Nietzsche is a more complicated case because of his anticipations of postmodernism) require a sense of a coherent vision, whose parts support one another and which also implicitly argues on the basis of life experience.

Related to all of these matters is the awkward issue, already discussed, of what in the end philosophy is intended to provide. Does it include truth? In much the sense in which we speak of moral realism or realism with respect to knowledge of the natural sciences, can we speak of philosophical realism? It does seem sometimes that philosophers contribute to our understanding of the world or of human psychology in ways that make some philosophies seem not discontinuous from the sciences. Alternatively we might look to philosophy for a logical analysis of, or an examination of meanings in, ordinary thought. The virtues to be looked for in this case will have more to do with clarity than with perspicaciousness or suggestiveness.

We need to insist that there is no reason to expect that simple answers to these questions will have any merit, or that the accomplishments of philosophies fit one general pattern. Battles between philosophical schools feature an array of procrustean beds. The point of view of this book is eclectic: to recognize one kind of excellence does not require us to slight others. In particular the logical achievements and accomplishments in structural analysis and in phenomenology of some recent Western philosophy should not blind us to the fact that there is great philosophy, much of it Asian, that includes a rich and suggestive moral psychology and a coherent vision of the formation of the self and the determination of desirable ways in which to live.

PART I

The Formation of Self as an Ethical Problem

1

THE PSYCHOLOGY AND
ETHICS OF SELF

Not only are ethical issues concerned with formation of self central to many Asian philosophical traditions, but they also are intimately connected with issues that I will take up in later sections. The scope of ethics is at stake, as is the nature of choice. A further complication is that the formation of self can be viewed as a single process that begins at birth or as a revisionary process that begins later, when someone experiences a need to be more enlightened, more pure, or more intelligently focused.

Let us begin with some obvious truths about the development of self and then move from these to philosophical issues. A human being in early infancy may already have certain features that are distinctive of her or his way of responding to events; these starting points of a developed nature are generally put under the heading of temperament rather than personality. Distinctive and characteristic ways of thinking and acting may well develop by the early teenage years. To say that someone at this stage has a fully developed personality—an articulated pattern of thought and behavior rather than mere tendencies—is not to say that this personality is not subject to change. What may lead to change will be discussed shortly.

The concept of character, as distinct from that of personality, places great emphasis on a person's reliable pattern of making moral choices and also in coping with difficulties in the pursuit of happiness. (To have no reliable pattern is to have no character, which is distinct from having a good character or a truly bad character.) An adolescent who has already developed a personality—let us say as an outgoing, relaxed, charming person—may yet not have a developed character, in the sense that he or she could go in more than one direction, as between being someone who is reliably honest and benevolent and has firm moral integrity, on one hand, and someone who is irresponsible and (when under pressure) deceitful, on the other. Character also, even when it has developed, can change.

If there are ethical issues pertaining to the formation of self in infancy or childhood, these principally concern parents, educators, and perhaps designers of society, rather than making demands on the infant or child itself. It is true that we sometimes speak of someone as a "good child," but this reports such things as an agreeable tendency to be cooperative and do one's best, along with early evidences of some generosity of spirit, rather than ascribing any kind of developed character. By and large we judge that infants and children are not in a good position to make decisions about the direction of their development of self.

This is a description in broad outline of the formation of self. Is it ever finished? The answer to this question (as we will see in Part II) arguably is "no." All the same, many people in their twenties have developed personalities and characters. Often this development is experienced as a result of a seamless process, including childhood advice from, or expectations on the part of, parents and teachers, and perhaps some thoughts of one's own that build on advice and expectation. Sometimes it will not appear so seamless: an early process that leads, let us say, to a somewhat developed personality and perhaps the rudiments of a character will be succeeded by a reflective examination of how things stand—and in which direction one wants to develop. There may be a change of direction as a result. In such cases it is tempting to think of what ultimately develops as a second nature.

The notion of a reflective phase of development that leads to a second nature is absolutely central to most classical Asian philosophies, as represented in such works as (to give a far from exhaustive list) the *Upanishads*, the *Bhagavad Gita*, most early Buddhist texts, and the *Analects* of Confucius. A good example, portrayed in mythic terms, is found in the *Katha Upanishad* (*Upanishads*, 55–66). Nachiketas, dissatisfied with his father's attitudes, is consigned to the kingdom of death, where it is revealed to him (before he returns to life) that the inner nature of the individual is identical with the divine reality of the entire universe. This revelation makes death seem quite different and calls for a different orientation in one's life. Nachiketas is then on his way toward becoming a different person.

A prominent example of a Western philosopher for whom second nature is central is Aristotle. Aristotle holds that the foundation of goodness is good habits. But a truly virtuous person needs a reflective second phase, in which habit is bolstered by understanding and also is modified so as to allow for the flexible responses required to follow the mean.

Needless to say, while many Asian philosophers and Aristotle have shared the concern with second nature, the advice as to what the goal should be (and how to get there) has diverged. Hardly any of the philosophers is prepared to endorse without qualification what might be termed ordinary human nature, which includes the tendencies (that arguably we all start out with) to have desires, seek pleasures, and think that we have real individual selves. But the degree of rejection varies greatly. There is a strong tendency both in classical Hindu philosophy and (for not entirely the same reasons) in early Buddhist philosophy to think that what most people would regard as normal human nature is driven by dangerous ignorance and indeed is sick, and that a strenuous effort to acquire a second nature is required in order to achieve a truly acceptable human life. Neither Confucius nor Aristotle is quite so deeply negative about the ordinary human nature, although both (in different ways) think that it can be improved.

All of these concerns suggest a range of topics that loom large in much Asian philosophy and also in Aristotle: what should be second nature, how does one work toward it, what contributions, if any, does it make to the directions of our lives, and does it have other benefits? It would be wrong to suggest that such topics are totally absent from recent Western ethical philosophy. But a fair assessment is that they have not been given attention in much of the best (and most highly regarded) work.

If virtually everyone's character changes, to some extent, during adult life, how do the changes take place? There is considerable consensus among psychologists and philosophers that a person's acts of will (to be a different kind of person) typically do not play a large very immediate role in change of character, and that when (and if) they do play any part at all they are likely to be indirect and gradual in their effects. The major role, as the "situationist" school in social psychology especially has emphasized, is played by the situations and routines that a person is placed in (or places herself or himself in). Along this line, the most important decisions regarding development of character that the average person makes are those of where to attend college, whether and whom to marry, and what sort of career to pursue. A simple example of the latter is a decision whether to become a debt collector or a social worker. Each of these decisions leads to a form of life that helps, sometimes gradually, to shape character and personality.

In his essay "The Sceptic," David Hume suggests that decisions to change one's character are likely to work, if at all, only by a change in one's routines and pursuits, and then the changes will be gradual rather than immediate (Hume 1985, 169). This pattern (while certainly not universal) fits that of many Asian texts. There is a pivotal decision: it may be to leave family and become a Hindu ascetic, or to join a Buddhist nunnery or monastery, or to become one of the students who lived and traveled with Confucius. The new pattern of life facilitates the change of self, but still it is a long haul.

The difficulty of willed change, especially of direct willed change, suggests that people generally have only a limited control over what their characters are or what they will be. This limited control puts into question whether they can be held responsible either for their characters or for actions that flow from their characters. In the *Treatise of Human Nature* Hume had considered this and had contended (1739/1978, 608) that people can be regarded as responsible even if there is not much control. I have argued (1991, chapter 3) that he was right.

Even if much that contributes to a good development of second nature is mediated by situations and routines that themselves may be as much a matter of luck as of choice, that fact scarcely deprives the result of ethical interest. Among the merits claimed in a variety of traditions for a good second nature are wholeheartedness, reliability, a beneficial influence on what a person actually does, and also the ongoing value of experiences that are connected closely with the second nature.

The forms that these experiences take vary from tradition to tradition, and also within traditions. In the Hindu tradition, for example, the *Upanishads* repeatedly insist on the psychological unity of a focus on, and identification with, an all-encompassing reality (Brahman), which goes well beyond ordinary wholeheartedness and is claimed to lead to experience of extraordinary value. The *Bhagavad Gita*, while not repudiating any of this, contributes a more varied picture of psychological options that will contribute both wholeheartedness and extraordinary value to experience. A central idea remains that loss of (individualized) self is in a way self-fulfillment. The apparent paradox is lessened if we realize that the texts balance two images of reality, one keyed to the viewpoint of an individual whose experience is not entirely pervaded by enlightenment and the other representing an ultimate metaphysical truth; the images contrast in much the same way as the commonsense and scientific images of the nature of a table (both true, but one arguably a deeper truth) famously compared by Arthur Eddington (1928, introduction). These are polyphonic intellectual systems.

Buddhist views of the self (and the metaphysics connected to this) are very different from those of Hindu philosophy, but here too loss of self is in a way self-realization. Compared to these Indian versions, Daoist and, even more so, Confucian models of the development of second nature seem less metaphysically driven and also less drastic. But they too, at the very least, are intended to substitute modes of life that are more focused and stylistically considered than the blooming, buzzing confusion of the average person's everyday life. Repeatedly it is suggested that this focus is validated by the experiential value of what will be achieved.

Here are three reasons why, in my view, the development of a self that will lead a life of value should be the central topic of ethical philosophy. One is that treating this topic as central makes possible a more rounded and realistic view of actual ethical life, including how decisions get made. The modern Western practice of wrenching these out of context can work fairly well for cases that represent a possible dramatic turning point in a life, as when serious wrongdoing is considered. In these the roles of habit and established ways of looking at things may not be completely eliminated, but as part of the story they can be minimized; and the result can be viewed, without major distortion, as a "one-off" decision. All the same, the agent's character development does provide constraints, even in these cases, on what is likely or even possible. Also, the need for the dramatic decision often turns out to be related to a pattern of prior choice: the situations in which people have to make stark moral choices are frequently ones they got themselves into. Comprehensive ethical judgment reasonably can be concerned with this pattern rather than merely with the pivotal moment of dramatic choice.

Most of the choices that people make in their lives, of course, are not as dramatic—or seemingly discontinuous from what came before—as those that are most used as examples in books on ethics. Often we find ourselves on a path of life, or immersed in projects and commitments of various sorts, and much of what we do is to carry on (pretty much as before) with minor deviations here and there. A great deal that is ethically important has this form. Philosophy that takes seriously the connection between what people do and their developed selves can best do justice to this. This is a strong reason for seeking an ethics that approaches longitudinally how people structure their lives.

A second advantage to treating development of self as a central topic is that, by encouraging us to see behavior in the context of individual character, we are better able to give room to the importance of style and nuance. This importance varies from case to case. In the ordinary murder it hardly matters how the deed is done. At the other extreme, style and nuance matter a great deal in acts of friendship or compassion. The latter do play a larger part in most of our lives than decisions of whether to murder, steal, rape, and torture do (however important and dramatic such decisions are), and a rounded ethics of actual life ought to have a place for them and for subtle factors that are important in them.

Third, there are issues of value that come to the fore when we move our attention from the broad nature of what is done to a closer view of how it is done. Much has been made of an alleged joyless hedonism of many modern consumers, in which an accumulation of pleasures is somehow not gratifying at any deeper level. But joyless moralism, in which people do their duty even though the salt has lost its savor, also can be a problem. There can be an important difference between two cases of what is in broad outline the same action, one done as duty dispiritedly or with clenched teeth, and the other done by someone who, so to speak, "gets into it" or finds it an enjoyable performance. It is well known that Aristotle is more willing to ascribe moral virtue to the second person, and Kant sometimes is interpreted as ascribing moral virtue only to the first. But the issue of value of life experience is separate from that of who gets moral credit. Even if we deny credit of a specifically *moral* sort to the second person—after all, Kant (1785/1981, 24) says that morality as a constraint is not needed by beings who have a holy will, and the second person on certain occasions may approach that ideal—we may think that it is much better to live like that. To have a fully realized second nature is presumably, after all, to have a life in which one is comfortable with oneself and one's actions, in which conflicts, ambivalent hesitations, and regrets are less likely than in most lives.

What is crucial here might be termed "naturalness" or "harmony." It plays an important part in the first of the two essays that follow, which is thirty years old and is keyed to Soothill's translation (for Oxford World Classics) of Confucius. Soothill renders *Analects* I.12 as "In the usages of decorum it is naturalness that is of value. In the regulations of the ancient kings this was the admirable feature, both small and great deriving therefrom. But there is a naturalness that is not permissible; for to know to be natural, and yet to be so beyond the restraints of decorum is also not permissible." The term *he* in *Analects* I.12, which Soothill translates as "naturalness," is translated by others (Arthur Waley and D. C. Lau) as "harmony."

A related passage is VI.16. Soothill renders this as "When nature [*zhi*] exceeds training, you have the rustic. When training exceeds nature, you have the clerk. It is only when nature and training are proportionally blended that you have the higher type of man." D. C. Lau (for whom it is VI.18) has "When there is preponderance of native substance over acquired refinement, the result will be churlishness. When there is a preponderance of acquired refinement over native substance, the result will be pedantry." Waley gives, "When natural substance prevails over ornamentation, you get the boorishness of the rustic. When ornamentation prevails over natural substance, you get the pedantry of the scribe."

In all of these versions, VI.16 is concerned with a contrast between something original (nature or substance) and an addition to, or modification of, it. An ideal balance between the two elements of the contrast is urged. It is not far-fetched to see a connection between this ideal balance and the harmony or naturalness (*he*) of I.12. Presumably what *he* involves is not merely this proper balance but also a relationship of the right sort between the agent and what she or he is doing: whether we speak of the ideal as harmony or as naturalness, it is to be at home in what one is doing so that it flows appropriately and is connected with who one is. The contrast is between *he*, on one hand, and perfunctory, awkward, tense, or grudging performances, clenched teeth, or ambivalent hesitation on the other. Life is likely to be far nicer if one maintains *he* in what one does, and moral behavior infused with *he* is arguably more reliable.

The second essay is concerned specifically with the roles of tradition and community in the formation of self, but secondarily develops an argument that Confucius offers a richer account of the formation of self than any Western philosopher (including Aristotle) does. The essay plays against one of the myths of modern Western individualism: that we create ourselves, as it were ex nihilo. (Sartre's early philosophical writing is a good source for this view of things.) No doubt the usually unreflective adaptation to circumstances and the charting of directions that play a large part in the development of self can be seen as a creative process. But, as Sartre himself increasingly recognized, it is governed by a variety of constraints and influences. My suggestion is that it is illuminating to take a closer look at what is often thought of as paradigmatic creativity, namely, creativity in the arts. This creativity typically flourishes within constraints; occasional dramatic violations of these constraints have to be seen as exceptions that prove the rule. It is hard to find any good art that has no relations at all to constraints or to a tradition, even if the relation is mainly one of reacting against. In much this way we can best understand the development of self within the context of the influences of family, community, tradition, and culture. Confucius supplies a better, fuller account of this sort than any other philosopher.

The Analects of Confucius

Because many readers will not be familiar with the *Analects*, it seems desirable to say a little about its setting and general character before moving (in the two chapters to follow) to more detailed discussion. Confucius (551–479 BCE) lived at a time when China, with memories of old empires, was disunited; rulers of kingdoms contended for dominance and sought for the secret of success. Confucius's interests were political and ethical, and hardly at all metaphysical (or religious in any sense related to creed). He was driven by an ideal of good government, which he saw as paternalistic and highly responsible. Rulers and an educated elite would be responsible for the well-being and, at least indirectly, the virtue of the people. There is some suggestion that good government is the secret of political success: when kingdoms contend, the people on both sides will want to live under a good ruler rather than a bad one, and this will have a great deal to do with the outcome.

Political and ethical questions are, in Confucius's view, intertwined, in that much of the work of politics consists of appropriate role modeling on the part of those in power, which will set the tone in a society. Rulers and officials of course should tend to the needs of the people, which requires some practical knowledge and skill (see I.5, XIII.5). But it also requires the unselfish determination not to cater to one's own satisfaction when the people are suffering.

It appears that Confucius's ambition was to provide crucial role modeling himself: to be entrusted with a high office in which he could demonstrate the power of goodness. In the meantime he taught numbers of students, who in some cases may have come to him to learn themselves the skills required for a career as a government official. The students lived with him and traveled as his entourage, all in all enjoying a relationship closer than that typical in modern universities. The *Analects*, put together after Confucius's death (the compilation we have may date from more than a century later), is largely the recreation of their conversations. Some of the students did gain coveted official positions, but Confucius himself never was offered one with any degree of real responsibility. Perhaps he seemed uncomfortably formidable. It is very likely that he died thinking of himself as in some respects a failure. Once, when he was very ill, the students around him dressed up as an official's retainers, an affectionate pretense that Confucius, reviving, found embarrassing (IX.11; see also IX.12; II.21; VII.32; XIII.14; XVII.7).

The *Analects* at first reading is a hodgepodge; although I want to say that, looked into more deeply, it is a great hodgepodge. Confucius's teaching included elements of ritual, classic poetry, remarks about historical figures, and comments on music, as well as subjects more easily recognized as falling within ethics or politics. Clearly, though, in a ceremonious society, a student's prospects for a career as an official would be strengthened if he were at home in ritual and knowledgeable about cultural traditions. Also it is clear that Confucius's view was that ritual, the classics, and music all played a part in the process of development into a good person that was both crucial to quality of life and requisite for truly acceptable performance as an official. So it all fits together, even though the integration of the work is at first far from obvious.

Two technical terms recur so frequently in discussion of this philosophy that they should be included in this prefatory note. One is *li*, which is propriety, and sometimes is more narrowly and specifically ritual propriety. As the essays that follow should make clear, this is a much more subtle and complex concept than one might initially suppose. We tend to think of propriety in terms of rule following. Confucius did take seriously some traditional rules, such as the one governing the length of mourning for a deceased parent; but *li* in his view included also matters of style, nuance, and demeanor, and allowed for large areas of judgment. In the last analysis one could have it only by a process of education and acculturation that made one a good sort of person.

The other term is *jen*, which has an early sense (see Hall and Ames, 143–46) of authoritative humanity and sometimes (especially in later texts) is translated as human-heartedness. The emphasis on *jen* in the Confucian tradition makes a difference to the shape of the ethics, much more perhaps than it does to its content. Cases of ethical failure that come to mind are likely to be seen under the heading of failure of (or lack of) humanity; this failure can be at least as evident in what we would consider to be private life as in the areas in which justice (a major Western preoccupation) is a prime consideration.

There may be an important difference between having *jen*, as an emotional component of human nature, and being able to focus and implement one's *jen*, which may require education or at least an effort at clarity. A distinction like this becomes a preoccupation of Mencius, Confucius's (fourth century BCE) great follower, whose philosophy will be part of the subject of part III of this book. To put Mencius's worry untechnically: someone can have benevolence as part of his or her normal humanity, but because of thoughtlessness, lack of moral imagination, or for other reasons not behave benevolently in most contexts. A major task of practical ethics, then, becomes the effort to focus, or as it were to unblock, the working of *jen*.

2

CONFUCIUS AND THE PROBLEM
OF NATURALNESS

There is a set of problems in ethics that concern themselves not so much with specific choices on special occasions, but rather with the style with which life is to be led. Examples may be found in the work of Nietzsche, Sartre, and Camus. What Nietzsche means by the *Ubermensch* is much more a matter of general style than of specific choices, and something similar is true of the "honesty" that Sartre considers so important, as well as Camus's "lucidity."

The majority of contemporary Western ethical thinkers tends, however, to ignore ethical problems that center on a style of life. There is a long and very powerful Western tradition, after all, that pictures ethics as the study of a certain type of choice: one in which good, evil, right, and wrong are at stake. According to this tradition, whether one decides to murder or not, or to lie or not, is typically an ethical matter. How someone spends money, or converses with friends, or has a manner that is cheerful and open rather than sullen and withdrawn is normally not a matter of ethics. Ethics thus focuses on certain special moments. The general tendencies of life are largely ignored, or are considered to lie outside of the subject.

This point of view is reflected in the types of example most commonly used, such as the following. Suppose you are a teacher who, on moral grounds, objects to being required to sign a "loyalty oath." Whether loyalty oaths are good or bad is not the question here. Suppose, for the sake of argument, that they are bad, and that no one ought to sign one or be required to sign one. Yet unless a sufficient number of other teachers in your institution or school system or state also refuse to sign, your refusal is likely to lead to the loss of your job and may also prevent you from obtaining another (Singer 1961, 158–59). Also, A owes money to B, and B owes money to C, and it is the law that creditors may exact their debts by putting their debtors into prison. B asks himself, "Can I say that I ought to take this measure against A in order to make him pay?" (Hare 1963, 90)

Nevertheless, some thoughtful people have a concern about ethics that goes beyond the typical concern of Western professional philosophers. Some thoughtful people worry, that is, not only about those dramatic choices that are so often considered paradigms of the ethical, but also about such broad matters as "the meaning of life," "honesty to oneself," being a "real" person, and so forth. There is a nightmare that lies at the heart of this concern. It is of a man who makes correctly all of the major decisions that are most commonly thought of as ethical. He does not cheat, or steal, or inflict pain needlessly, and so forth. He does not prosecute debtors and refuses to sign loyalty oaths. However, his life in most respects is unexciting and drab. In late middle age he wakes up to the fact that his life "lacks meaning," or that there has been something (which seems at least to border on the ethical) lacking in him, or that he has made a number of choices (which he had not thought of as ethical choices, or perhaps had not thought of as choices at all) very badly. This is, in its way, a philosophical nightmare, since the agony is related to the man's having had a poor conception of what ethical problems are.

It would be generally agreed, by those who entertain the nightmare, that the way to avoid living it would involve, broadly speaking, having a good style of life. There is no unanimity about what is essential to having a good style of life. One concept that often recurs, however, is that of "naturalness." There is a sort of person nowadays who is very sensitive to ethical problems, but who also is inarticulate and philosophically untrained. People of this sort often say, "The important thing is to be natural."

In this chapter I will examine naturalness in relation to the thought of the most outstanding philosopher who has dealt with it, Confucius. This examination should accomplish three things. First, Confucius's thought clearly reveals the ambiguity of the term "naturalness." Second, Confucius's conception of the most desirable kind of naturalness sheds light on his conception of *li* (propriety), and is relevant to the general problem of moral decision in difficult cases. Third, Confucius's discussion of naturalness will provide us with a useful approach to the larger question, "What is most valuable?"

In book I, section 12 of the *Analects* Confucius's close follower Yu distinguishes between two kinds of naturalness. He remarks, "In the usages of decorum it is naturalness that is of value. In the regulations of the ancient kings this was the admirable feature, both small and great deriving therefrom. But there is a naturalness that is not permissible; for to know to be natural, and yet to be so beyond the restraints of decorum is also not permissible."

(At this point—1998, thirty years after this essay was first published—an interjection is needed. The translation used is that by W. E. Soothill [Oxford World Classics], which has many felicities. Its translation of *he* as "naturalness" seemed to me to serve nicely to subvert the contrast, which became so influential in the 1960s, between the natural and the artificial. The even older, but still good, translation by James Legge renders *he* as "natural ease." Arthur Waley's, which many sinologists favor, and also D. C. Lau's give *he* as "harmony." But what is "harmony"? Any plausible answer will point to an accord between words and behavior, on one hand, and inner impulses, on the other, so that there is an absence of inner conflicts. Thus the meaning of "harmony" converges with that of "naturalness.")

In a later section of this chapter I shall examine the naturalness that Yu praises here. There is an air of paradox about it that requires examination, since clearly it is a naturalness that would strike most Americans (and many Chinese) as quite artificial. After all, Yu is speaking of the "usages of decorum," that is, of intricately ritualized polite behavior. The naturalness that he praises is naturalness that participates in this behavior and presumably is expressed in it. The question that we must answer later is, how can highly ritualized behavior, which requires much training, practice, and self-control, be said to involve "naturalness"?

The second kind of naturalness that Yu distinguishes is more closely related than the first to the concept of self-expression. Everyone, even a cultivated Confucian gentleman, has desires and impulses that, if they were expressed freely, would ruffle the surface of human relations and perhaps in some cases would weaken the bonds of civilization. Almost everyone, for example, has moments of hostile feelings toward someone near him or her.

To express such feelings may seem "natural." Why "bottle it up"; why be inhibited? Yet from a Confucian point of view, this "naturalness" is "not permissible." The reasons for this are not entirely social. It is true that there is a danger to society if large numbers of people express all of their feelings too freely. There is also, however, a danger to the integrity of the individual. As we shall see, the view is that someone's chance of becoming a remarkable and "superior" person will be ruined by this kind of naturalness.

Some people speak of a third kind of naturalness, or rather a third sense of "natural," pertaining to someone's original tendencies and capacities. To be "natural" in this sense is to act in accordance with one's original bent. What is natural in this sense plainly depends on one's original tendencies or thoughts. Someone who believes that the mind at birth is a blank tablet, lacking even innate tendencies, will discount the possibility of naturalness in this sense. Someone, on the other hand, who follows Mencius in thinking of *jen* (human-heartedness) as being present in original nature, and who in addition believes that *jen* is the principal ingredient of an ideal moral nature, will feel that naturalness in this third sense is very close to the naturalness that Yu praises.

Arguably, Confucius's view lies between these two extremes. He clearly did not hold a blank tablet view. Thus he could say, "By nature men nearly resemble each other; in practice they grow wide apart" (XVII.2). On the other hand, Confucius places great emphasis on training, culture, intelligent discrimination, and refinement, qualities that could not be a part of original nature. He points out (VI.16) that "When nature exceeds training, you have the rustic. When training exceeds nature, you have the clerk. It is only when nature and training are proportionally blended that you have the higher type of man." (Waley has "When natural substance prevails over ornamentation, you get the boorishness of the rustic . . .") This statement suggests that Confucius's ideal of naturalness (the naturalness that Yu praises) is quite distinct from naturalness in the sense of simply following original nature.

A kind of naturalness that one may argue is distinct from the three thus far distinguished is the naturalness praised by Daoist philosophers. This Daoist naturalness is quite complex and most accurately should be considered a cluster of senses of "natural" rather than a single sense. Philosophical Daoism was not a monolithic movement, and even within a single work (e.g., the *Zhunghzi*) a reader can find shifting areas of emphasis. Nevertheless Daoist conceptions of naturalness do have characteristic foci. I may briefly and simply summarize these as being spontaneity in behavior, simplicity in social life, and harmony with the fundamental tendencies of the universe.

Daoist naturalness certainly is not naturalness within "the restraints of decorum," which the Daoists considered ridiculous and artificial. The naturalness of the Daoists also did not involve giving general vent to feelings. The Daoists were not wild men: indeed, they believed that certain common feelings, such as anxiety, should be as much as possible eliminated rather than expressed. Arguably also, the naturalness that the Daoists recommended is not simply a return to one's original nature, since the original nature of everyone includes a tendency toward anxiety and other feelings of which the Daoists disapproved.

Many of the same comments apply to the naturalness that in the 1960s beatniks often recommended, ideas reflected in the beliefs of others who find social conventions intolerably artificial. This naturalness is not naturalness within "the restraints of decorum." It does not involve giving general vent to feelings; such activity would not be "cool." It, too, is not simply a return to one's original nature, which includes tendencies toward anxiety and noncool behavior. It also is not the same as the naturalness of the Daoists. There are a number of major differences: one is that beatniks did not in general express a responsiveness to the world of nature at all comparable to the responsiveness of the Daoists. Another is that there was no parallel among beatniks to the extraordinary sophistication underlying the naturalness of the great Daoist philosophers.

At this point I have distinguished at least five senses of "naturalness" that have enjoyed some currency. Undoubtedly there are more. It should be clear that if someone says, "The important thing is to be natural," the ethical claim is highly ambiguous, and there is a wide range of possibilities as to the style of behavior recommended.

Let us examine further the sense of "naturalness" in which Confucius considers naturalness desirable. In *Analects* XII.8, Chi Tzu-ch'eng, an official, remarks, "For a man of high character to be natural is quite sufficient; what need is there of art to make him such?" The reply of Confucius's disciple Tzu-kung is quite instructive: "Your Excellency's words are those of a noble man, but a team of four horses cannot overtake the tongue. Art, as it were, is nature; as nature, so to speak, is art. The hairless hide of a tiger or a leopard is about the same as the hide of a dog or a sheep." (Waley: "Culture is just as important as inborn qualities. . . . Remove the hairs from the skin of a tiger or panther, and what is left looks just like the hairless hide of a dog or sheep.")

It is not made clear what is Chi Tzu-ch'eng's idea of "natural": whether it corresponds to "original nature," or is a proto-Daoist idea, or some amalgam of the two. Whatever it is involves a contrast between art and what is "natural." By "art" Chi Tzu-ch'eng presumably means manners, the approved styles of ceremonial behavior, and perhaps more broadly refinement and culture.

Tzu-kung's reply rests on a subtle point. As the example of the leopard and the sheep shows, what is natural is relative. What is natural for a leopard is not natural for a sheep. The point of the example is *not* that some men have fundamental and original natures as opposed as those of a leopard and a sheep. Confucius, after all, remarks that "By nature men nearly resemble each other; in practice they grow wide apart." Thus, if the example is meant to indicate that some men are as different from one another as a leopard is from a sheep, the difference is meant to be construed as one resulting from practice rather than from (original) "nature." This interpretation is bolstered by the connection that Tzu-kung establishes between art and nature. The word "art" has connotations of something that is learned; and to say that "art is nature" suggests that what a man learns may well affect what is natural relative to him.

It still may seem paradoxical to speak of naturalness in a sense in which "nature is art." The paradox disappears, however, once we stop thinking of education as merely placing a veneer over original "nature." Once we realize that education can transform what a person is, we realize that it can in a sense transform people's natures. What "comes naturally" is very much a product of training and habit.

The point can be elucidated by means of an analogy with the case of artistic creation. Because of myths about the naturalness of artistic creativity, many people expect that the production of great art is an uninhibited act of self-expression, that it involves the second kind of naturalness that Yu distinguished, the naturalness that he said "was not permissible." There undoubtedly are cases of which this is true. But the cases in which it is strikingly not true, however, are much more common. Many people have been shocked, for example, to learn of the time and effort that Beethoven put into painstaking revision of his compositions. The flow of notes in Beethoven symphonies had seemed so "natural."

The work of composers such as Bach, Haydn, and Beethoven, not to mention Stravinsky and Schoenberg, is a product of ingrained self-discipline. This is not to say that all of the compositions of all of them required painstaking revision. Some of them sometimes composed quite spontaneously and did little revising. But any spontaneous composition could occur only by virtue of the quality of spontaneous thought having been severely channeled by training and discipline. The spontaneous production of something stylized can occur only if what is stylized has become "what comes naturally."

This point holds also for writers, poets, philosophers, and so forth. Indeed, it touches on one of the most difficult things about learning to be a competent writer, poet, philosopher, historian, or literary critic. Unless the student is unusually gifted, at the beginning of the learning process the "natural" mode of production is loose and sloppy. An essential part of education requires going against the grain of what is natural. At the same time the student must not only learn to create a different style, but must also force herself or himself to assimilate this style, to the point at which it is "what comes naturally." This requires, especially in the early stages, extreme self-restraint and inhibition. It is no wonder that graduate school training seems to many students to involve the intellectual counterpart of having one's feet bound.

The result of a successful training program is thus a new "nature" and a new kind of "naturalness." The writer, artist, or composer who has become disciplined and skillful will in general develop something of a characteristic "voice" or style. Modes of expression that fit this characteristic style will come to seem "natural"; they will come to be "natural."

Thus, the flow of notes in compositions of Bach and Beethoven does, within the context of the works, sound "natural." Furthermore, if Bach or Beethoven were somehow to revert, in a portion of one of his works, to the manner of composition characteristic of an untrained musician, this would not seem "natural" in relation to the rest of the work. If the composer were to vent his feelings musically in an undisciplined way, this too would not seem natural, and indeed it is hard to imagine how Bach or Beethoven would do such a thing. It so clearly would not be natural for them.

The naturalness of the skilled composer is an analogue to the naturalness that Yu endorses. There is one major difference. The naturalness reflected in the work of a skilled composer, or an artist or literary critic, is a "compartmentalized" kind of naturalness. It represents the result of education in one area of a person's life. Confucius and his followers tended to think of education in much less compartmentalized terms than Western thinkers have.

They also assumed that the type of education that we recognize as relevant to musical or literary style is equally relevant to the style of a whole life.

The point can be put this way. Western educators devote a great deal of thought to how a pupil may become a skilled composer, or skilled in prose composition, or skilled in historical work, or for that matter a skilled mathematician, businessperson, or engineer. There has been no widespread and thorough attempt to relate this education to the style of a person's life at those moments when she or he is not exercising the special skill. (It is true that some Western philosophers have spoken of this; and also that many American schoolchildren, for example, are purportedly taught to be good citizens and to adjust to one another. But such training is generally conducted in such a simpleminded way as to discredit all such enterprises. The central point is that, besides its being quite rudimentary, it generally is detached from and unrelated to the training in special skills that our education emphasizes.)

Chinese views of education have tended to be opposite to this. Training in literary skills, for example, was not conceived as entirely detached from the education of the whole person. We take for granted the phenomenon of the literarily accomplished person who is exceedingly childish. In traditional China, such a person would be considered to represent a failure of education.

Confucius clearly thought that he was teaching his pupils more than just specialized skills. As H. G. Creel (1949, 95) puts it, "He considered the study of literature a part, but only a part, of the education of a gentleman. More basic was the cultivation of character. . . ." For Confucius the "art" that a good education should impart was more than the art of being a skilled literary man or a skilled government official. It was an art reflected in a pupil's whole character and style of life.

With this in mind, we can clearly perceive Confucius's estimation of various sorts of naturalness. "Naturalness that is not permissible" for him would represent falling back to a lower style. The process of becoming a Confucian worthy is in large part the process of creating an advanced style of life by means of training and effort. If someone who is in the midst of this process acts "natural" in the sense of "letting oneself go," he or she is forfeiting the benefits of education. For someone who has already become a Confucian worthy such behavior no longer by any stretch of words can be said to "come naturally."

To be natural in the sense of acting out one's original nature can have good features, especially if original nature involves *jen*. (If original nature involves *jen*, then a highly developed nature should retain features of original nature. Mencius, who stressed this view, held that "The great man is he who does not lose his child's heart" [a, book VI, B. 12, 322]). However, to be natural in this sense in a thoroughgoing way would again for Confucius (and perhaps also for Mencius) involve forfeiting the benefits of education. It would involve acting like a rustic.

To be natural in a Daoist or beatnik manner would represent, in part, a repudiation of good education. It would implicitly deny the value of those complex styles of behavior that, through education, can become natural. It also, incidentally, would implicitly deny "nature" in the sense of original nature. Tendencies toward anxiety and other noncool emotional states are arguably part of original human nature. Daoists considered that the true path involved entirely suppressing these emotions, but Confucius instead favored harmonizing and controlling them. As *The Doctrine of the Mean* says, "When men try to pursue a course, which is far from the common indications of consciousness, this course cannot be considered The Path" (128).

The naturalness that Confucius favors represents the thorough assimilation of a higher style of life that, however, is grounded in original nature: it is not "far from the common indications of consciousness." This higher style of life is closely related to Confucius's conception of morality. In order to understand this, we have to examine Confucius's conception of *li* (propriety).

The term *li* is very often discussed in relation to established rules governing ritual behavior or moral choice. Certainly *li* is very closely related to rules and traditions. Commentators who stress this side of the Confucian conception of *li* inevitably interpret Confucius as a basically conservative figure. However, a case can be made for saying that Confucius's *li* involves much more than simply a close reliance on rules and traditions. Creel (1949, 85) has made this case. He argues that Confucian *li* involves not only a knowledge of the traditional practices of society but also "the ability to modify them as circumstances and common sense might require." Evidence for Creel's view is found throughout the *Analects* in Confucius's general avoidance of pat solutions and in his willingness to adjust to a student's personality what he says to that student. Confucius does not stress rote learning of an established and precise code of behavior. Indeed, he appears to regard this kind of thing as dangerous. "The honest countryman is the spoiler of morals" (XVII.13.). Conversely, he prided himself (XVIII.8.) on his flexibility: "With me there is no inflexible 'thou shalt' or 'thou shalt not.' "

If Creel is right, and Confucius's *li* requires more than just the application of established rules, then we face intriguing questions concerning moral decisions. How do we decide in a difficult case what is right? How do we achieve *li* in a case in which traditional rules may need to be modified? We may attempt an answer as follows. First, an important element in *li* has to be *jen*. The person of true propriety has to be basically benevolent. She or he also has to be impartial and open-minded. Thus, "The master was entirely free from four things: he had no preconceptions, no predeterminations, no obduracy, and no egoism" (IX.4).

However, *jen*, impartiality, and open-mindedness are not always enough. Some moral problems involve many conflicting considerations and (to use Ross's language) many conflicting prima facie duties. In such cases well-meaning and impartial people may feel at a loss for a solution. Confucius as much as any philosopher recognized this. It was for this reason that he considered education and culture relevant to moral development. Some of the elements of education and culture that Confucius stressed—for example, music—might seem unrelated to morality. But Confucius remarks, "Let the character be formed by the poets; established by the laws of right behavior; and perfected by music" (VIII.8).

The ideal product of good education in any case cannot be merely someone who by precise calculation knows what is good. Precise calculation is impossible with regard to a problem that cannot be solved simply by means of established rules. Furthermore, the education that Confucius himself provided was quite unlike a technical education and clearly was designed to produce people who were not merely moral technicians; what Confucius requires of a superior man, rather, is that he gravitate to the right moral solution, to the appropriate action in a difficult situation. What he "feels like" doing is what is right. Something like this is indicated by Confucius's claim that "At seventy I could follow the desires of my heart without transgressing the right" (II.4).

In other words, the person who truly possesses *li* is the one who naturally makes the appropriate choice. Only she or he can be counted upon to make the right choice in those difficult situations that are not clearly covered by established rules. Also, there is a sense in which only someone with Confucian naturalness will behave really appropriately in those ritual situations that are covered by established rules. This is because, for Confucius, the manner of performing an action is at least as important as the broadly defined character of the action. Thus, "In the usages of decorum it is naturalness that is of value."

Confucius's naturalness is the key not only to an ideal moral nature but also to an ideal psychological harmony. The ideal person is sincere, having a thoroughgoing harmony among thoughts, words, and actions. This harmony among thoughts, words, and actions is comparable, to use the aesthetic analogy again, with the harmony among the works of an accomplished and mature composer. Just as almost any composition by Beethoven has that in it which enables the trained listener to recognize it as something by Beethoven, so ideally any word or action on the part of an accomplished Confucian worthy should have that in it which makes it recognizably related to the entire character.

Confucius considers the value of this higher naturalness to be quite considerable. Furthermore, it has the special feature of being an "inner" value and is thereby much more clearly within the control of the individual who has it than the "outer" values associated with wealth, fame, community standing, and love. The Confucian worthy who values most of all his or her naturalness need be less concerned about chance events than most people are. Thus, "The noble man is calm and serene, the inferior man is continually worried and anxious" (VII.36).

Confucius's discussion of naturalness thus offers much more than just an analysis of what is meant by "being natural." It is highly relevant to the problem of moral decision in difficult cases. It also suggests important answers to the questions "what is valuable?" and "what is most valuable?" Since John Stuart Mill, many British and American philosophers have discussed these questions in ways reminiscent of economics: in terms of the accretion of experiences or pleasures by faceless consumers. The notion that important values can be achieved only by a change of character has not often been explored. Thus, in this and other areas, discussions such as Confucius's can help to remind contemporary British and American ethical philosophers of what they have been missing.

3

TRADITION AND COMMUNITY IN THE FORMATION OF SELF

Call the world if you Please "The vale of Soul-making".... There may be intelligences or sparks of the divinity in millions—but they are not Souls till they acquire identities, till each one is personally itself.

John Keats (1970, 249–50), from a letter to his brother and sister-in-law in Kentucky, 1819

This chapter will explore the role of tradition and community in the process in which a human being becomes "personally itself." The argument will be (1) that tradition and community are constitutive as well as causal factors, so that they will contribute to elements of the soul or self that is formed, (2) that how they do this has a great deal to do with the excellence of the result, and (3) that Confucius gives an exceptionally good account of this in the stages corresponding to advanced education. All quotations in this essay from Confucius are from the Arthur Waley translation.

Our exploration will begin with the early stages and the development in childhood of the foundation of self. Then we will examine the development in teenage and early adult years, and how someone becomes a really good person. Finally, we need to pay some attention to general issues concerning the unity of the self and also creativity. To become personally oneself is an exceptionally important activity, and if done well can be a creative achievement; we will need to examine the role of tradition and community in creativity generally.

The Development in Childhood of
the Foundation of Self

Erik Erikson (1968, 160) has observed that "the community often underestimates to what extent a long intricate childhood history has restricted a youth's further choice of identity change." Aristotle would not have been surprised by this observation. The *Nicomachean Ethics* is full of comments on the ethical importance of early upbringing and on how it should be managed. The *Analects*, in contrast, has relatively little that is explicitly on the subject. If we ask why this is so, when Confucius has so much to say about the advanced stages of ethical development, a variety of answers suggest themselves. One is that teachers and writers, including philosophers, often do not say what does not need to be said: what it can be assumed that virtually everyone in the audience already knows. It simply may be that early upbringing had become more problematic in Aristotle's Greece than it was in Confucius's China. Also, Confucius himself functioned primarily as an educator, all the while in search of other roles. His students were no longer small children when they arrived, and it would be natural for him to have much more to say about the stage of their ethical development in which he had a major role than about much earlier stages. Finally, it is natural to regard early childhood ethical development as the province of the family. Confucius has a great deal to say on the subject of family life and its importance. But this concern with family life is compatible with regarding some matters as best left to the judgment of parents.

The broad outlines of what Confucius and his circle thought family relations should be are evident, as are the social ramifications of proper family structure. The *Analects* quotes Master Yu as saying, "Those who in private life behave well towards their parents and elder brothers, in public life seldom show a disposition to resist the authority of their superiors" (I.2, 83). Proper family attitudes are the trunk of goodness.

Aristotle is far more specific on early childhood training techniques. "We ought to be brought up in a particular way from our very youth, as Plato says, so as to delight in and to be pained by the things that we ought . . ." (II.3, 1744). Our more mature delight and pain are the result of childhood management (by parents and others) of pleasure and pain, which in a rather Pavlovian manner establishes predispositions to feel pleasure and pain at certain things or thoughts. This management is central to early childhood education. "In educating the young we steer them by the rudders of pleasure and pain . . ." (X.1, 1852).

This observation about pleasure and pain is linked to an emphasis on habit as a factor in the foundation of goodness. In much of our adult life we behave characteristically, expressing established predispositions. As Aristotle says, we become just by doing just acts and temperate by doing temperate ones (II.4, 1745). Childhood patterning reinforced by pleasure and pain is crucial.

It would be tempting to regard the right set of habits as the core, and perhaps nearly the whole, of personal goodness. But Aristotle knew that this would be an exaggeration, for two reasons. One is that even someone who is a creature of habits can encounter major temptations, in which habit-violating actions promise great pleasure (or at least the thought of them is very pleasant). Even Pavlov's dogs might well break their training under such circumstances. One element of protection in Aristotle's view seems to be a habit of associating incontinent or antisocial behavior with pain, which can add a painful element to what would otherwise be pleasant thoughts of habit-violating behavior. Plainly this element can be supplied by persistent measures that make incontinent or antisocial behavior in early childhood come out to be, on balance, painful, thus creating a habit of painful thoughts to be associated with it. This is the most plausible explanation of what Aristotle has in mind by the "rudder of pain."

A second reason that habits, including habits of connecting painful thoughts with certain kinds of transgressions, can never be entirely protective is that they will have power chiefly when someone is faced with familiar options in familiar kinds of circumstance. Their power, conversely, will be limited when the choice is among alternatives that may not be readily classifiable (so that someone may not identify what he or she is about to do as a transgression), or when the agent is disoriented by unusual circumstances in which the choice is presented. Familiar modern examples are choices made during wartime, or after social upheavals, or by people who have moved into occupations whose rules are not clear. Various psychological experiments, the most famous of which are the ones initiated by Stanley Milgram, have shown that a majority of people (most of whom must be presumed to have been moderately decent in ordinary life) will do appalling things in circumstances so unusual that ordinary standards might seem not to apply, especially if someone who seems reliable suggests to them that what they are about to do is really quite normal (see Milgram 1974; also Haney et al. 1973). The desire to ingratiate oneself, to be agreeable, appears to play a part in these cases. Perhaps this kind of thing is part of what Confucius had in mind in his observation that "The 'honest villager' spoils true virtue" (XVII.13, 213)? To be reliably good in familiar everyday situations is not necessarily to be a genuinely good person.

Aristotle certainly would have been familiar with Plato's thought experiment in the Myth of Er of Book X of the *Republic* (St. 619, p. 877). Er is reported to have had a near-death experience in which he saw the spirits of the dead, in the underworld, choosing new lives. One, who had completed a decent life in a well-regulated city, chose the life of a tyrant. Yielding to this glittering (and ruinous) temptation might seem inexplicable; but Plato remarks of the man, "His virtue was a matter of habit only, and he had no philosophy." There is nothing to suggest that Aristotle differs from Plato on this issue. A good set of habits, including the habit of having painful thoughts on appropriate occasions, will constitute the foundation of personal goodness in Aristotle's view and will not constitute goodness itself. The habits are a prelude to philosophy and are required in order to hear the philosophy in the right spirit.

Aristotle's last word on the subject in the *Nicomachean Ethics* lays this out. "The soul of the student must first have been cultivated by means of habits for noble joy and noble hatred, like earth which is to nourish the seed. . . . The character, then, must somehow be there already with a kinship to excellence . . ." (X.9, 1864). The phrase "kinship to excellence" is meant, I think, to do justice to the phenomenon of the very good child, who has not fully become a very good person, but who is clearly on her or his way and already has qualities that resemble those of a very good person.

How do we create such very good children? It is here that Aristotle deviates most sharply from what Confucius almost certainly would have said. Aristotle insists that what are required are right *laws*. Sparta is referred to as a place where they take these things seriously, rather than allowing (as in most states) each man to live "as he pleases, Cyclops-fashion, 'to his own wife and children dealing law' " (X.9, 1864–65).

It is well known that Confucius did not place emphasis on law as a contributory factor in social harmony or ethical development. He remarks, "I could try a civil suit as well as anyone. But better still to bring it about that there were no civil suits!" (XII.13, 167) Criminal law similarly is marginalized. "Govern the people by regulations, keep order among them by chastisements, and they will flee from you, and lose all self-respect" (II.3, 88).

Crime and wrongdoing have to be seen as (by and large?) symptomatic of social evils such as poverty. Ordinary people who are daring and are suffering from great poverty will not long be law-abiding (VIII.10, 134). The ruler who wishes to create a law-abiding polity in which the people trust their rulers has a first priority of seeing that the people have enough to eat (XII.7, 164; see also XII.9; XIII.9).

None of this should be read as a rejection of law or, for that matter, of legal punishments. "Where gentlemen think only of punishments, the commoners think only of exemptions" (IV. 11, 104). This statement certainly suggests that Confucius believes in applying the full force of the law on some occasions. It may be linked to Confucius's scorn for those who are capable of spending a whole day together without ever once discussing questions of right and wrong, who "content themselves with performing petty acts of clemency"(XV. 16, 196–97).

A plausible interpretation of Confucius's position is that law should be, both socially and ethically, a seldom-used tool of last resort, and that in any society frequent and heavy-handed legal compulsion is a sign that the ruling group is either ineffective or full of corrupt desires (cf. XII.18) or both. An analogy might be with a teacher's use of discipline in a schoolroom full of young children. It can be a sign of inexperienced or poor teaching if discipline is constantly accentuated; conversely, a skilled teacher who is like a polestar (see II.1) to the class will normally (i.e., barring unusually difficult conditions surrounding the classroom) have little need for this.

Thus, there is every reason to think that Confucius would have been incredulous at Aristotle's suggestion that law should have an important role in the education of young children. A more fundamental difference is that Confucius clearly regards as very important the role of the ruler as an attractive model of what a person should be, like the polestar (II.1, 88). When the ruler of Lu suggests that he could kill those who do not have the Way in order to encourage those who do, Confucius immediately counters by emphasizing the way in which a ruler's goodness can modify the nature of the people (like wind over grass): "If you desire what is good, the people will at once be good" (XII.19, 168). "If the ruler himself is upright, all will go well even though he does not give orders" (XIII.6, 173). Conversely, we see Confucius's harsh diagnosis of the ruler of Lu's trouble with thieves: "If only you were free from desire, they would not steal even if you paid them to" (XII.18, 167). The negative moral force of the ruler's greedy desires is part of the problem. To put Confucius's message in a contemporary framework: conspicuous greed among the upper orders creates an atmosphere of greed that encourages crime among those below.

The general analogy between rulers and parents can be taken as informative in both directions. Good parents, like good rulers, influence their charges by their moral force as role models. Confucius presumably would have regarded punishment in both domains as an undesirable last resort.

It is important not to assume that the contrast here is clearer than it is, or to oversimplify. I am not suggesting that Confucius would totally reject Aristotle's line of thought about the rudders of pleasure and pain. One should bear in mind that pleasure and pain can be conveyed even to young children in a variety of ways: silent reproach from someone who is loved can lead to a train of painful thoughts, and enthusiastic smiles can be wonderfully pleasurable. Thus there is no reason to associate habituation linked to pleasure and pain with only the least subtle (and often most counterproductive) measures that might be employed. The chief difference between Aristotle's and Confucius's moral psychology, as it pertains to young children, is, I think, the latter's emphasis on the educational use of role modeling. It is plausible to say that, in Confucius's view, the greatest contribution parents can make to the ethical education of young children is to make them want to become people of an ethically developed sort. Adult goodness, in this view, typically owes a great deal to imitation, as well as to habituation that may be reinforced by management of pleasure and pain.

Implicit in the Confucian model is that tradition and community values enter the lives of young children primarily through their parents. Community values do not by themselves constitute goodness; think of the "honest villager." But Confucius would certainly have regarded these rudiments of everyday virtue as a major approach to goodness. An unwillingness to engage in deceit, dishonesty, and violent behavior is, to say the least, required for goodness. It is arguable also that effective agency requires relationships within a community (see Wong 1988, 327 ff.). Community values provide categories that structure one's experience of human actions (see Kovesi 1967). A sometimes derided function of parents is to convey to children how their actions might seem to others in the community. This can be seen as basic education in the categories of social life.

Beyond this, the lessons of community values can be refined in the development of reflective culture. We can acquire a more subtle sense of the varieties of harm that we should not inflict on others, avoiding actions that might not strike the "honest villager" as wrong. There also can be a growing awareness of connecting elements in what appears to most people to be a hodgepodge of recommendations (cf. "the one thread" in *Analects* IV. 15, 105; XV. 2, 193).

The role of parents in introducing traditions to young children is more complicated and also is often less conscious. Perhaps the rudiments of a culture are conveyed in the songs and stories that children learn. Clearly there are lessons in how to live, exemplified in the behavior of heroes and heroines of these stories, in comments on everyday occurrences, and of course in the ways in which parents themselves behave. A complication is that the sum of these messages will inform the child not only about cultural norms but also about cultural anti-norms. One learns about the available repertoire of ways of being a bad (or merely not-so-good) person. Thus, the child who is developing a self learns early that there is a limited menu of major options. These will add up to a very large number of possibilities, all the same, partly because it is always possible to combine features taken from more than one model of life, and mainly because of the possibility of idiosyncratic variation on a basic orientation. Furthermore, there can be unusual cases in which someone, strongly driven by a sense of vocation that is almost impossible to formulate, creates a not entirely coherent self that in major respects does not approximate any existing models. Thus, it was possible to become a lonely, emotionally troubled genius in the European middle ages. But it became much more possible in the nineteenth century.

It is arguable that people's personalities usually are largely determined by the time they pass from childhood to adolescence. Some philosophers have thought this, most notably Sartre, who believed that a basic choice of self in childhood structures a person's choices throughout her or his life, rendering people largely predictable (see Sartre 1943, 453 ff.). The freedom that many people associate with Sartre's philosophy involves either subtle variations on what is dictated by the basic choice in childhood, or (more importantly) the ever-present possibility that one could reconsider that choice and adopt different patterns of behavior (something, however, that, in his view, is very difficult and may require psychoanalytic help).

It may be, as I suggested earlier, that people's personalities usually are largely determined by the time they pass from childhood to adolescence, and that their characters are not. A certain temperament and style of interacting with other people, along with a way of pursuing one's projects and goals, can be compatible with great goodness and also with moral depravity. If we adhere to psychoanalytic models, whether Freudian or existential, it is easy to regard the formation of self as largely complete by the onset of adolescence. If, on the other hand, we think of virtue or its lack as a crucial element of self, it becomes clear that much remains to be decided.

Becoming Really Good

One suggestion that Confucius, like Aristotle, thought of education in real goodness as something that took place against the background of a partly formed self is the exchange between Tzu-kung and Confucius reported in I.15 (p. 87) of the *Analects*. Tzu-kung begins with "Poor without cadging, rich without swagger," to which Confucius counters "Poor, yet delighting in the Way; rich, yet a student of ritual." Tzu-kung then picks up the theme, quoting the *Songs*: "As thing cut, as thing filed, / As thing chiseled, as thing polished." Confucius is delighted by the acuity this displays.

A number of Confucian themes are captured in this small space, and they are worth noting. First of all, the extreme allusiveness of the dialogue answers to a basic Confucian conception of what constitutes effective teaching. It must present only, as it were, a corner of the subject, leaving the student to complete the rest (cf. V. 8, 109; VII.8, 124). Confucius never engages in the "spoon-feeding" that is characteristic of so much American undergraduate teaching. If the goal is to develop really good people, his teaching strategy makes a great deal of sense, in that it engages the student and forces the student to be active rather than passive. We have already seen that passive absorption of an ethics does not guarantee reliable goodness, and it is plausible that only someone who comes of himself or herself to certain conclusions is likely to internalize them properly.

Second, there is a wealth of meaning in Confucius's initial reply to Tzu-kung. "Poor, yet delighting in the Way" may remind us of Confucius's view that it is unreasonable to expect the poor very generally to be law-abiding in times of great poverty, especially when they receive poor examples from above. This view is a generalization about human nature under pressure to which there are implicit exceptions. (There is some parallel to Plato's presentation of the Myth of Gyges in Book II of the *Republic*: there it is suggested to the reader that people who find a ring of invisibility, and realize that with it they could do anything with impunity, could not be trusted, but the reader is meant to think that this would not be true of Socrates.) A truly good person of course would be law-abiding and would continue to delight in the Way, even in poverty.

"Rich, yet a student of ritual" reminds us that ritual may seem more important to those in dependent positions than to those who are wealthy and powerful. (One might think of the ways in which rudeness has sometimes been taken, in some societies, as an aristocratic privilege.) Ritual is never completely and finally mastered, particularly in that it includes implicit attitudes and messages conveyed by posture of the body, facial expressions, and by the timing of one's movements. The way in which such nuances can be important is conveyed by Confucius's comment (II.8, 89) that demeanor, above and beyond specific actions, is crucial in the treatment of parents. Therefore, a good person will remain a student of ritual.

This is consonant with Confucius's repeated insistence that he himself had much (in general) to learn from others (cf. VII.3, 123; VII.21, 127; IX.7, 140). Perfection is never presented as a realizable goal. It is a hallmark of a gentleman that he "grieves at his own incapacities" (XIV. 32, 188).

It is important that the central message of I.15 is conveyed by a quotation from the *Book of Songs*. That collection might seem to most modern readers to have a folk song–like quality and to be without any significant philosophical or ethical content. (This quality is brought out nicely in the translation by Arthur Waley, and in some ways even more so in the translation by Ezra Pound.) Yet the masters of allusiveness found much of ethical importance in this source. A good student might be expected to know the *Songs*, as Tzu-kung did, and to be able (quite rapidly) to cite the right text in relation to a line of thought. This element of cultural tradition, in short, was seen as a wellspring of ethical insight.

Finally, we have to take seriously what Tzu-kung saw in the song he quoted. It refers, as did the earlier sayings, to the ethical ideal. The process of becoming the best kind of person involves something akin to cutting, filing, chiseling, and polishing. (We might speak of fine-tuning, but the point is essentially the same.) What is required, in short, is nothing like a conversion experience or a drastic realignment of character. Rather, it is a slow and subtle process of refinement, which can be viewed as a number of kinds of adjustment (like cutting, filing, etc.) rather than a single unified change. Refinement will work, of course, only if what is refined is already near to true goodness:

there must be the right kind of partly formed self at the outset of this stage. The *Songs* and ritual both play a part in the creation of this protoself, but that does not mean that they cannot also have a role in its further refinement.

There may be a natural progression. At one point Confucius says, "Let a man be first incited by the *Songs*, then given a firm footing by the study of ritual, and finally perfected by music" (VIII.8, 134). One of the uses of the *Songs*, apart from their implicit messages, is to incite emotions (XVII 9, 212). Ritual, on the other hand, comes after groundwork (III.8, 95–96).

What music does is more subtle. Good music can be delightful. But the quality of music also is ethically and politically important. Confucius, like Plato, thought it to be important to insist on the right sorts of music. He wanted to do away with the licentious tunes of Cheng (XV. 10, 195–96), which presumably were like the Lydian and Ionian harmonies that Plato (*Republic*, Book III) thought so little of. It is important when Lu reforms its music (IX.14, 141–42).

We know that Confucius himself played the zithern (XVII.20, 214) and that he made evident his enthusiasm for good music (cf. VII.13, 125; VIII.15, 135). All the same, music means "more than bells and drums" (XVII.11, 212). It may be that Confucius's view of the power of good music is like the view of aesthetic goodness developed by I. A. Richards (1925; see also Richards 1932). This is that the mark of aesthetic goodness is a work's function in rendering the psychological system (especially the attitudes) of one who appreciates it more balanced and nuanced. We know that a view in some respects like this was taken seriously in Confucius's circle. The disciple Tzu-yu, given command of a small walled town, teaches music and promotes musical performances (XVII.4, 209–10). Confucius teases him about it, comparing it to using an ox-cleaver to kill a chicken, but has to admit that there is some reasonable basis for Tzu-yu's policy.

We can appreciate best the roles of tradition and community in the Confucian process of refining goodness if we contrast Confucius's view of the transition from conventional goodness to real goodness with that of the *Nicomachean Ethics*. The two views are often considered to be similar, in that neither Aristotle nor Confucius (despite his references to the "one thread") regards the best choices as algorithms derivable from fundamental principles or standards. Nor does either place emphasis (as many Western philosophers, including Kant, have) on a motivation to follow certain familiar general rules as a key element in personal goodness. Further, the Confucian *Doctrine of the Mean* is similar in many respects to Aristotle's account of the mean. Nevertheless, there are important and interesting differences in the two accounts of what is required for genuine goodness.

Aristotle, as is well known, emphasizes judgment of particulars (cf. VI.11, 1805–6). Experience and maturity help to develop this ability. "Therefore we ought to attend to the undemonstrated sayings and opinions of experienced and older people or of people of practical wisdom not less than to demonstrations. . . . [E]xperience has given them an eye they see aright" (1806). We need to become good judges not only of particular cases (in areas of life that are not simply rule governed) but also of our own characteristic failings and distortions of judgment. Aristotle recommends that, in attempting to reach a mean between excess and defect, we adjust our aim slightly further (than we might) away from the extreme to which we are predisposed, as a way of compensating for personal bias (II.9, 1751).

The image is of continuing education in problem solving. One's basic orientation was provided by the early stage of ethical education, which besides establishing good habits would have made one hate what should be hated, admire what should be admired, and so forth. Advanced ethical education is seen as primarily intellectual. Aristotle shares this with Plato, one difference being of course the greater role for Plato of mathematics in this intellectual development (whereas for Aristotle sensitivity to particulars and to the ways in which they are connected assumes paramount importance). Clearly both Plato and Aristotle believe that a genuinely good person internalizes goodness in ways in which a conventionally good person does not, but this emerges as a natural result of superior intellectual development supervening on a sound basic orientation.

One way of beginning to see the contrast between Confucius and Aristotle is to establish a model of the situation in which one must make a decision. For Aristotle, there will be a range of alternatives, along with one's ability to discriminate among them and to be aware of one's own characteristic weaknesses of judgment. Perhaps friends have advised one about some of these. The important thing is to judge well. It may be unrealistic to think of an optimal solution, but one must choose well enough. Aristotle seems to be a believer in what recently has been termed "satisficing."

In Confucius's model, there is more than one person playing this game and more than one possible point of view on the outcomes. A gentleman (II.14, 91) "can see a question from all sides without bias. The small man is biased and can see a question only from one side." To appreciate more than one point of view is typically to realize that there are pros and cons. Confucius looks at these (IX.7, 140), suggesting more of a view of superior ethical judgment as (at least sometimes) a form of negotiation within human relationships than Aristotle provides. Even rulers must win over the people. Among the three evils described in III.26 is "high office filled by men of narrow views." (The alternative translations "not tolerant" or "intolerant" support the same point, if one bears in mind that to be tolerant is to take account of and to accommodate other views.)

Training in ritual and in music can be conducive to not having narrow views, especially in that ritual and music often (although not always) involve performance by more than one person, such that one must relate one's actions and demeanor to those of others. Training in ritual and music is important in other ways. Once we stop thinking of ethical deliberation as necessarily a search for single optimally correct solutions, the role of nuances—especially the style with which something is done—can seem important. The right kind of training in ritual and music is training in style. It can lead to a harmonization of subtle gestures and of the attitudes that they express. Harmony (I.12) is crucial in the practice of ritual. Solutions to ethical problems typically are performed as well as thought, and some harmonization of style with others (along with responsiveness of ethical judgment) is part of reasonable accommodation.

This belief in harmony is consistent with a belief in the "one thread" of the *Analects*, which, like *li*, should not be thought of as like an ethical principle that serves as an algorithm for (or a precise test of) ethical solutions. A better analogy is with a theme, which in various contexts can be expressed in more or less good ways.

We are now in a position to see more clearly the contrast between Confucius and Aristotle as regards the advanced stage of development of self, and also to see how Confucius's emphasis on tradition and community is implicated in this contrast. Confucius and Aristotle share an assumption that advanced ethical education, in order to be effective, must take place against the background of an already somewhat developed good character. Ornament and substance, Confucius says (VI.16, 119), must be duly blended. I have suggested that Confucius and Aristotle also share the view that ethical judgment often looks for good, rather than perfect or optimal, solutions.

Within this shared framework, Aristotle gives us a picture of the search for good solutions that is literally timeless. The Aristotelian would-be good person of course does (or should) have experience of how various policies work out and situations develop. But she or he will act in a way that is not portrayed as dependent upon, or stylistically tinctured by, the ways in which others have acted before. Neither will cultural accomplishments of the past, comparable to the *Book of Songs* or (see *Analects* II.21) the *Book of Documents*, play a part in readying someone to behave as a very good person.

Tradition is, in Confucius's presentation of the development of a good self, not only a source of inspiration and advice but also (more important) a source of modeling. The right kind of parent-child relation, in his view, has this character. One develops a self that of course is separate but is not entirely separate: there will be elements reminiscent of parents, who in turn had developed selves that included elements reminiscent of their parents, and so on. Rituals and music have an authority that derives in part from the ways in which they encapsulate styles of behavior and of feeling from the past. In listening to the music, or in performing the music or the rituals, one enters into (to some degree) these styles and makes them part of oneself.

Community also assumes a prominent role in the Confucian presentation of the development of a good self. In the foreground of the picture are the ways in which choice occurs within the context of a variety of points of view, which should be taken account of and often should be to some degree reconciled. Confucian development of the self also is very much in the context of what David Hume (*Treatise*, book 2, part 2, sec. 5, 365) called mirroring fellow minds. Other people's opinions of us need to be taken seriously. Even if they fail to appreciate whatever virtues we have, they still may have noticed something in us that requires work; or it may be that we need to work on the ways in which we communicate to others. Finally, goodness can infect a community. Moral force, Confucius says, "never dwells in solitude; it will always bring neighbours" (IV. 25, 106). This is one of the reasons that it is goodness "that gives to a neighbourhood its beauty" (IV. 1, 102).

The themes of the ethical importance of tradition and community have not been entirely absent from Western philosophy. Alasdair MacIntyre is an example of a contemporary philosopher who takes both seriously and has interesting things to say about them. David Wong's argument that effective agency requires relationships within the community also has been mentioned. Less recently, both Hume and Hegel come to mind as philosophers who assigned great importance to community. I want to suggest, though, that Confucius is uniquely good in his articulation of a moral psychology that explores the role of both tradition and community in the advanced stages of development of a very good self. He also offers a model in which tradition and community are not merely causal contributors but also are constitutive of the self that develops.

In Confucius's view, the self that a person develops (assuming that things go reasonably well) will be based on a primitive layer of imitation of parents (who have imitated their parents, etc.), as well as of behavior that has been encouraged by parents. Are these things merely causes of the person one becomes? It is hard to deny that they become, generally speaking, constitutive. Often, that is, an adult will be acting, thinking, and talking much as her or his parents did, or in a manner retained and refined from childhood. It may be too much to speak of survival of some lives in other lives, or of children in adults. But much like quotations within a text, the adult self will include elements taken from outside or taken from earlier stages. Something like this is true also of the borrowings from tradition (e.g., *The Book of Songs*) and from the community-based interactions involved in ritual.

The distinction here between what is constitutive and what is merely causal is neither sharp nor precise. Certainly it would be rare for an element in someone's character or psychic life to be exactly the same as one in a parent or a traditional source. But there can be a degree of resemblence comparable to that between elements of different stages of the same person's life, and if the degree is fairly high, we would be inclined to speak of more than a merely causal relation.

Clearly, if there are such strong connections, the quality of the sources matters a great deal. The child of thugs has much to overcome; although interesting forms of departure, yielding good results, are possible. We are not condemned to be thoroughly like our parents, and what is present at a primitive layer of self can become inverted in subsequent development. Nevertheless, it is—from a Confucian, and indeed from almost any point of view—a great advantage in life to have good parents. Similarly, rituals of cruelty and absorption of soft and sentimental music can be (in the Confucian view, and in many others) major handicaps in the development of self. Even if we are not immediately aware in every case of their roles in the selves that develop, we can see that there is a case for regarding the qualities of ritual and of music as ethically important.

Elements of recognition of this importance can be found in many philosophies, including Plato's. The citations thus far should make clear, though, that Confucius is exceptional in the detail and persistence of his comment on these factors in the development of self. This, plus the complexity and subtlety of what he has to say, constitutes one of the excellences of his philosophy.

The Unity of the Self, and Creativity

The remainder of this chapter will discuss some general issues concerning the self and also the creativity that can be at work in the development of self. It might be raised as an objection, either to Confucius (as I have portrayed him) or to my own view, that to regard a self as typically constituted in part by elements derived from outside sources is both to undermine (or deny) the unity of the self and to slight the creativity involved in becoming "personally oneself." I want to suggest that such objections would reflect widespread misunderstandings, both of the self and of what creativity is.

Let us begin with the self and explore a view that seems to me very plausible; it cannot be attributed to Confucius, but does seem at least to be consistent with what he says. Call it the self-as-collage. It holds that typically an adult's self can be viewed as layers that represent the absorption (or sometimes, rejection) of various influences at various stages of life, going back to early childhood. Different layers of the self will be evident under different circumstances. How this happens depends very much on the individual. Some people, for example, are much more prone than others to be childlike in moments of relaxation or distress.

This is not to suggest that any of the layers of a person's self can be regarded as *merely* a contribution from an outside source (e.g., a childhood environment). For one thing, the degree of acceptance or rejection can vary. Also, more important, different people absorb influences in different ways. Rarely or never will a source of self be, so to speak, absorbed whole without at least some subtle modification. The selectivity of being influenced, along with the stylistic contributions, ensures that even what is very imitative will have some degree of individuality. It will be generally impossible to disentangle a personal (possibly genetic) contribution from what is owing to outside sources. And then, of course, much of the process of being influenced is not all that imitative. People frequently "take off from" what they admire. Further, the modification of sources and of layers of the self is ongoing and never ended. (This continual development is a large factor in what will be discussed later in the book as the fluidity of the self.)

In the end, whether an interpretative model such as the self-as-collage succeeds or fails depends very much on the light that it sheds (or does not shed) on particular lives. My sense is that it functions well in relation to the lives with which I am best acquainted, including my own. To speak for myself: increasingly I am aware at some moments of patterns of thought and reactive behavior that are uncannily and uncomfortably like one or the other of my parents. At other moments I find myself thinking and acting in ways that can be identified with middle class groups in the place where I grew up, Chicago, and with that time. In the midst of more subtle personal interactions there is sometimes a sense of spirit possession by a style that can be associated with the college where I was a graduate student, and (again) with that time. No doubt there are many other elements in the collage. To mention one: it is often observed that one of the results of long and reasonably successful marriages is increased similarity in responses, so that two people can come to have much the same outward look. This might be classified within demeanor, but there is much psychology that goes with it.

On the surface, this model may seem to destroy all thought of the unity of self and also to fail to leave room for character. This would be a mistaken response, for a number of reasons. First, the unity of self should not be thought of as like a single tune that is endlessly repeated throughout a life. Nor does character require that someone be predictable on any given occasion. Indeed, I have suggested elsewhere (Kupperman 1991, 15) that it can be part of someone's character that under some circumstances a style of behavior becomes not altogether unlikely. An example is a person who is capable of great cruelty: this does not imply that we can predict cruel behavior on any given occasion, but means that it sometimes is much more likely for that person than for most people.

For almost everyone there will be multiple themes, various concerns, and styles of thought and behavior that can vary drastically with context. This last point is brought out effectively in Erving Goffman's classic study *The Presentation of Self in Everyday Life*. What is recognizably the same person can be very different in different settings.

The question then becomes how well these themes, concerns, and styles of thought and behavior are integrated in a life. A highly unified life will have recurrent themes, stable major concerns, and recognizable links among styles of thought and behavior in various contexts. Other lives may have rapidly changing themes, diffuse concerns, and real discontinuities among styles of thought and behavior. In addition, behavior in some contexts may serve to undermine the purposes of behavior in other contexts. The two great nineteenth-century philosophers who are often labeled as "existentialist," Kierkegaard and Nietzsche, can be read as emphasizing the importance of having a unified self organized around a relatively small number of major projects (Nietzsche) or one central religious project (Kierkegaard). It may be that what they emphasized was already beginning to be increasingly problematic. Certainly, as modern industrial and consumer society develops, it can be taken less for granted that the influences of early childhood will be similar to later sources of self, and more diffusion of attention and interest becomes likely. Further along, increased mobility and patterns of distraction (nicely captured in Don DeLillo's novel *White Noise*) help to create the self of postmodernism.

The unity of self, in short, is a matter of degree; and it may be that a high degree of unity is (for many people) much more difficult to achieve than once would have been the case. There is no reason, though, why someone whose self is a collage of quite various elements cannot achieve a reasonable degree of unity, forging connecting links and imposing some degree of consistency on the layers of self. This process has to be understood against the background of the limits of what it is possible to achieve, through acts of will, in the management of a self. "Probably for most of us," Jonathan Glover has observed, "self-creation is a matter of a fairly disorganized cluster of smaller aims: more like building a medieval town than a planned garden city" (Glover 1988, 135; see also Glover 1983, Meyers 1989). Even limited goals, also, are normally not achieved instantly—or even quickly—by acts of will; results, if any, will be very gradual and usually require some management of the circumstances in which one places oneself, as well as one's routines.

None of these observations, understood properly, poses any challenge to the concepts of character and integrity. To have character (or a strong character) does not imply that one is exactly the same at all moments of life; but arguably it does imply that one is much the same when it really counts, and that one is reliable in important matters of the treatment of other people or the accomplishment of central projects. The account presented earlier in this chapter suggests that at least two layers of self are especially involved. A relatively primitive early layer (or layers) that includes habits and attitudes toward others that are reasonably cooperative and "decent," along perhaps with habits of persevering toward personal goals, will be important. So also will be a more sophisticated layer that includes abilities to make allowances for nuances and for unusual circumstances (especially in orienting onself toward a mean in making a difficult decision), and also the ability to be skeptical of authority or of pressures to go along with others in order to be agreeable. These layers can be integrated in a style of life that is reasonably consistent where it counts. Many people do it.

A truly integrated self nowadays may seem like a creative achievement. Let us look at creativity and at the insane (but alluring) idea that true creativity is ex nihilo. The only cure is to look at examples of people who actually are creative and (even better) to listen to them. Igor Stravinsky has remarked that "The more art is controlled, limited, worked over, the more it is free." He insists that limits are required for creativity. "If everything is permissible to me, the best and the worst; if nothing offers me any resistance, then any effort is inconceivable, and I cannot use anything as a basis, and consequently every undertaking becomes futile" (Stravinsky 1970, 85).

This comment suggests that there is more than one way in which creative efforts, including those involved in self-creation, can use the surrounding culture and its traditions. These can be useful as starting points to draw upon and be inspired by (as Stravinsky used his Russian predecessors and selected early composers, such as Gesualdo and Pergolesi, whom he admired). But traditions can also be starting points against which one reacts and that thus provide a kind of creative leverage. Tradition, in Stravinsky's view, is "entirely different from habit. . . . A real tradition is not the relic of a past that is irretrievably gone; it is a living force that animates and informs the present" (75).

The point is not merely that creative things can be done with (and within) a tradition. It is also that it is impossible (or at least virtually impossible) to do creative things without a tradition. The creativity that is important in developing a self, to adapt Stravinsky's model, will always occur within a context (supplied by tradition and by the surrounding community) that will provide themes, the beginnings of elements of style, perhaps menus of options, and quite possibly loci of resistance. Despite the influences and all of the other causal factors, there will be moments of (a degree of) self-creation, in which one accepts, shapes, modifies, or tries to reject elements of what one has begun to be.

The result will be to be "personally oneself." This self-creation is something that is often done in a haphazard and fairly thoughtless way, but it can be done intelligently and well. Confucius offers an exceptionally rich moral psychology that offers guidelines on how to accomplish this.

4

THE FORMATION OF SELF

Afterword

What lessons are we to draw, apart from the general recommendation that issues of development of self should be central to ethical philosophy? Here are three specific suggestions for the practice of contemporary philosophers. One is to use a wider variety of examples, resisting the imbalance that results from almost exclusive use of cases of dramatic, "one-off" choice. Choices that make sense only within a pattern of habit or commitment need more attention. Most fundamentally, of course, the problems of someone who wishes to make changes in who she or he is (or who ought to be encouraged to have this wish) need to be taken more seriously.

Second, examples need sometimes to be contextualized. There is a natural temptation to seek brevity and also the generality brought by abstraction. Ethical philosophers now so regularly succumb to this temptation that a reader who comes from outside the field might think that contemporary ethics is meant to govern a universe of stick figures. Biographical and literary contextualization can help to remedy this problem. It is instructive that three great ancient ethical philosophies, to be found in the *Analects* of Confucius, the *Dialogues* of Plato, and early Buddhist texts, are presented in the context of what amounts to a biography of a central figure. In all three, biographical details help to complete the meaning.

Third, if development of self is the central problem of ethics, then empirical evidence, including that provided by modern social psychology, is highly relevant. The time has passed when philosophers of science could be largely ignorant of all of the sciences and writers of books in aesthetics could have only a superficial knowledge of any of the arts. In a comparable way, philosophers of ethics need to know something about the human sciences. The insights that these provide complement, and in no case that I know of conflict with, those that can be derived from the wisdom of a philosopher like Confucius.

What Confucius and other members (such as Mencius) of the Confucian school have to offer is presented in a way that is heavily contextualized in a time and a cultural setting. Many details will seem to a contemporary reader to be both exotic and philosophically irrelevant. Nevertheless, at the core is a set of philosophical judgments (whose interconnections and also relation to experience constitute an argument) about the formation of self that largely survive decontextualization. Any philosopher who wishes to take seriously what has been argued here to be central to ethics is best advised not to start from scratch, when so much insightful work already has been done. Standard current advice is to read Aristotle and David Hume. This is all for the good, but can be improved. Confucius and his followers make a contribution that, in its complexity and subtlety, cannot be disregarded and should form part of the starting point of any work in this area.

PART II

The Fluidity of Self

5

DEBATES OVER THE SELF

The preceding part, on the formation of self, in effect assumed a philosophical position with regard to the self: that it is created and modified in the course of living. Something like this would be widely accepted, at least in the twentieth century, in relation to the self that we think is expressed or revealed in everyday experience. There is, however, a long-standing philosophical problem of whether there is a self underlying everyday personality that is *not* created or modified in the course of living, but rather is entirely the same through a lifetime and perhaps beyond. Some traditional philosophies, both in the West and in India, have held that there is such an enduring, stable self.

One form in which this might be claimed is in terms of the Western substance/quality distinction: the personal qualities that develop and change belong to a substance that itself remains the same. You remain you as a substance, even if you look different, your personality has changed, and most of your memories have gone. We cannot of course, in this view, have direct knowledge of substance through the senses or introspection, so that the view might seem to lack experiential content. (This inaccessibility of substance is also the explanation given of why the bread and wine of the Eucharist, when it becomes the body and blood of Christ, appears to the senses as having all of the characteristics of bread and wine.)

Another form is to claim that behind the individual self (in Sanskrit, *jiva*) there is a psychic core—accessible in the right kind of meditation—that entirely lacks any changeable or individual chararacteristics. This inner, personal reality, *atman*, logically must be the same in anyone. From this it is not a long step to the conclusion that *atman* equals Brahman (the divine reality of the entire universe). In other words, everything, including individual human beings and the gods and goddesses that figure in popular religion, is in its ultimate reality merely an aspect of Brahman. This is the central claim of the *Upanishads*. (For an exceptionally clear discussion of the *Upanishads*, see Dasgupta 1962, chapter 2.) The claim that *atman* is Brahman is, as already noted, thought of as consistent with the view that there is another framework, legitimate but not that of ultimate reality, in which there are individual humans, some of higher caste or more enlightened than others, and so forth.

The traditional stable, enduring inner self has been challenged many times, notably by David Hume in Book I of the *Treatise of Human Nature*, and by the early Buddhist doctrine of *anatman* (literally, no *atman*). Little or nothing that follows hinges on which side one takes. This part in particular is concerned with the fluidity of the self that reveals itself in everyday experience, and I think all (or virtually all) of it is compatible with the idea that there is an *atman* or a hidden inner substance that never changes.

Nevertheless, it is worth making two remarks. One is that the persistent intuitive plausibility, in either Western or Indian culture, of the traditional view must have a great deal to do with the persistent, entrenched sense that (whatever changes) you are you—and also with our very assured sense of our own personal identity. This sense of identity makes it appealing to suppose that there is a *something*, perhaps deeply hidden, that literally stays the same (in what the eighteenth-century philosopher Bishop Butler called a "strict and philosophical" sense of sameness).

The second point is that the phenomena that make the traditional view appealing can be explained at least as well by Immanuel Kant's idea that the "I," in relation to the world we experience, is a synthesizing concept that is not *of* an item that can be experienced, but rather represents a synthetic unity of the thoughts, experiences, and so forth, that a person could normally judge (given our conventional standards of personal identity) to be "my" thoughts and experiences. In other words, it is an idea that we impose on experience rather than drawing it from any content of experience. To posit that each person has an "I" that unifies the history of what we normally regard as an individual is consistent, then, with the denial that "I" has any nature or content that needs to be stable and enduring. "I" becomes a psychic place marker, in this respect comparable to "here," "now," and "this."

Kant himself did not think that this was the whole story of self. Is there something else, behind experience, perhaps in a "noumenal realm"? How could we know? The general comment of the fourth-century BCE. Daoist philosopher Zhuangzi (also known as Chuang Tzu) is both characteristic and apposite: "It seems that there is something genuinely in command, and the only trouble is that we cannot find a sign of it" (*Zhuangzi* a, 51).

The Challenge to Character

Let us return to what is expressed or revealed in everyday experience. We can recognize that all of us do change throughout our lives in character and in personality, not to mention in the experiences and the thoughts that we have. We have to live with psychic fluidity. Is there a self to be fluid? It all depends on what we are willing to consider as one. In the early Buddhist classic *The Questions of King Milinda* (vol. 1, 63–65), the analogy of a chariot is suggested; the chariot is not the wheels, the spokes, and so forth, but is the system of which these are parts. This suggests that we can speak of a self (a field in which the synthesizing "I" is at home) that is a psychic system (rather than some element or core that might be directly experienced), bearing in mind that the nature and constitutents of a given system can keep changing. Similarly, the great Hume scholar Annette Baier has repeatedly suggested (see Baier 1979) that Hume, after rejecting the stable, enduring self in book I of his *Treatise of Human Nature*, spends much of books II and III examining a different kind of self, which he views as a social construction that, like the Buddhist self, is subject to change.

These philosophical paths—an early Indian and a later Scottish one—lead to a fluid self. Here are two sets of ethical problems—very different from one another—that the fluidity of the self generates. Let us assume it true that even the most stable person changes somewhat throughout adult life, so that, in the (very narrow) sense of "same" in which Heraclitus said we cannot step in the same river twice, we cannot meet the same person twice. How then can we hold people responsible for what was done or promised by their former selves? Questions of this sort seem fanciful to most people when the changes are slight. But they seem very serious when the change is drastic. As I write this, a young woman, who in prison became religious and appears genuinely to have transformed herself, has been executed in Texas for the brutal murders of two people. Many of her symphathizers cannot shake the sense that she had become in some sense a different person, one who no longer had a firm connection with the brutal murders.

With some change inevitable, and drastic change imaginable, how can we take responsibility for what we are to do or think in the future? It may be a very different person, with our name, who will have to live up to this responsibility. Again, worries of this sort become more serious when there is reason to think that drastic changes are a strong possibility. Some would urge that this is often the case when what we are supposed to be responsible for is far (e.g., thirty or forty years) in the future.

More generally, we might wonder whether our concept of *character*, which some writers (including me) hold should be central to ethics, rests on a fiction.

Admittedly, assigning someone a definite character of some sort does not preclude change, but to have a character does require a degree of stability, which perhaps never can be guaranteed. Is talk of character a way of papering over variations, fluctuations, and so forth? Does it (as might be asked also of the traditional stable, enduring self) represent more the simple expression of a wish, and a requirement we impose on life, than a reality?

There is also room for a practical worry about whether an ethics of character, if it ever has been workable, can continue viable in a postmodern era, in which both ideas and social arrangements (as individuals take on multiple roles, played out within the context of rapidly shifting arrangements) accentuate the fluidity of the self. Goffman's *The Presentation of the Self in Everyday Life* examined the very different styles of behavior exhibited by a group of people when, on one hand, doing their jobs and interacting with people who might not know them very well, and, on the other hand, when with friends and family. It is hard to read Goffman's perceptive analysis without thinking that what he is examining is a split in the self rather than merely a divergence in the presentation of the self. His subjects led a life in the Shetland Islands in the 1950s that would seem very simple to most people living today in London, Paris, New York, or Los Angeles, especially considering what feels like both a quickened pace of technological development and of bureaucratic expansion (i.e., of procedures that require bursts of conformity in form filling and record keeping) in industrialized societies. The split in self artfully revealed by Goffman now might look like fissures running in many different directions, and the stability of any set of adjustments would be less than it was. There is also the increased role of multiple distractions, messages coming from all directions, most of which cannot really be attended to. All of this is what I mean by the postmodern world. In it, the idea of a self so unified that it can be thought of as having a character, and as generally acting in character, might seem highly nostalgic. The worry is already evident in Kierkegaard: "Can you think of anything more frightful than that it might end with your nature being resolved into a multiplicity, that you really might become many, become, like those unhappy demoniacs, a legion, and you thus would have lost the inmost and holiest thing of all in a man, the unifying power of personality?" (Kierkegaard 1843/1959, vol. 2, 164).

The other set of problems concerns what may be the positive side of fluidity of self. Perhaps the self, as well as being fluid, can be seen as having many levels, some of them much closer to current experience and adjustments than others; and perhaps what flows does not flow away, but remains within the self, at some barely accessible level not closely connected with immediate experience? If so, then the thought is that there may be levels of the self, in most people's lives not playing any obvious role in current experience and behavior, that could be sources of energy and creativity. Beneath discursive thought and the judgments of immediate experience there could be, as it were, an underlying chaos that is capable of producing major benefits. The great work that, in my view, develops an anwer of "Yes" is the Daoist *Zhuangzi*. The second of the two essays that follow examines this in the context of Zhuangzi's emphasis on spontaneity and his ideas about the education of emotions.

Two Daoist Texts

The *Tao Te Ching* (also known as *Daodejing*) looms large in the first of the two essays that follow, and the *Zhuangzi* (also known as *Chuang Tzu*—in this case I adopt the newer romanization) is at the center of the second. These are widely considered to be the two foundational texts of Daoism (Taoism), although they are not entirely alike. Some readers may find it useful if a little is said in advance about Daoism, and about the special characteristics of these two works.

The most elementary point is that Daoism centers on the *dao*, normally translated as "way." The term is available (much like such terms as "democracy" and "freedom") to people who have widely divergent views of what they are talking about, and Confucius repeatedly speaks about the dao, meaning roughly an appropriate path of life. In Daoism there is a much stronger emphasis on the connections between humans and nature, and especially on the idea that there are rhythms and structures (which largely or entirely comprise the Daoist dao) in the natural order of the world that we ought to attune ourselves to. Man is small and nature is large, and much of the flavor of this point of view is conveyed in those traditional Chinese landscapes in which tiny human figures can be discerned amidst spectacular scenes of mountains and water.

The *Tao Te Ching* was traditionally thought to be the older of the two great books, and to be the work of the legendary Lao Tzu, a contemporary of Confucius. It is now judged by scholars to date from about two hundred years (or more) after the time of Confucius, and which of the two Daoist classics is prior is not entirely clear. It may well be that there were Daoists before there were great Daoist texts. Characters who sound like Daoists appear in the *Analects* (XIV. 41; XVIII.5–7), but then these passages may date from a good deal later than most of the *Analects*. All the same, these characters might be regarded as proto-Daoists who represent a tradition within which the *Tao Te Ching* developed. Victor Mair holds (*Tao Te Ching* c, 120) that it is "the result of a period of oral composition that lasted approximately three centuries (from circa 650 to 350 BC" and that the text was "essentially completed by the end of the third century BC"

The *Tao Te Ching* has three major foci: mystical, personal, and political. It seems to me to articulate a sense of a mystic general order of reality, a primal source of nature (the dao), more than the *Zhuangzi* does, although there are passages in the *Zhuangzi* that can be read in that way. The poem traditionally numbered as I (*Tao Te Ching* b, 53) sets this tone: "There are ways but the Way is uncharted . . . things have a mother and she has a name."

The personal message of the work has a great deal to do with the ideal of responsiveness to the dao. One aspect of the rhythm of the world is a kind of Newtonian law that actions generally lead to reactions: to push at the world, as striving people do, is generally counterproductive. It also exacts a toll: striving leads to tension and anxiety (and sometimes danger), as well as to frustration. This why the Daoist-sounding characters who appear in the *Analects* are reported as both scorning and pitying do-gooders such as Confucius, and presumably why they have dropped out from normal society (in which there are pressures to strive). The interplay that the *Analects* reports is striking: Confucius (always anxious to learn, and to expose himself to other points of view) wants to talk to them, and they want to avoid him.

Dropping out from ordinary society may be in the direction of countryside, where a harmony with nature can seem more directly feasible. It might involve instead an urban pretense of mental illness, as in the case of the "madman of Ch'u" (*Analects* XVIII.5), who as represented sounds as if he has his wits about him. A tension within Daoism, with its high rating of harmony, is that a harmony with the dao is difficult or impossible to combine with a harmony with (the increasingly artificial) human society. There may be a trace of this idea in the poem of the *Tao Te Ching* traditionally numbered 20. The narrator says that

> The reveling of multitudes
> At the feast of Great Sacrifice,
> Or up on the terrace At carnival in spring,
> Leave me, alas, unmoved, alone,
> Like a child that has never smiled.

Further on he describes himself as "melancholy. / Restless like the ocean . . ." (*Tao Te Ching* b, 72).

In an ideal society, such as may have existed in the remote past, there would be no such problems. The entire society would be in harmony with nature. People would not have consciously articulated virtues. They simply would behave naturally in a harmonious way. The appearance of articulated virtues thus was a symptom of a falling away from this natural order. Not only are the virtues deformations of nature, but they also lead (given the logic of the dao) to vices that are their opposites. The Daoist view of history (as it has been thus far) is in a way an inverted Hegelianism: syntheses have been falling apart, and giving way to opposed pairs of thesis and antithesis.

One of the subtleties of this perspective is that it mixes a general empirical view of the way pushes and pulls interact in the workings of the universe with what amounts to a logical point. Virtue concepts logically cannot originate unless decent behavior (of the general sort they relate to) no longer can be entirely taken for granted. Beings of a holy will (to borrow Kant's phrase) not only will not need morality; left to themselves they cannot even think it up. Once virtue concepts are originated, on the other hand, the logical space (so to speak) for vices also has been created—and the real vices will not be far behind.

The political philosophy (which some scholars regard as a later accretion) that goes along with this concept of virtue centers on the idea of a ruler whose role consists of constructively doing nothing. Attempting to dominate the course of events will be counterproductive. The idea, as I interpret it, is that in a way a great deal can be accomplished through creating an atmosphere and a sense of an agenda—by what amounts to subtle and hidden nudging—so that whatever is visibly done is done by people who think that it was their own idea. The poem traditionally numbered 17 (*Tao Te Ching* b, 69) speaks of

> him who is highest,
> The people just know he is there . . .
> But once his project is contrived,
> The folk will want to say of it:
> "Of course! We did it by ourselves!"

Number. 43 (*Tao Te Ching* b, 96) speaks of the benefit

> Of something done by quiet being . . .
> Accomplishment apart from work,
> Instruction when no words are used.

The *Zhuangzi* has much less to say about politics; and, if its repeated musings about nature are taken as mystical, the mysticism seems more diffuse than in the *Tao Te Ching*. The work also can seem to point in a number of directions at once. (For an interesting account of this, see Van Norden 1996.) One pronounced element is an emphasis—from the opening passage of chapter 1 onward—on the differences in the world as taken from different perspectives. This emphasis amounts to a metaphysical view that has strong affinities with what in contemporary Western philosophy would be termed anti-realism. It may help the reader approaching the *Zhuangzi* for the first time if I say a little about this view.

Metaphysical anti-realism is the view that there is no single definitive way the world is: there is no optimally correct account of any reality. Instead there are a variety of perspectives, some of which may have more to be said for them than do others. A metaphysical anti-realist, in short, need not be committed to the kind of simple relativism that denies that any consistent perspective or account can be said to be better than any other. Indeed as one well-known anti-realist, T. S. Kuhn (1970), insisted (denying that he was a relativist), nature cannot be put in an arbitrary set of conceptual boxes. Anti-realism thus is consistent with the claim that there is progress in the sciences, but it would be committed to denying that there is some ideal terminus. The *Zhuangzi*, with its constant emphasis on shifting perspectives, consistently can hold that it provides a philosophical perspective superior to those of its rivals. But there is no suggestion that this amounts to an optimal view of reality, and indeed one of the striking features of the work is Zhuangzi's openness and willingness to declare uncertainty.

One major difference between the anti-realism exhibited by the *Zhuangzi* (as well as the Daoist-influenced anti-realism that found its way into Zen Buddhism), on one hand, and recent Western anti-realisms, on the other, is this: the *Zhuangzi* is less concerned in the end with the metaphysics than with what it sees as its ethical and practical implications. There certainly is a subtle and interesting metaphysics in the work, but much of it is held off at arm's length. This is partly because, if there is no final truth, then nothing Zhuangzi can say about reality can claim to be final truth; it is merely a partial insight, superior perhaps to its rivals but not the last word. As in the case (chapter 2) in which Zhuangzi dreamed he was a butterfly (but perhaps it is a butterfly now dreaming that it is Zhuangzi) we do not know enough.

The ethical implication of anti-realism is seen (both by Zhuangzi and by Zen Buddhists) as openness and lack of seriousness. This can be trained. One Zen method, of curing the tendency of unthinking realists to look for literal truth, is to present puzzles (e.g., "What is the sound of one hand clapping?") in which it should be evident even to the slowest that there is no literal truth available. The Zen Buddhist literature in this way gravitates toward moral psychology, while the metaphysics is dramatized rather than argued for. The *Zhuangzi*, though, does present a developed metaphysics, and conversely has nothing at all specific to say about training techniques or about the moral psychology of becoming less serious. Nevertheless, the ethical implications of metaphysical anti-realism are almost constantly uppermost in the text, not least in the manner in which it is written.

There are other elements important to the ethics of the *Zhuangzi*. The value of spontaneity and emotional freedom (discussed in the second of the two essays to follow) is one. Related to this is the focused and skillful behavior that is made possible by this freedom and the corresponding elimination of emotional distraction.

One way in which the ethics is presented is in a series of fanciful portraits of people who have developed in the way recommended. Those portrayed generally are in humble circumstances, and in some cases are grotesque or have previously lost limbs as a legal punishment for wrongdoing. The effect is often colorful and amusing, but at the same time an idea is conveyed of what is possible if one abandons pretentiousness and artificiality and educates one's emotions. Confucius (along with his favorite student, Yan Hui) appears as a character in the *Zhuangzi*. Unlike the representations of proto-Daoists in the *Analects*, though, this is parody. Confucius is represented as earnestly trying to grasp the point of the Daoist dao, but not quite getting it.

6

FALSITY, PSYCHIC INDEFINITENESS, AND SELF-KNOWLEDGE

The poem of the *Tao Te Ching* that traditionally has been numbered 18 (and in the new translation by Mair is 62) describes in an amusing and cynical way our descent from primitive integrity. After the mighty Way declines, kindness and morality take its place. The advent of wisdom and shrewdness/intelligence (Mair has cunning and wit) is accompanied by a great *wei*. Some translators (e.g., Legge and Blakney) render this as hypocrisy; Mair has "falsity" (see *Tao Te Ching* a, 61; b, 70; c, 80). These are different views of the territory of what is not genuine or is insincere, and it is this territory that I wish to explore. Someone who is false to others may well be false to herself or himself, so that we may pursue the links among hypocrisy, self-deception, and insincerity, as well as the connections between these qualities and the genuine ones (if there are any) of which they are counterfeits.

The least interesting part of this territory is falsity that is fully conscious hypocrisy or dishonesty. Bloggs tells us that he has done X when he knows full well that instead he has done Y, or he misdescribes his attitudes or a pattern of his behavior, knowing that he is misdescribing. The motives for this kind of deception are usually clear enough: they may have to do with a desire for popularity, or respect, or not to be bothered or pressured. The context is usually Bloggs's awareness that there are certain things, such as kindness, morality, wisdom, and intelligence, that are thought highly of and that he has been falling short. None of this generates philosophical puzzles.

Sometimes Bloggs convinces himself, as we say, of the story he is telling us. This is more interesting. How could Bloggs start out knowing the truth, and in the end forget or blur it? Or, even if we cannot specify a time at which it is clear that Bloggs fully knew the truth, we might posit that in some sense he did—and does—know the truth. Or, at least, the truth is readily available to him, and it is as if he chooses not to know. So *he*, who knows (or knew, or could know) the truth, is deceiving himself as well as us, even though in his case the deceiver and the deceived are one and the same person. That is the philosophical problem.

It should be pointed out that this summary is too neat for the continuum of real-world cases, in which Bloggs may "sort-of" know that the story he is telling us is not an accurate one; he may think, though, that the story is not too misleading (or that it is, but that it really makes no difference), or it may be that at some moments he is very well aware that the story he has been telling is inaccurate but that at other moments he convinces himself, and so on. There are many patterns of self-deception, not merely one. Rather than pursue this, though, we will return to the philosophical puzzle of how the truth can be available to Bloggs and yet (at least seemingly) not known by him.

We can approach this puzzle by means of some comments on a recent book, Stephen White's *The Unity of the Self*, which approaches self-deception in a way that has become increasingly influential and also links to the topic an interesting (and I think wrongheaded) account of the psychological context of responsibility. White sees a person as an interacting system of homuncular subsystems, which are conscious but not self-conscious. This way of viewing a person will seem bizarre to some, but the idea of homuncular subsystems (as pioneered by Daniel Dennett and William Lycan) has played an important part in the recent philosophy of psychology literature; and, as some commentators point out, Freud's account of self-deception is in a way an account in terms of homuncular subsystems. If the subsystems, while meeting the standards of consciousness, are not self-conscious, there is a sense in which none of them avows (to use a word crucial in Herbert Fingarette's account of self-deception) the truth, which they are shielding the system from. This, at the least, lessens the apparent paradox in self-deception.

White's account of responsibility is more novel. It centers on the ascription to any individual of an ideal reflective equilibrium (IRE), which is "the most coherent extension of the subject's noninstrumental or intrinsic desires that the subject could and would produce . . . in eliminating conflicts among his or her noninstrumental desires" (White 1991, 202). This account prepares the way for the following dilemma. If someone acts on a desire, either that desire is or is not in that person's IRE. The former case is like that of a psychopath, in that blame can find "no footing in the person's motivational makeup." In the latter case the agent is like someone who is compulsive: both act on a desire whose motivational strength is out of proportion to its evaluational strength. In this case, then, like that of compulsive behavior, blame seems irrelevant and unnecessary (White 206, 268).

White's solution to this dilemma, which grounds ascriptions of responsibility in the importance and value we give to authorship of actions, seems to me ingenious and plausible. But the dilemma itself can seem plausible only if we can accept an exceedingly simple a priori psychology of human desire. Some sense of empirical complications is required if we are to begin to understand self-deception and more generally the *wei* referred to in the *Tao Te Ching*.

This discussion must include profuse apologies. First of all, I am not a psychologist. And, in any event, it would be impossible to develop an adequate account of human conative attitudes in a single, not very long chapter. Second, the psychological inadequacy of what I will say is conjoined with crudity at one important linguistic point. The recent philosophy of psychology literature is marked by reliance on a small number of simple category words, so that the single world *desire* is used—artificially and contrary to ordinary usage—for a wide variety of positive conative attitudes. Reliance on an artificial all-purpose use of the word *desire* would be disabling in an essay that centered on Buddhism. Here it is merely embarrassing, but convenient; and I will follow in this usage the authors I am commenting on.

The most important thing that White's attractively simple model of human motivation leaves out is the indefiniteness of many desires. (This is the conative counterpart of the image of a speckled hen, of which one can ask futilely, "How many speckles are there?") It also leaves out the fluidity of desire. Most of us do not know, much of the time, entirely what we want; and any attempt at arriving at an IRE will depend in part on how the questions are put and the context in which they are raised. Most of us also are suggestible in at least some of our desires. How else could philosophers such as Charles Stevenson ascribe with any plausibility emotive effects to ethical judgments? It is now a commonplace among psychologists (see Funder 1983) that almost everyone often is, at least to some slight degree, "situational" in her or his behavior, which means that context (including other people's recommendations or expectations) influences behavior. As Robert Solomon (1996) points out, character (to the extent that one has one) is played out in human relationships in such a way that different traits are expressed, stimulated, or inhibited in different company. Roles that one is expected to play also can make a difference. In some cases the influence on behavior is a matter of conscious compromise, but often it is a matter of the modification of desire or the shaping of unformed desire.

A dramatic illustration of the point is the Stanford prison experiment (see Haney, Banks, and Zimbardo, 1973). College-age subjects were randomly assigned roles as prisoners and guards in a simulated prison. Guards became arrogant and brutal, and prisoners became apathetic and demoralized. The experiment had to be cut short because of the surprisingly quick, thorough, and excessive adaptation of the subjects to their roles, which suggested risks of psychological damage. What were the real desires of the pretend guards and the pretend prisoners? It is far from clear that there is a definite answer to that question or a single-solution IRE for each of them.

It should be added that the indefiniteness and fluidity of many desires is linked to an indefiniteness and fluidity in most people's sense of self, which allows them to dream or fantasize about themselves (i.e., someone they identify with) doing things that are drastically out of character. Part of the key here is Kant's idea that the self is a constructed, synthesizing concept by means of which the mind's "I" spreads itself on a range of experiences, thoughts, and actions. Not only do we unhesitatingly identify people as the same even after they have switched political, moral, and religious allegiances, but also people very often have no difficulty in thinking that they would be the same despite drastic changes in values. This conceptualization gives us a self that is fluid and to which it is difficult to assign definite character.

It then does not seem all that puzzling that we hold people responsible for things they did that, in some sense, they wanted to do. Even if it makes sense to speak of the operative desire as part of their current IRE, blame can nudge them in the direction of a new (and better) IRE. Even if we can say flatly that they have a current IRE that does not include the operative desire, we still can hope to nudge them in the direction of an IRE that includes desires that are strong and reasonable enough to outweigh or control the wayward desire.

The fluidity of the self also provides the key, I think, to accounts of self-deception that are superior to White's homuncular analysis. Here I follow Mark Johnston (in McLaughlin and Rorty, 1988). I accept his argument that the phenomena of self-deception are better viewed in terms of "subintentional tropisms" than in terms of homuncular subsystems. Whether these tropisms can be grouped under the heading of wishful thinking is a complicated question, into which I do not propose to go. There may be forms of self-deception that are to the general category as nightmares are to dreams, and even an elastic treatment of "wish fulfillment" may not do justice to the varieties of self-deception.

A deeper question is whether the fluidity of the self, marked by psychic tropism and shifting influence of situations, allows for any knowledge that can be contrasted with self-deception. Some readers may think of Sartre here and may think of remarks in the section on "bad faith" in his *Being and Nothingness* that indicate an answer of no. Those who have read to the end of the book know that Sartre's answer is in a way yes. We can work toward our own answer in the second half of this chapter, at the same time considering Sartre's view and also the Confucian view of the virtuous person's self-knowledge.

First, though, we can return to the poem of the *Tao Te Ching* with which we began. One way of reading it is as a caution against positing too simply a self-knowledge that can be contrasted with self-deception. At the very least, the poem gives an account of what is presupposed by (and must be in place for) self-deception. But the poem also can be taken to suggest that conventional attempts to overcome self-deception bark up the wrong tree and that indeed one should not be (so to speak) barking up any tree at all.

One analytical point the poem makes is that the motivation for falsity, at least in normal cases, presupposes normative standards. It is imaginable that Bloggs might represent himself as X when really he is Y even if X is not thought better than Y, but it does not seem likely. (And thus what is arguable is that self-deception could not exist as a culturally recognized practice— although there could be isolated cases—if there were not normative standards that people would like to satisfy.) If X is thought better than Y, then Bloggs has a clear incentive to convince the rest of us that he is X rather than Y. To the extent that he accepts, or at least goes along with, this normative judgment, he also has an incentive to convince himself that he is X rather than Y. Eliot Deutsch (1996) has a point when he suggests that if a self-centered and ungenerous Bloggs describes himself as generous, this can be understood (if one knows how to interpret it) as expressing a desire to be generous . . . as he is. Bloggs may, as we say, fudge the evidence, even when he is reviewing it for himself, or he may manage to forget or not to notice key bits of evidence. Herbert Fingarette's (1985) notion of "avowal" is useful here: whatever Bloggs may have once known or noticed, or have been in a position to know, need not be avowed by him. However we tell the story, normative standards can provide strong motivation for Bloggs's self-deception. When the mighty Way declines, people no longer behave toward one another in a natural, unselfconscious manner; instead, there are good ways (kind, moral) and bad ways of acting. Bloggs will try to convince himself, as well as others, that he is a kind and moral person.

A key element in this story is that Bloggs not only is motivated to misrepresent himself, but also that misrepresentation has become possible in a world in which people are busily representing themselves. This is a world of wisdom and intelligence, or cunning and wit. Perhaps, before the mighty Way declined, people did not try to formulate who or what they were, either to others or to themselves. They simply were. Now they are busily presenting avowals, which very possibly vary according to mood, circumstance, and audience. Presumably Goffman's (1959) finding that what is displayed can be different within a circle of intimates from what it is for a wider public could be paralleled by differences in avowals. Any inner narration of one's thoughts and behavior can differ from the avowals presented to various groups, but it would be surprising if it were not influenced (at least for most people) by the outward avowals.

Inner presentations can fulfill a variety of functions. They can be reminders of what one thought one was doing or choosing, something especially useful for those of us who are easily distracted or confused. It scarcely need be said that, before the Dao declined, this help would have been much less needed, especially if one assumes that *then* behavior was natural and unreflective. A second function of inner narrative may be to give a sense of structure and meaning, and hence of value, to what is going on in one's life (see Arendt 1958, 181–88; MacIntyre 1978, 202 ff.). This function obviously supposes that normative categories have emerged and that we live in a world in which we can ask if a life is meaningful. A third function is that of nudging desires, as well as behavior, in the direction indicated by the inner presentation. We need to bear in mind that (as Johnston emphasizes, and perhaps overemphasizes) a great deal of self-deception is wishful thinking, that people usually want to be what their self-deceptive inner presentations suggest that they are. For that matter, in many cases people seem "sort of" to know that the inner presentation is not entirely true, but they think that there is some truth to it and that, with effort, it could become more true. The inner presentation can be a way of nudging one's desires and one's character in a certain direction.

One should not entirely fault this presentation. If it is true that desires are (for almost all of us, most of the time) both indefinite and fluid, then a little self-deception in some contexts might be a good thing. This would be a little like the cases in which unwarranted self-confidence turns out to enable someone to achieve more than what she or he otherwise would have done. In short, there is room for a case that a limited degree of self-deception can have advantages, and philosophers such as Amelie Rorty (who presents self-deception as being a good adaptive strategy at times) and Bas van Fraasen (who links it to courage) have made such a case. (See the essays by Rorty and van Fraasen in McLaughlin and Rorty, 1988.) Indeed, self-deception need not be fantasy: it can be recognition (and exaggeration) of what is already there, encouraging a person to build on that. It is relevant to note that, from the point of view of a puritan or a Jansenist, any statement "I am a good person" will be this kind of self-deception.

In a world in which desires are indefinite and fluid, various forms of nudging can be useful. What was it like before the mighty Way declined? One hesitates to answer, in part because there is a great deal about which the *Tao Te Ching* is far from explicit. But part of the answer surely is that desires were still. Indeed—if one pays proper attention to the ordinary use of the English word *desire*—one would have to say that, strictly speaking, there were no desires. So what is there to nudge? Also, in this prelapsarian world, inner presentations would be neither possible nor useful. Why would anyone want to mar the unity of praxis by introducing the double-mindedness of self-representations as accompaniments of thought and action? Hence self-deception could not exist.

Is Self-Knowledge Possible?

Of course, self-deception does exist in our world. To the extent that it is undesirable, and can be viewed as a blemish on human life, there are two main ways of responding to it. One is to view it as a poor way of playing a game that cannot in any case be won and should not be played at all. As we have seen, that is the view of the *Tao Te Ching*. Skepticism about self-representation also emerges in the famous chapter on bad faith in Sartre's *Being and Nothingness*. The alternative way of responding to self-deception is, of course, to insist that the game of self-representation can be won, or at least played successfully, and that there is self-knowledge that can be contrasted with self-deception.

Sartre's skepticism in chapter 2 of *Being and Nothingness* is based on the ascription of nothingness to the *pour soi*. Anyone who tries to fit his or her true nature to a formula is willfully disregarding the fact that choices that do not fit the formula are possible. Thus self-representation is an attempt to evade the discomfort and responsibility of freedom. Insofar as freedom involves anguish, each of us would like to say, "This is the way I am; I cannot be anything else." But even if the formulas we use for ourselves are honest in the sense of fitting accurately what has been the pattern of our thought and behavior, this "good faith" is in a way just a subtle form of bad faith, because it denies something important about us: our ontological openness and our freedom.

This is a beguiling argument, presented by Sartre with considerable panache. It is not easy to discuss, in part because (like much in Confucius, Hume, and Nietzsche, to mention other great philosophers who are also not easy to discuss) it is a mixture of analytic and empirical (psychological) points. One analytic point is that if there were such a thing as self-knowledge, it would involve not only description or analysis of facts but also decision (or something related to decision). That is, to say I am an X kind of person not only makes a claim about the way I am thinking and behaving, or have been thinking and behaving, but it also implies a decision to continue thinking and behaving in an X kind of way, or at least the absence of a decision to stop. I have explored this point elsewhere at some length (Kupperman 1984–85). If decision, or a failure to decide, is an essential component, then it is fair to ask, "By what necessity does she/he have to decide to continue as an X kind of person (or fail to decide not to continue)?" There is also the question of how bindingly one can decide what one's decisions will be next week or next year. All of this suggests that, when a person defines himself or herself, what is presented as definite is in reality up for grabs; it also suggests that what is a matter for decision is being dishonestly presented as merely a matter for description.

The ontological openness or "nothingness" of human beings is presented by Sartre simply as an insight, but clearly it is related to what I have called the "fluidity of desire," for which there is considerable psychological evidence. However, two problems suggest themselves. One is that (as already noted) many psychologists will agree that most people are "situational" in their behavior, and on this account alone, fluid in their desires. But most need not equal all. It may be that people vary enormously in the degree to which they have Sartre's ontological openness; and for that matter it may be that an individual can vary within a lifetime, becoming, say, more rigid in her or his old age. In short, it could be that there is a continuum of degrees of "nothingness," with the average conformist teenager at the high end and perhaps someone like Cato the Elder at the low end. (Public figures who are eager to please also could be toward the high end; Kierkegaard sometimes joked about people losing their selves, but when it happens it is no joke.) One need not look at the low end for someone as distinguished (and odd) as Cato the Elder; some literary characters seem to fit the pattern of *en soi* more than *pour soi*, in a way that suggests the question of whether there are any real people like that. In a very revealing remark, Sartre (1962) commented that he did not believe there could be real people like some of Faulkner's characters. It would be interesting to unpack the basis for this skepticism and to assay the role of empirical evidence.

A related problem is that if Sartre wishes to maintain that it is always possible for Bloggs (or anyone else) to do such and such, we need to look at various senses of the word *possible*. Does saying that it is possible that Bloggs will do X mean that we cannot have 100 percent certainty that Bloggs will not do X? In this sense, perhaps it is possible that President Clinton will suddenly order a nuclear attack on Great Britain: as astonishing as this would be, it is difficult to see how we can rule it out with absolute certainty. But perhaps this is more a comment on human knowledge, and specifically on the kind of knowledge provided by the social sciences, than on anything else. (It is often said that the social sciences are much better at predicting mass phenomena than the actions of an individual. A standard example is the ability to predict, within some limits, the number of dead [undeliverable] letters that will be posted in London in a given year; this prediction, however, does not yield complete certainty about whether the next letter I post in London will be able to be delivered. Neither does the National Safety Council's ability to predict traffic fatalities during the next holiday weekend include an ability to predict whether Bloggs will be one of them.) There is a sense of "possibility," in short, in which we say (of an individual's future behavior), "Anything is possible"—in relation to what we can know. The thesis of ontological openness seems to lose something in interest if it is interpreted in relation to this sense of possibility.

Another sense is one linked to phrases such as *real chance* or *live option*. William James (1947) first pioneered the use of the phrase "living option" in a discussion of religion. There are some religious allegiances that might be living (or live) options for me, in the sense that it would not be entirely surprising if I considered them as possibilities (and not "beyond belief" that I ultimately adopted them); in this sense, it would not be a live option for me to become a Mithras worshiper or a Sikh. What does this mean in terms of probabilities? One would certainly say that the probability of my becoming a Mithras worshiper or a Sikh is vanishingly small. But is there any basis for saying that it is zero?

Enough has been said to make it clear that the concept of live option is hardly a scientific one, especially if one's idea of science is modeled on the physical sciences. (But perhaps the social sciences in general fall short of being "scientific" by that standard?) Nevertheless, the concept is a useful one in accounts of human choice. The most obvious points to begin with are that no one's live options are, at a given time, unlimited, and second that someone's live options can change drastically with circumstance. Even the conformist teenager, whom I placed at the upper limit of ontological openness, will not have a live option of becoming a Mithras worshiper, at least if he or she lives (let us say) in Iowa in the late twentieth century. But the same teenager, transported in time and place to the heyday of the Mithras cult, could become an enthusiastic Mithras worshiper. If we look purely at moral choices, a number of studies, including Stanley Milgram's *Obedience to Authority* and Hannah Arendt's *Eichmann in Jerusalem*, indicate that for most people the range of possible live options can be very wide.

What might serve to limit someone's live options? As the example of the Iowa teenager and Mithras worship suggests, one limit might be that some putative possibilities are seen (in the situation one is in) as too outlandish, too difficult to present persuasively. Plato, in the myth of Er in book X of the *Republic*, suggests another source of limits. Commenting on the story of a man who had led a virtuous life within a well-ordered community, and in the underworld chooses his next life to be that of a tyrant, Plato (st. 619; vol. 1, 877) deconstructs the man's previous "virtue" as a matter of habit but not philosophy. The idea seems to be that education can provide some understanding of values, or of the reasons for moral norms, such that a properly educated person will not regard morally unacceptable choices as live options.

Something like this appears to be central to Confucianism. It enables Herbert Fingarette (1972) to title the second chapter of his book on Confucius "A Way without a Crossroads." Before we discuss Confucian moral education, and the kind of self-knowledge for which it would seem to clear the way, it is worth taking another look at Sartre. He too, after all, seems to allow for a kind of self-knowledge, at least as a knowledge of limited personal live options.

Sartre's view is that someone's live options are structured by two phenomena of childhood. One is simply the emergence of a sense of self. He speaks (1950, 19–20) of "the fortuitous and shattering advent of self-consciousness," illustrating it by means of a long quotation from Richard Hughes's novel *A High Wind in Jamaica*. The other is the formation in that self of an "original project," which as circumstances develop will yield particular projects (and presumably, as circumstances change, will yield new projects).

A simple example of the intersection of original project with particular decision is the case in which Sartre, out for a long hike with companions, has to decide whether to stop to rest (Sartre 1943, 453 ff.). Sartre yields to fatigue but recognizes that there is a sense in which he did not have to; he could have continued with his companions to the designated resting place further ahead. The question, Sartre says, really should be

> Could I have done otherwise without perceptibly modifying the organic totality of the projects which I am; or is the fact of resisting my fatigue such that instead of remaining a purely local and accidental modification of my behavior, it could be effected only by means of a radical transformation of my being-in-the world?

What is at stake is Sartre's original relation with his body, and more generally with the in-itself of the world via his body. Particular actions, mannerisms, and gestures fall out from the original project: "A gesture refers to a *Weltanschaung* and we sense it" (ibid. 457).

An original project, Sartre says, is not a deliberate choice: "This is not because the choice is *less* conscious or *less* explicit than a deliberation but rather because it is the foundation of all deliberation and because as we have seen, a deliberation requires an interpretation in terms of an original choice" (ibid. 461–62, italics Sartre's). However, the original project can be deliberately reconsidered, either in the context of existentialist psychoanalysis, or perhaps by an adult who has the power and insight to rethink the orientation that had been conditioned by childhood circumstances. (This seems to be one of the themes of Sartre's *Saint Genet.*) Insofar as existential psychoanalysis is available to everyone, we can say of anyone that she or he does not have to be like that. But how "genuine" or strong a possibility this points toward may vary from individual to individual.

In any case, *Being and Nothingness*, taken as a whole, points toward a kind of self-knowledge that differs from the dishonest good faith of chapter 2 in embodying recognition of a component of commitment, and the accompanying possibility of change of commitment. Bloggs can say: This is the kind of person that I appear to have chosen myself to be; insofar as I intend to carry on being that kind of person, I can say that that is what I am like, although I have to recognize that I could (in some sense of "could") choose to change. Self-knowledge, in this view, is not a matter of finding a summary formula for a series of choices. It is rather like linking a number of dots on a page and suddenly discovering a picture and deciding that one does not mind living by that picture, or that one feels unable to change one's orientation (which is not the same as saying that it is impossible). In a classic case of existentialist psychoanalysis, that of "Ellen West," chronic overeating was analyzed in terms of a project of "the metamorphosis of life into mold and death" (Binswanger 1958, 318).

That an original project, which usually is then decisive throughout a person's life, is adopted in childhood is an empirical claim, one that calls for research on the formation and role of childhood self-images. Sartre did not do this research, and, in that I also am not a research psychologist, I will not argue for a view of my own on this topic. Some philosophers have suggested, though, that willed change of character is highly difficult, or is likely to consist at most of limited modifications of a basic structure rather than fundamental redesign (see Hume 1739/1978, book 3, parts 3 and 4, 608; "The Sceptic," 169 in Hume 1985; Glover 1983; Glover 1988, 135, 136, 179). This observation fits common sense and, if true, supports the view that who we are is largely formed in childhood. It may be, though, that what is largely formed are patterns of attention and emotional response, attitudes toward our bodies and other people, and so on; and it may be that what is largely formed in an individual will be consistent with a variety of moral policies, ranging from the virtuous to the vicious. In other words, it is possible to believe that a large part of who someone is will be formed by the end of childhood, and also to believe that whether that person is good or not will typically not have been determined by the end of childhood. (For relevant discussion, see Kupperman 1991, appendix B.) Both of these beliefs seem to me to be plausible. They will look inconsistent only to someone who assumes that moral virtue is a matter of deeply embedded instinct (rather than one that requires moral judgment), or that moral virtue simply depends on one's being a "nice" person or having been brought up to respect the right set of moral rules. Confucius's observation (*Analects* c, XVII.13) that "The 'honest villager' spoils true virtue" is a pungent comment on the latter assumption.

Let us agree with Confucius that a pattern of doing the right thing in ordinary circumstances is not enough to make someone genuinely a good person, and with Plato that it may take something as extraordinary as a ring of invisibility, or a choice of reincarnation—or life under an evil regime, or participation in an experiment such as the Stanford simulated prison or Milgram's—to find out. What would make someone a reliably good person in all of these circumstances? It may well be that we do not have enough hard evidence to answer this question with great confidence. One study, of Gentiles who risked their lives to save Jews during the Holocaust, suggests a conclusion that may be disconcerting to those who would like the answer to involve roots in a community. Nechama Tec puts first among the common features of the "rescuers," "They don't blend into their communities" (see Block and Drucker 1992, 6; also Tec 1986).

Probably most of us would like the key ingredient of genuine goodness to be the one Plato spoke of: philosophy. However, our response may depend on whether we take "philosophy" to refer to formal training in the subject or merely the acquisition of a reflective sense of personal values and the ability to engage other points of view. If it is the case that there is some form of cultivation that can turn an adolescent with a wide range of moral possibilities into a genuinely good person, then this cultivation must have, as one of its accomplishments, that some immoral things will seem personally unthinkable even when all those around one are saying, "Go ahead; it's the normal thing to do; it's really nothing." How philosophy-based this process of cultivation must be is a question I will not attempt to answer. Indeed, the appropriate answer might vary from individual to individual. Rather, we can look at the form genuine goodness will take. This will bring us back to the topic of self-knowledge.

The connection is that genuine goodness, by definition, includes a strong tendency to act virtuously even in situations in which it might no longer seem the "normal" or "expected" thing to do. The data—from My Lai to Stanford—indicate that habits and a conventionally acceptable upbringing are not enough. Sometimes the virtuous person must think, "I am different from the others; *my* values dictate different behavior." However it is arrived at, one element of this virtue is what might be termed a "sense of self": an awareness of oneself as a distinct individual, with her or his own values. In a television documentary on the My Lai massacre, a soldier who had refused to participate (to outward appearances an uneducated man) said retrospectively, "*I* don't do that kind of thing." This expresses a moral commitment, but it is also an element of self-knowledge. Knowing who one is in some form is implicated in genuine goodness.

So let us look again at self-knowledge. Thus far the image of it we have developed is that (pace Sartre) it includes an element of awareness of one's own psychic fluidity, and (insofar as self-knowledge is not merely knowledge of oneself up to this microsecond) an element of something like decision—either a decision to continue more or less as one has been, or at least the absence of any decision to the contrary. One respect in which this image still seems to me to be seriously defective is that, despite the factor of something like decision, it offers us (as the fruit of self-knowledge) a largely static picture of a person's thought and behavior patterns. It is instructive then to look at the self-knowledge reported by Confucius in the *Analects* (V. 27): "The Master said, In a hamlet of ten houses you may be sure of finding someone quite as loyal and true to his word as I. But I doubt if you would find anyone with such a love of learning." The Confucian self is always in process, at least to the age of seventy (and very probably beyond). Confucius's self-knowledge is presented in terms of the leading vector of personal change.

The key assumption behind this image of psychic fluidity is that of the fallibility even of a very good person. One always can learn. Furthermore, even a very good person repeatedly will encounter situations that function as a challenge to self-examination. Mencius presents this fact dramatically: if he encounters someone who treats him in an outrageous manner, the superior man "will turn round upon himself—'I must have been lacking in benevolence and courtesy, or how could such a thing happen to me?'" Hence, Mencius (b, book IV B. 28, 134) says, "While a gentleman has perennial worries he has no unexpected vexations." (Legge has, "The superior man has a life-long anxiety and not one morning's calamity.")

There is another dimension in the Confucian account of self, as Roger Ames (1996) points out. The social context and interrelationships of individuals are an integral part of the story. In this context, the dilemma of the person of superior merit, such as Confucius himself, whose merit is not generally recognized, is in a way a dilemma of self-knowledge. It may be (as in Sartre's discussion of bad faith) that there is no straightforward solution that is ideal: for the unrecognized worthy to act as a high official would be presumptuous, but to act as a nobody would be (and should be) felt as demeaning.

Even if we focus on the individual, a final point is that what counts as self-knowledge depends on the focus of the inquiry. There is more to any person, including her or his response to various kinds of foods, emotions on seeing various kinds of imaginative enactments, and so on, than anyone could possibly have a firm grasp of. Self-knowledge must be predicated on a selective emphasis. The self-knowledge of Sartre and of psychoanalysts focuses on sources of desire, aversion, awareness, and inattention. Confucian self-awareness focuses on factors decisive to a person's goodness, and also to that person's effectiveness in the social and political world. The two are closely connected. Mencius (book IV, A. 12, 123) links being true to oneself with the ability to move others (by winning their confidence and trust).

Charles Taylor (1989) recently has argued that values provide the orientation or framework within which a person's sense of self assembles itself. This is more clearly true of ethically oriented self-knowledge than of psychoanalytic self-knowledge. To the extent that it is true, ethical reflection is part of the process of achieving self-knowledge. And, as Confucius's remark about learning suggests, it is arguable that neither process will ever be complete.

7

SPONTANEITY AND EDUCATION OF
THE EMOTIONS IN THE *ZHUANGZI*

A working title of this chapter had been "A Cicada Propounds Three Theses About Zhuangzi." This title had been intended not only to be modest, but also to allude to the perspectivism with which the *Zhuangzi* opens. Part of the greatness of the *Zhuangzi* is that it is rewarding from so many perspectives. This is not accidental: the strongest vein of skepticism in the *Zhuangzi*, if I am right, is skepticism about meanings, including skepticism about interpretations of itself. It would go against the spirit of the work to pretend to supply a definitive or a "very best" interpretation. It also would do violence to the deliberate openness of many of the meanings. In what follows, I will point toward a reading of three major elements of the work. In each case, a brief statement of an interpretation will be followed by explanation and elaboration. The longest of the three sections will be the third, concerned with the project of educating the emotions, partly because it seems to me that the most difficult and contentious issues lie here. All references will be to the translation of the *Zhuangzi* by A. C. Graham.

Transforming the Reader

The underlying project of the *Zhuangzi* is, as Robert Allinson says, self-transformation (Allinson 1989). This statement must be qualified. The author's project in producing the Inner Chapters—his project for himself, that is—very probably is not what we would normally term self-transformation, at least if that phrase is taken to refer to a drastic change in what one is. We are to assume that the author already has been transformed. Of course, there will be further changes: there is no suggestion of a static ideal. But it seems likely that the point of producing the work, for the author, had a great deal to do with a free play of spontaneous psychic forces, the sort of thing indeed that is celebrated in various forms throughout the book. In chapter one (47), the possible use of an unmarketable calabash is described in terms of floating away over the Yangtse and the lakes. This is a good metaphor for the use to which the act of creating the *Zhuangzi* put an unmarketable wisdom.

What Allinson is right about is the nature of the project for us, the readers, that must be central to any plausible account of the meaning of the book. We are encouraged to see the attractiveness of styles of life of which we very probably have no personal experience. At the same time, the folly of styles of life in which we very probably participate is gently exposed. There is no sustained exhortation. But the implication clearly is that one would be better off if one approximated the free and spontaneous life that is presented as a possibility.

The word "approximate" is important here. There is no suggestion that there is a single version of the very good life to be followed. Perspectivism applies to styles of life. Not only is it the case that what is good for a loach or a gibbon would not be good for a human being, and vice versa (57), but also there is no suggestion that Cook Ding, the demonic carver, could just as well have the psychological skills of Chu Boyu or that Chu Boyu could be a demon carver (63–64 and 71–72). In chapter 5, Confucius is made to say that (spiritual) Power can stand out without shaping the body (80–81). It is consonant with this that Power would not obliterate the various psychological leanings that are at the root of our individualities, and hence that Power could be expressed in a variety of styles of life as well as in a variety of physical forms.

Also a wonderful style of life, like the wonderful dancing of a Margot Fonteyn or a Rudolf Nureyev, is not adequately captured in words. Someone who studiously masters a description is not thereby in a good position to approximate the quality of the life. One reason for this (which will be explored in the next section) is that while nuance, generally speaking, does not have a major role in morality, it does have a crucial role in the nonmoral assessment of styles of life. As Camus (1955, 50–51) points out, someone who takes a very impressive life as an example to be followed risks having a life that is, in fact, ridiculous.

A digression on philosophical method is appropriate here, after the jarring note of quoting Camus in an explication of Zhuangzi. There is a dilemma inherent in comparative philosophy as practiced by Western academics who attempt to understand and explicate Asian philosophies. On one hand, any approach that attempts to suggest that Asian philosopher X is really just like Western philosopher Y is almost certainly going to be too primitive, giving us a cartoonlike image of X and ignoring X's intellectual and cultural context. On the other hand, Western readers of comparative philosophy are likely to approach any Asian philosophy as something like a second (rather than a first) philosophical language, for which at least some rules of translation into familiar terms would be useful. A deeper problem is the following. Experience suggests that one better understands any philosopher, Western or Asian, if one has been thinking independently about similar problems: this parallelism of thought enables one better to see the point of various remarks, assumptions, and philosophical moves. If so, then an effective Western student of comparative philosophy will be functioning, in some small way, as a Western philosopher herself or himself. Use of an alien philosophical framework, thus, will facilitate interpretation of an Asian philosophy (which is something positive), while at the same time multiplying the risks of error and distortion (which is something negative).

These risks exist, of course, even with regard to texts that are, broadly speaking, within one's own philosophical tradition. At the root is the fact that interpretation of a text is itself an activity for which there can never be entirely strict rules, and that always calls for leaps of judgment. Because of this nature of interpretation, many literary critics have argued in recent years that (while some interpretations are clearly better than others) there can be no such thing as a definitive set of meanings of any text.

If the writer of a text already believes that there are no definitive meanings, or has intimations of it, there are a variety of ways in which she or he can react. Someone who is disturbed by the fluidity of interpretation can attempt to counteract it by thickening the content at key places, say by laborious definitions of key terms and articulations of central claims, or by elaborate notes that say, "What I really mean is." Someone who is resigned to the fluidity of interpretation may be far less strenuous in these matters. A writer who glories in the fluidity of interpretation, on the other hand, may act out a complicity with it, at key places saying, "Perhaps this is so; perhaps it is not," and by constantly suggesting the possibility of variations of perspective. This is the strategy of Zhuangzi.

This strategy is one reason for the humor, the jokiness, that runs through the *Zhuangzi*. Another reason has to do with the project of transformation of the reader. If one were to want to change a group of people so that they become devotees of a religious or political cult, then it might seem appropriate to pull hard on their attitudes to life and to give them formulas for what they should be loyal to. Zhuangzi's ideal and project of transformation are of very different sorts.

A fuller characterization of this ideal and project will be pursued in the last section of this essay, but for present purposes it is enough to dwell on Zhuangzi's emphasis on freedom and spontaneity. It most certainly would not be appropriate to pull people hard in the direction of such a good, or to give them formulas for what are in the last analysis qualities that people have to come to of themselves. One may nudge them in the right direction and gently ridicule what they presently have. A strong pull would be counterproductive and also would risk substituting a more virulent form of something unnatural for what people start out with.

Non-Moral Improvement

The transformation at the heart of the *Zhuangzi* cannot be understood in terms of moral improvement. To move in the direction of being more like a sage may well not involve becoming a morally more virtuous person. But it will involve having a better life.

This may well seem confusing as it stands, and it has led to a lot of confused talk about relativism. P. J. Ivanhoe (1993a) has done, it seems to me, an exemplary job of clearing away mistakes in this area. But it may be useful to look at the philosophical roots of the confusion. We can begin with a basic distinction, between morality and other aspects of a life that may be judged as better or worse. Failure to observe this distinction has led to the worst mistakes.

The distinction in question is a modern Western one, which arguably reflects interest in morality as an instrument of social control—and perhaps even more strongly, reflects interest in carving out a territory (sometimes loosely identified with an area of privacy, or the part of life in which hypothetical imperatives alone govern) in which life can be better or worse that should *not* be viewed as subject to social control. It is often observed that no closely corresponding distinction occurs either in classical Greek or in classical Chinese philosophy, although this does not imply that we will be unable to find places in which an ancient Greek or Chinese philosopher treats certain matters in much the way in which we treat what we regard as moral matters. Arguably, for example, Confucian philosophy regards failure to mourn a dead parent for more than a few days much as we regard gross immorality.

One mark of what we consider to be immoral is, as John Stuart Mill (1861/ 1979, chapter 5, para. 14) observed, we think it deserving of punishment: if not actual legal punishment, then punishment from the force of society's condemnation or the internalized punishment of the malefactor's sense of guilt. There are some forms of behavior that we dislike or think tasteless, to which a normal response is instead distaste, contempt, or shunning (see Mill 1859/1978, 77); the judgment that something is immoral is more akin to impulses to hit out. We can add that much of traditional morality focuses on actions that directly harm others. (Mill's revisionary proposal, in *On Liberty*, was that we narrow the boundaries of morality so that it focus on nothing but these, thus preventing "the tyranny of the majority.") A morality can be most effective in discouraging such actions if it is able to be taught in the form of broad general rules that are able to be understood even by the very young and the very poorly educated. Nuances and subtleties thus cannot have a major role at the core of a viable morality. There is a contrast here with what a philosopher such as Aristotle or Camus can advise with regard to the most desirable kinds of life, in which the importance of nuances must be acknowledged and we cannot expect much show of precision.

P. F. Strawson (1961) has pointed out that there also is a great difference between the allegiance claimed by a social morality and that claimed by what he terms "individual ideals." A social morality demands exclusive loyalty: one cannot make sense of the idea of a life genuinely governed by two conflicting moralities, whereas Strawson sees no comparable difficulty in the idea of a life governed by two conflicting ideals.

Most recent Western ethical thought has centered on the dialectical interplay between, on one hand, the society's control (legal, political, and moral) of the individual, and, on the other hand, the individual's right to preserves of independence. This focus has made it difficult for many philosophers to appreciate the distinction that has just been sketched: the temptation is to treat morality as the whole of ethics. But when, say, Aristotle argues that the contemplative life is the best for a human being, his thesis cannot be mapped onto what we think of as the territory of morality. There is nothing immoral, even in our terms, in a decision to lead an undemanding and humdrum life rather than to engage in the most desirable forms of human activity. (When we advise people not to drop out of college, we do not tell them that it would be morally wrong.) Similarly, it is impossible to get any sense of what is going on in the final chapter of G. E. Moore's *Principia Ethica* if one thinks that it is about morality.

The *Zhuangzi* is, as far as I can see, not about morality. There is no clear suggestion that the sage either would violate, or would be sure not to violate, those socially sanctioned rules of conduct that most closely correspond to what the modern West thinks of as morality. There are, it is true, passages like the one in chapter 6 (91), in which Yan Hui is described as having "forgotten about Goodwill and Duty." But this forgetfulness certainly cannot be construed as a decision to violate moral norms, and (for all that we are told) is compatible with a pattern of behaving in compliance with moral norms but not as a result of thinking *about* the norms. One reason for reading it as compatible is the passage earlier in the same chapter (90) that observes that fish forget all about each other in the Yangtse and the Lakes, as men forget all about each other in the lore of the Way. The fish are not constantly bumping into each other, and it makes no sense to imagine the men as in anything like a Hobbesian state of nature.

The transformation at the heart of the *Zhuangzi*, then, is not necessarily or primarily a moral transformation. It is primarily in how one thinks and feels about the world, and in the behavior that expresses this. A key assumption is that even someone who loyally complies with all of the major recognized social norms, a "good" person, can have an inadequate and unsatisfying style of life, and should be motivated to transform herself or himself. There may be cases, of course, in which someone's inadequate and unsatisfying style of life includes what we would term immorality, and that enlightenment would have as one of its by-products the elimination of the motivation for this immorality. This is not precluded by the *Zhuangzi*, but as far as I can see the work does not advertise increased moral virtue as one of the possible rewards of transformation.

Becoming Spontaneous

The transformation at the heart of the *Zhuangzi* concerns primarily one's emotions and also the connections between emotions, on one hand, and motivation and conduct, on the other. We can approach this by way of examination of something that figures repeatedly in the *Zhuangzi*, and that has been treated as a puzzle by some Western philosophers: spontaneity. What is spontaneity?

There are two connected ideas here. On one hand, there is a spontaneity that (at least arguably) is necessarily a feature of all human thought and action, so that one must come to thoughts and actions spontaneously or grind to a halt. On the other hand, there is a sense (which is clearly uppermost in the *Zhuangzi*) in which some people are more spontaneous than others, and indeed some are so lacking in spontaneity that their lives are deeply flawed.

Let us look first at the thesis that we are, so to speak, condemned to spontaneity. A general form of this thesis is the claim that no set of rules by itself univocally compels the next step (partly because of the openness of interpretation), which is a major theme of Wittgenstein's *Philosophical Investigations*. Less generally, we may look at three theses: (1) The next thought is not compelled; (2) Desire does not compel preference, and (3) The next action is not compelled. All three theses arguably can be found in Kant, and the interested reader can trace discussions of spontaneity in Henry Allison's *Kant's Theory of Freedom* (1990). But Kant is not the only Western philosopher with a strong interest in spontaneity, an interest that has led to some fissures in philosophical analysis.

We may begin from the point that, even if there are constraints (related, say, to space, time, and the categories) on anyone's system of thoughts, these constraints do not in general govern the order of one's thoughts, and they most certainly do not determine whether, at any particular moment, one has a thought at all (rather than having one's mind blank). In addition, if one looks at the actual functioning of people's minds, it is striking that the stream of thought very often includes seemingly random, unbidden thoughts. There is Mozart's famous remark, quoted by Daniel Dennett (1984, 13), about his musical ideas, that they come from one knows not where. Remarks about the mysterious sources of ideas abound in the *Zhuangzi*. For example, "Pleasure in things and anger against them, sadness and joy, forethought and regret, change and immobility, idle influences that initiate our gestures—music coming out of emptiness . . . no one knows from what soil they spring" (50).

Some unbidden thoughts may be merely inconsequential; others may represent a hostility or a greed that is not one's dominant or considered attitude. There is a great temptation to say of the latter, as Mozart said of his musical ideas, that they are not my thoughts. This temptation is all the greater in that one repudiates such thoughts, and very probably would rather not have them.

This unwelcome spontaneity may impinge on one's sense of self. One major American philosopher of recent years, Harry Frankfurt, has devoted himself to resolving this tension. He has argued, with great skill and panache, that the self is formed as a result of higher-order desires that have the effect of either incorporating or rejecting the first-order desires that one may happen to feel (Frankfurt 1988). This process leads to the image of a coherent self as an island in the larger sphere of one's mind: beyond the self, much of the mind may be ugly or chaotic.

I have argued elsewhere (Kupperman 1991, chapter 3) that this is too intellectualized a picture of how people arrive at a character or a nature of their selves, and that such factors as habit can play a major role. But there is another objection that could be leveled equally at Frankfurt's and my accounts. It is that we are attempting to analyze and reconstruct something that verges on the pathological, a partitioning of the mind that easily can cut people off from the most interesting forms of spontaneity. In dreams and creative activities, it will be said, the boundary markers are down. Zhuangzi would surely concur with this objection. It is one of many reasons that dreams and transformations play such a role in suggesting the possibility of variations of perspective. This is the strategy of Zhuangzi.

We also can lead a coherent life without either cutting ourselves off from some of our desires or straightforwardly ratifying every one of them in our conduct. We may prefer not to act out a desire in any direct way, and neither our desires at the moment nor our previous behavior dictates what our next action will be. That neither preference nor action need be governed by desire is a major theme of many moralities, including Kant's. But it must be seen as the beginning, rather than the end, of a train of thought for Zhuangzi.

Here is an analogy that may help us to approach the problem of the relation between desire and preference. Commentators on the architecture of Sir Christopher Wren sometimes focus on the problem of the church steeple, which is round, before it tapers to a point, and is mounted on a square tower. The problem is in managing the transition from the square tower below to the roundness of the steeple without its seeming visually abrupt. This transition can be made through intervening (and visually intermediate) layers of construction between the squareness and the roundness. The steeple might be given an octagonal base or one that is square but scalloped at the corners; the base might have more than one level, each one closer to round than the one below it. Wren, to the best of my recollection, never solved the problem twice in the same way, and his solutions are invariably both subtle and beautiful.

Similarly the transition from desire to preference should not be abrupt and jarring. Otherwise, as Zhuangzi (67) makes Confucius (i.e., the half-bright Confucius of his stories) remark in another context, the "tension might show in one's face." One respect in which the analogy breaks down, though, is that the nature of one's desires, unlike the squareness of church towers, is not typically a given. Desires can be modified or eliminated, and by now, studies of Buddhism have made us used to the idea that the best solution to the problems of life is the elimination of desire. Might Zhuangzi's solution be, so to speak, a beautiful spire that is mounted on nothingness?

It is difficult to answer this question with great confidence. But we should be cautious of imposing alien philosophical frameworks—Indian as well as Western—on Zhuangzi. We also need to be cautious in our handling of the English word "desire." It is often used (the word "cravings" running second) as an English translation for what Buddha recommended that one eliminate. It is also used in much recent analytic philosophy for motivational thrusts in general, so that "desires" is treated as roughly synonymous with "wants" or "would like." This use reflects the crudity of a great deal of contemporary "philosophy of mind." Annette Baier (1986) has pointed out (to my mind convincingly, at least as regards the meaning "desire" has had) that the meaning of "desire" is more narrow and specialized. The proper object of desire, she suggests, is "a thing or person in some future close relation to the desirer" (Baier 1986, 60 n.8). To this one might add that mild wishes are not likely to be called desires, and what gets translated as "desires" in Buddhist texts are at home in cases in which not getting what one would like is tantamount to suffering. The word can look out of place, conversely, in cases in which the response to not getting what one wanted is one of relative indifference.

Thus, even if it is true that Zhuangzi to some extent anticipated the advent in China of Buddhism, it would not follow that the spire of preference is mounted on nothingness. It can be mounted on wishes and urges that do not amount to desires. Indeed there is a passage (97–98) that suggests that Zhuangzi's preferences, rather than resting on nothingness, rest on primal psychic chaos. (One may speak here of the shifting inclinations provided by one's *qi*—one's vital spirit—that may differ from conscious preferences in such a way that we risk frustration whether or not these conscious preferences are satisfied.) We will return to psychic chaos shortly.

My immediate suggestion is that both the basic Buddhist injunctions regarding the management of emotions and the respects in which Zhuangzi may have anticipated the advent of Buddhism are easily lost in translation. The word "desire" has become so problematized that even recent writings in English that center on the word can be, as it were, lost in translation from English to English. It does look as if Zhuangzi wants us, at the very least, to lessen the urgency of our desires. Thus he remarks that "wherever desires and cravings are deep, the impulse which is from Heaven is shallow" (84). This remark is consonant with the suggestion (82) that it is best that a man "does not inwardly wound his person by likes and dislikes, that he constantly goes by the spontaneous and does not add anything to the process of life." This way of living is spoken of as being without "the essentials of man," which strongly implies that it must be learned and that the learning will require effort. What is required is a "fasting of the heart" (68), which paradoxically is a source of increased energy, in that one is put in touch with "the tenuous which waits to be aroused by other things."

So much for Zhuangzi's view of desires. What of preferences? It might look as if his recommendation is that there be none. Graham translates one passage that way: Confucius is made to say appreciatively to Yan Hui, "you have no preferences . . . no norms" (72). However, the discussion of the self might give one pause. Without self there is "no choosing one thing rather than another" (51). Zhuangzi's view of the self is not crystal clear; I think that one can read without irony his observation that "It seems that there is something genuinely in command, and the only trouble is that we cannot find a sign of it" (51). Hence, I read him as holding that there is a self, and of course we choose one thing rather than another. In any event, the *Zhuangzi* is full of characters held up to our admiration who are doing what, in some sense, they prefer to do and are moving toward outcomes they prefer. One might, for starters, think of Cook Ding (63–64), who clearly prefers not to wear out his chopper.

My interpretation of Confucius's appreciation of Yan Hui is that Yan Hui's choices are not governed by the rigid dictates of any code ("norms") and that Yan Hui does not have preferences that are so strong that he is really disappointed if they are not fulfilled. In this sense he does not "wound his person by likes and dislikes" (82). The transition between desires (or wishes and urges), on one hand, and preferences, on the other, is made smooth by the fact that, first, both elements are light rather than heavy and, second, that desires of any gross or antisocial sort (that might cause real trouble and tension if formed into preferences and acted out) have been lessened or transmuted by "fasting of the heart."

This interpretation still does not get us far. There is more to Zhuangzi's education of the emotions than fasting of the heart, and the account we have given thus far of the shaping of preferences does not explain the nature and importance of the spontaneity that is recommended. It is time to look at the puzzling series of semimagical presentations of self described in chapter 7, second series. Huzi presents himself to a demonic shaman first "as I am when I hold down the impulses of the Power," then as he was when "names and substances had not found a way in, but the impulses are coming up from my heels," then "the absolute emptiness where there is no foreboding of anything" (which Huzi achieves when he levels out the impulses of the breath), and finally himself as "it is before ever we come out of our Ancestor . . . I attenuated, wormed in and out, Unknowing who or what we were." The shaman is misled the first three times, and terrified the last (97).

One thing we might get from this sequence is that the psychic nature toward which the *Zhuangzi* points is both complex and fluid. We may be tempted, in general, to read any discussion that recommends what sort of person one should try to be in terms of a static picture of a soul, a sort of spiritual x-ray. This stasis never entirely works: even the kind of harmony of psyche that is sketched in Plato's *Republic* or the very different spiritual stability praised in Kierkegaard's *Fear and Trembling* has to be understood in terms of sequences in which checks and balances or appeals to what is highest come into play. My suggestion, though, is that it works even more badly for Zhuangzi than it does for Plato or Kierkegaard. Some of Huzi's self-transformations might seem to refer to earlier stages of spiritual transformation, but the point to bear in mind is that they are still present as part of what he is. He is still—as people say—"in touch with" the impulses of very early childhood, which worm in and out, with no essential connection with any sense of self. To be in touch with these impulses is to be aware of them, to accept them for what they are rather than attempting to squash them, and sometimes (but I think not always) to ratify them in one's preferences and to act on them.

There is a much later Zen story in which a Zen master, challenged to perform a miracle, says, "My miracle is that when I feel hungry I eat, and when I feel thirsty I drink" (*Zen Flesh, Zen Bones*, 91). I think that the *Zhuangzi* points in this direction. Education of the emotions here includes being aware of, and comfortable with, basic wishes and urges, including even those that a small child would have. It also includes one's sometimes acting on them, again easily and comfortably, even in some cases in which norms of good manners might seem to dictate otherwise. It should be emphasized that the Daoist sage is not someone who always acts on impulse or, in the vernacular of the 1960s, "lets it all hang out." But he or she will be someone whose preferences will not be at war with basic wishes or urges.

This psychic connectedness with early and primitive levels of one's mind has been emphasized as a factor in artistic creativity by Anton Ehrenzweig, who links finished works of art with a "deceptive chaos in art's vast substructure" (1967, xii). In Ehrenzweig's view, both the artist and the scientist deal with apparent chaos, which they integrate through unconscious scanning (ibid., 5). One mark of the process of unconscious scanning may be a blank stare. (One is put in mind of the vacant stare that David Hume's friends, including D'Alembert, cautioned him about and that made Rousseau especially edgy [Mossner 1970, 477].) Unconscious scanning "in contrast to conscious thought which needs closed gestalt patterns—can handle 'open' structures with blurred frontiers which will be drawn with proper precision only in the unknowable future" (Ehrenzweig 1967, 42).

Ehrenzweig draws a number of lessons from this for the education of artists. Students must be taught, he argues, "not to wait for their inspiration and rushes of spontaneity, but to work hard at being spontaneous through choosing tasks that cannot be controlled by analytic vision and reasoning alone." The objective constraints that are inherent in the tasks will trigger spontaneity (Ehrenzweig 1967, 146). This is, in fact, a perfect description of the work and professionalism of Cook Ding, who does not need a rush of creative inspiration to be spontaneous.

Anyone who reviews the literature referred to in this essay must be struck by the fact that no one attempts to provide a clear and direct explanation of what spontaneity is: not Zhuangzi, not Kant or Henry Allison, and not even Ehrenzweig. Here is such an attempt. Spontaneity, in the sense in which everyone has it, is the occurrence of a thought or an action, or the formation of a preference, in a descriptive and explanatory context in which it is anomalous. (I use the word "anomalous" in the sense it has in Donald Davidson's "anomalous monism" [see Davidson 1970].) Spontaneity, in the sense in which some people are much more spontaneous than others, has to do with the relation between one's preferences and actions, on one hand, and the layers of one's mind (going back to childlike wishes and urges), on the other. For some people there is rather little relation: they are governed by norms of conduct and of what they should prefer, and may be hardly aware of psychic elements that run in different directions. Ehrenzweig sees this lack of relation as characteristic of the kind of artist we would term "academic," who composes or paints by the rules. Someone who has a more easy and satisfying relation with these psychic elements, and is able to act in a way that is not only anomalous but also expressive and free from tension, is very spontaneous. For most of us it is not easy to be that kind of person. But Zhuangzi, who is not at all a relativist about values, clearly thinks that it is much better.

8

FLUIDITY AND CHARACTER

Afterword

The portrait of self that has emerged is that it never is (or can be) entirely definite or stable, and normally can be seen as both fluid and multilayered. Further, the essay on the *Zhuangzi* argued that there are emotional and creative advantages to embracing the fluidity of self and adjusting one's thought and conduct so as to remain in touch with the more primitive levels of its construction. Are these advantages balanced by costs? The major ones to worry about are connected with the ability of a fluid self to take responsibility and to maintain a recognizable character.

It is important to be clear about the nature of the discussion that follows. Much contemporary philosophy is heavily influenced by admiration for the "hard" sciences, along with a sense that philosophy at its best must emulate both the precision and the abstraction that are characteristic of some of them (especially mathematical physics) at their most successful. The kind of investigation of possible workings of a system of concepts, attitudes, and habits of mind that follows, though, is much more like engineering than it is like the sciences. It will be concerned with tensions rather than impossibilities. A good result would be much more like a conceptual counterpart to the invention of the flying buttress than like a proof or logical derivation.

What, in this analogy, is under pressure (chiefly from the fluidity of self) is character. Good character does not require that those who have it never change, but it is widely held to require constancy, a point especially emphasized by Jane Austen in her novel *Mansfield Park*. Constancy, on any reasonable understanding, does not require that one never change one's mind, even on major political or social issues or in such important personal matters as whether to accept a marriage proposal. Like the concept of character itself, it is mainly concerned with matters of trust and responsibility and the core requirements of a reasonable moral code, as well as the pursuit of central life projects, and has little to do with tastes in poetry or personal adornment (matters that normally are viewed as well outside the sphere of morality or "the plan of life"). What constancy does require is a high degree of predictability in decisions involving trust and responsibility or core requirements of morality, and a degree of stability in one's basic attitudes and feelings toward others.

In the latter it is close to the concept of sincerity, which is more longitudinal than is generally realized. To be sincere is more than to have feelings and attitudes at a given moment that match one's words at that moment. If tomorrow's attitudes are very different, that normally (barring a wrenching and difficult reconsideration overnight) is an indication that one was not sincere. Those whose attitudes and feelings fluctuate are incapable of sincerity. In short, constancy and sincerity do not require that a person never fall out of love, or change her or his mind on what government policy should be; they do require that changes not be abrupt and capricious.

This analysis confirms that fluidity of self is a threat to character, but also makes clear that the nature of the threat depends heavily on the form that fluidity takes. Someone who can be in the mood for pizza and then abruptly change her preference to Chinese food, or whose tastes in music fluctuate from day to day, can have a character that is strong and good. Fluctuations in the attitude toward promise keeping are quite another matter. This suggests that good character requires that the fluidity of self be controlled in certain crucial areas of life, while it is not a problem in others.

A puzzle remains: what or who is doing the controlling? If we have jettisoned the stable enduring self of tradition, an ultimate source perhaps of control over behavior and the progress of our thinking, then how can control be understood? We need to contrast two models of control. In one, the self is a committee of homunculi, representing distinctively different sorts of interests; one of them (call it the ego) weighs these concerns and arrives at and enforces a decision. In the other, the self is seen as a congeries of occurrences (e.g., experiences, feelings, thoughts) and processes; some thoughts trigger processes that involve feelings of discomfort or distaste, along with counterthoughts along the lines of "This is not the kind of thing that I do." If these negative responses are not immediately effective, there can be a sustained process of a psychological sorting out that substitutes other thoughts or lines of thought for the original ones when they occur. These other thoughts can include reminders of policies and commitments (including commitments to other people or to moral responsibilities, or to decisions as banal as that not to overeat).

Willpower (something very important to good character) can be seen, within this second model, as a collection of such processes of control. The genuine feeling of effort that we sometimes have on such occasions might suggest the idea of something like a psychic muscle. But what we have evidence of is simply that such processes occur, and that training and habit have a great deal to do with how likely (and how effective) they are for any given individual.

These processes of control are the psychic analogue to the flying buttress, helping character not to buckle under the pressure of fluidity of self. This, I think, is the general line of solutions to the tension between good character and fluidity of self, but it is not the case that all solutions along this line are equally desirable. In particular, there are dangers in control that is too strong or that encompasses too much of life. At one extreme is the rigid person—unbending and inflexible—who is not open to new ideas and is incapable of reconsidering old ones. At the other extreme is someone who is excessively open, too ready to compromise with or adapt to whatever may present itself, whether it is a fascist dictatorship or a new style in music.

Plainly one needs to aim at a mean. But, as anyone familiar with texts such as the Confucian *Doctrine of the Mean* or Aristotle's discussion of the mean in book II of the *Nicomachean Ethics* knows, finding the mean has much less to do with moderation (and much more to do with reflective judgment of particulars) than one might initially suppose. To find the mean, for example, between rashness and cowardice is in some cases (when the possible gains outweigh the risks) to advance into danger much like the rash person, and in others (when the risks outweigh the possible gains) to avoid danger much like the coward. Thus courage (the mean) is not a matter of following a rule or a middle path, but rather requires intelligent judgment of cases, along with an appropriate secure comfort with reasonable risk taking.

The mean between rigidity and excessive psychic fluidity also requires sensitivity and judgment. A crucial element is a thing's weight in morality, central personal relationships, or in the core purposes of one's life. Many things, including one's response to beauty in the world, can have great value in someone's life and yet normally very little weight in the aforementioned areas. Here fluidity carries few risks. Abrupt and capricious changes (say in someone's tastes in novels or poetry) may be counterproductive, not lending themselves to cumulative processes of appreciation. But if these are well away from the central areas of life, they hardly constitute a weakness of character. In general, interest in the new or a willingness to experiment hardly would detract from character. Experiments in cruelty or irresponsibility of course would be a special case.

It is no accident that the Daoist examination of psychic fluidity traditionally has had strong associations both with people's aesthetic relations with the world and also with a celebration of emotionally free private life. These are areas in which spontaneity and creativity can contribute a great deal. Arguably they can contribute much also to morality, especially when style of performance matters to moral quality, or when the two obvious alternatives that present themselves turn out to be inferior to more complicated ones that might come to the mind of someone with moral imagination. All the same, in much of morality—as in most decisions of whether or not to murder, torture, rape, or steal—creativity and spontaneity play little part and hardly seem called for. They loom larger as virtues of private life than of the public realm.

Nevertheless, fluidity can have a use in the public realm. This usefulness is connected with two worries. One is that an established code, unthinkingly accepted by the great majority of ordinary decent people, might turn out to be seriously inadequate. Examples are codes that allowed for slavery, for the imprisonment of debtors, or for limiting opportunities along gender lines. The moral corrections of recent centuries should give us pause, in that people (perhaps our ancestors) that seemed decent in most areas of life subscribed to what we now judge to be unthinkable. In this light, it is hard to be complacent that the morality endorsed by most of us is flawless.

The second worry is that even models of morality that center it on rules must allow for judgment and interpretation as part of the process of relating rules to specific cases. (Models of morality that relate many cases to the idea of a mean, as we have seen, assign an even larger role to judgment.) Someone who follows a conventional code that usually does not work badly may sometimes fail to appreciate the distinctiveness of a situation at hand, and may not be open to the thought that this situation should be treated differently from others. This necessity of judgment may be part of the thought behind Confucius's remark that "The 'honest villager' spoils true virtue" (*Analects* c, XVII.13), even if the primary meaning has to do with the unsatisfactory nature of conformist motivations.

Hence, it is important that we be able to change our minds either about specific cases that seem to call for moral judgment or about established moral principles. Intelligent judgment is crucial. One risk of openness that is not accompanied by intelligent judgment is that people will convince themselves that the sort of thing they had thought was wrong—but now everyone seems to be doing it—really is all right in the new world order of fascism, or Stalinism, or the world of aggressive corporate finance, or whatever. In this direction lies corruption. Faced with cases of this sort, we may be tempted to insist that the best, the safest, policy is to follow established morality. But what do we think then of the first people who reflectively and painfully decided that slavery was morally unacceptable, or of those disruptive ones who first insisted that women should have equal opportunities?

This line of thought may seem remote from the subject of psychic fluidity, but it is not. I have argued, in effect, that some degree of resistance to psychic change in areas of self related to morality and to core personal relationships and projects is important to character. But if the degree of resistance is too high, the open-mindedness lacked by the "honest villager" and by those who continued to endorse slavery will be impossible. There is every reason to expect, also, that the people who are not always dogmatic about morality, and who when it is appropriate are open to reconsideration, will be those who manifest some openness and fluidity that will enrich other aspects of their lives.

Similar comments can be made about adherence to core personal relationships and projects. Arguably, there can be value in being open to the thought "This isn't working." It is hard to deny that midcareer shifts or divorces are ever justified. All the same, if the thought "This isn't working" comes too easily, as perhaps it has for some who have many careers (in which there is not time to attain real proficiency), this suggests excessive psychic fluidity. Again, judgment is crucial, especially the ability to judge when sticking with the established situation can have rewards and when it would be absolutely intolerable.

Good character does not require that one never act out of character or that there not be areas in life of the sort of spontaneity that can involve unpredictability. Nor does it preclude second thoughts about the dictates of morality or about central personal relationships. What it does require is stability where it matters. The contrast drawn has been between a unity of self growing out of fixity and stagnation, on one hand, and a limited unity of self that displays control over one's thoughts and behavior and may require will power, on the other.

PART III

Choice

9

CHOICE AND POSSIBILITY

The subject of choice has been dogged by cases like the following. Snurf suffers from a powerful addiction, which makes it utterly predictable that in three hours (when his previous dose has worn off) he will again inject his drug of choice. Meanwhile, Snurf is deliberating over whether to do this: reasons against it come to his mind and seem persuasive. Over the three-hour period the inner debate evolves. More and more arguments come to mind that it would do no harm to take the drug again, or that now is not the time to stop. The objections begin to seem weak and pointless. At the end of the three hours Snurf makes his decision; he takes the drug.

This process has the felt character and appearance of a choice, and yet it is very tempting—because the outcome is entirely predictable—to say that this appearance is an illusion. Snurf did not really have a choice, we might say. To have a choice is to have the possibility of going either way, and the possibility that Snurf would not take the drug was only apparent.

The denial of choice that this line of thought represents can be evaluated in two different ways. First, is it true that Snurf did not have a choice, even though "phenomenologically" it seemed a choice? It should be noted that the inclination most of us have to deny that Snurf really did have a choice may be strengthened by the fact that we think of drug addiction as not close to the core of what Snurf is: it seems more like a physiological vise, which could be removed if Snurf is cured.

We might hesitate more over the following case. Schweitzer is offered a huge reward if he does something shabby or unworthy; there are plausible reasons for accepting, and he deliberates for some time, finally saying "No." But anyone, let us suppose, who knew Schweitzer could have confidently predicted that he would decline. Schweitzer himself might say in the end, "I had no choice." But we might be torn, saying, "In a way he did, and in a way he did not."

Now one of the differences between the two cases is that the second has a closer relation to character than the first. A possible move is to hold that, even if behavior is causally determined, it still counts as the agent's choice if the causality is routed through the agent's character. Because it genuinely grows out of character, it does count as her or his choice. This escape route looks more clearly available for Schweitzer's case than for Snurf's.

A second difference is that in the real world, if we cannot identify powerful physiological forces at work, we tend to regard human decisions as at best highly predictable, not as entirely predictable. People, even ones we know well, sometimes surprise us. Thus our ordinary thought about choice and possibility (which I want to suggest is divided and confused) allows us to think, "Well anything is possible." If we are a bit less likely to say this in Snurf's case than in Schweitzer's, our hesitancy may be a tribute to the contemporary influence of the idea that human beings are—underneath it all—physical systems and that in some cases, like Snurf's, this fact can be the whole story of how someone behaves. Is this a coherent response? Possibly not.

The second issue that grows out of the denial that Snurf had a choice, then, is this. Should we take Snurf's case as in some sense paradigmatic, and say that the only difference between his and more ordinary decisions is that the physiological mechanisms that determined his behavior were more apparent and easier to appreciate than is normally the case? Is the only difference between Snurf's and Schweitzer's cases that we already know what makes Snurf tick, and we must await progress in the human sciences (or in neurophysiology) before we have similar knowledge of what makes Schweitzer tick?

Anyone who is persuaded by this line of thought will accept determinism (that our behavior is entirely determined by antecedent factors). This acceptance can lead to the further step of holding that we never really have choices, especially if a philosopher rejects the escape route of making exceptions of cases in which the causal route from antecedent factors to decision goes through what we would think of as the agent's character. The "hard determinist" can contend that when we eventually come to understand ordinary decisions as well as we understand Snurf's, we will come to treat them all in the same way.

It might seem relevant that in the current state of the human sciences it is hard to claim 100 percent certainty for any prediction of Schweitzer's behavior. Something like 99.9 percent seems more the norm for highly confident forecasts. This limitation may contribute to the current popularity of "soft" forms of determinism. They appeal to a double vision: when we fully understand human behavior, all decisions may seem much like Snurf's, but in the meantime some futures seem open—and we can gesture at the factors that make that seem the case and hold that these constitute something like freedom. As a result of such considerations, someone who accepts determinism, with its accompanying pressure to hold that we never really have choices, may well be inclined to say that of course, in a sense, we do have choices. This is a philosophical neurosis of common sense.

The question of choice constitutes a large and daunting subject. Can we assume that the human sciences in the future will become capable (or at least in principle are capable) of predictions at the level of confidence displayed by some of the textbook predictions of physics and chemistry? Or is there something in the human subject matter that renders this level of certainty impossible? If the human sciences do become as rigorous as physics and chemistry, will we abandon our current conception of choice?

Let me suggest that at this point there is hardly a compelling case for determinism, which can be taken as an idealization of hopes for great success in the human sciences (or for all significant uncertainties to be removed by advances in neurophysiology). Nor is there a compelling case against it. We may well, in the interim before more light is shed on the issue, wish to have a provisional sense of "choice," one that does not take sides on determinism. Such a sense conceivably could survive even if determinism is firmly established or refuted.

The essay that follows suggests such a sense, in which "choice" is linked to "possibility" in that to have a choice is to have more than one possibility. It is arguable that in this sense (whether or not determinism is true) Snurf does not really have a choice, however it may feel to him at the time. Perhaps Schweitzer also does not genuinely have a choice, if yielding to temptation goes against his developed nature and if there is no inclination to reconsider that nature or to make room for an exception.

When do we have choices? A short answer is that they are far more abundant before someone has formed a character than is likely afterward. The life of a teenager is full of choices. But even someone with a developed character can reconsider or can think "Just this once." Further, a character should not be thought of as a detailed blueprint for everything that comes up in life. Someone whose character is to be honest will not have a choice when there is a clear-cut issue of honesty, unless of course she or he is at that moment genuinely prepared to reconsider the policy that the character subsumes. But sometimes it will not be clear whether a decision does involve issues of honesty: there can be borderline cases or ones requiring interpretation, in which an honest person could act in more than one way. Even if there is a clear-cut issue of honesty, there may also be more than one option that includes honesty.

In short, to have a developed character does not preclude having choices. Increasingly, though, these choices (as when there is more than one option that includes honesty) will be ones of style or nuance rather than involving a dramatic parting of ways. Some choices that a teenager makes can be put under the heading of "What kind of person am I to be?" Dramatic moral choices will generally have this character. Someone with a developed character may well find that she or he "has no choice" on such occasions.

Mencius

Two of the four philosophers discussed in the essay to follow, Hume and Kant, will be familiar to many readers; and Confucius already has been introduced in this book. Something should be said about the fourth philosopher, Mencius, a follower of Confucius who lived in the fourth century B.C.E. Mencius's philosophy shares a number of features with Confucius's thought. These include a parallelism of political and ethical concerns, the insistence that the personal goodness of those at the top is the key to social improvement, and the assumption that at the heart of personal goodness is basic humanity that has been made sophisticated by learning. The book of Mencius contains less emphasis than the *Analects* on the educational role of the arts of refinement—ritual, the classics, and music. Mencius also tends to be more pointed and assertive in his approaches to rulers whom he wishes to convert to a reign of goodness.

There are in addition two features of Mencius's thought that seem highly distinctive. (My remarks will be brief; for a magisterial study of Mencius, see Shun 1997.) One is that Mencius, in the course of presenting a view of goodness, has some interesting things to say about energy. The two topics seem related, in his view, in that the development of true goodness involves a psychological freedom (and lack of inner conflict) that liberates energy, and conversely goodness that is expressed energetically has more to be said for it.

At one point Mencius (b, book II, A. 2, 77), eschewing false modesty, comments on his own "flood-like *ch'i*." "Ch'i" (qi) is translated by Shun (1997, 68) as "vital energies." Part of what nourishes these is a heart/mind that is unmoved, in the sense of not being divided or uncertain in its orientation. But Mencius offers elaborate comments on the management of vital energies.

The second feature is that Mencius offers a sustained, explicit argument for a thesis about human nature. (For scholarly background, see Graham 1990; for convincing argument that Mencius indeed does have a conception of a common human nature, see Bloom 1997.) Mencius's claim is that innate benevolence is part of human nature. The argument centers on a thought experiment (b, book II, A. 6, 82), a case in which one can imagine that there is no obvious self-interest involved on either side of a decision. Someone sees a child about to fall into a well; would not virtually anyone (regardless of the normal nature of that person's conduct) save the child? The assumption is that various nonbenevolent impulses (including ones that we might regard as selfish) that are also within us can influence much of ordinary behavior, so that one needs a special case (in which these other impulses may be thought of as not in play) in order to isolate this special element of human nature. Hume (1751/1975, 226) executed a very similar maneuver two thousand years later with his example of deciding not to step on someone's gouty toes.

The argument also requires an explanation of why the degree of benevolence actually exhibited in human behavior varies so widely. Part of the reason lies in the effects of individual circumstances. Mencius (b, book VI, A. 8, 164–65) offers as a metaphor the state of Ox Mountain, whose trees were constantly lopped with axes; new shoots are eaten by cattle and sheep, and finally the mountain is bald. Innate benevolence is never guaranteed to be decisive in anyone's conduct, and to have much influence needs to have scope and opportunity and to be encouraged.

Because of his claim that benevolence is innate, Mencius is often contrasted with Xunzi (Hsun-tzu, third century BCE), who represents a rival form of Confucianism that emphasizes that human nature requires control through the processes of cultivation and through law. The simplest expression of the contrast has been that Mencius believes that human nature is good and that Xunzi (Hsun-tzu) believes that it is bad. But this amounts to caricature, in that Mencius never denies that humans have nonbenevolent sources of motivations, nor does he deny the importance of cultivation; and Xunzi for his part clearly assumes that there are elements in human nature that can lend themselves to cultivation. Xunzi's view in a way is that morality is an acquired taste (see Ivanhoe 1993b, chapter 3). There are important differences, but there is not diametric opposition.

A similar point can be made about Mencius's (and more generally the Confucian) relation to Daoism. Mencius does say (b, book IV, B. 16, 130), for example, that "You can never succeed in winning the allegiance of men by trying to dominate them through goodness." He also observes (a, book VI, B. 12, 322), that "[t]he great man is he who does not lose his child's-heart." (Lau has "retains the heart of a new-born babe.") It would be wrong to see Confucians as opposed to spontaneity, although clearly it is more circumscribed for them than it is for, say, Zhuangzi.

10

CONFUCIUS, MENCIUS, HUME, AND KANT ON REASON AND CHOICE

Herbert Fingarette (1972, 18) has suggested that Confucius is interestingly and dramatically different from Western thinkers in that he omits "the whole complex of notions centering around 'choice' and 'responsibility.'" This is one of a number of provocative and valuable points that Fingarette makes about Confucius; but, like the *Analects* itself, this statement is subject to interpretation. One might distinguish between the strong interpretation—Confucius does not think that the people he talks about make what we would term choices—and a more moderate interpretation— of course Confucius thinks that people make what we would term choices, but they are not or should not be (in some sense, to be explicated) "real" choices. In what follows I will discuss the concept of choice in order to ex- plicate the difference between the strong interpretation (in which the claim about Confucius would be false) and the moderate one (in which it is true). I will then broaden the discussion to include a comparison of how Mencius, Hume, and Kant treat choice, as opposed to Confucius's treatment. As part of this comparison, I will contrast the roles that reason seems to be assigned in choice by these four thinkers.

Before beginning, I should like to make some remarks about how this investigation fits into the growing discipline of comparative philosophy. First, the student of comparative philosophy can expect to find some interesting similarities between Asian and Western philosophies, but must be cautious about them. For there are differences not only in substantive claims and em- phasis but also in the ways in which key terms must be interpreted. For example, it is often said that Confucian ethical philosophy contains no concept closely parallel to the Western concept of "morality" (as a special realm of emphatic normative judgments, in some accounts closely linked to generali- zations), although there certainly are subtle and enlightening discussions in the Confucian canon of problems that we would term moral. In much the same way, we cannot count on philosophers such as Confucius and Mencius to have concepts that correspond closely to the traditional Western concepts of reason and choice.

Thus, step one toward a more sensitive discussion of Confucian and Western treatments of reason and choice is the understanding that we must not expect Confucian and Western philosophers to be answering exactly the same questions. Step two is to refrain from thinking of Eastern and Western philosophies as two tightly unified philosophical traditions. For the West itself does not subscribe to a single conceptual map. Thus, the very differences between Confucian and Western ethics with regard to the concept of "morality" that have already been pointed out can also be argued to obtain between, say, Aristotle and Kant. And the differences between the conceptualizations of reason and choice in Hume and Kant may be as great as those between Hume and the Confucians. Nor does the East subscribe to a single conceptual map. We need not even assume that, because Mencius is a Confucian and in many ways identifies his position with that of the master, his conceptualization of what in ordinary English would be termed "choice" is identical with that of Confucius.

Choice

Here is a provisional definition of "choice." X has made a choice in situation S if and only if more than one course of action was possible for X and X decided among these possibilities. This definition is provisional, in part, because it leaves open the question of the sense in which we can speak of a course of action as "possible" for an agent. If what is meant is "causally possible, given all antecedent conditions," and if determinism is correct, then it follows from the definition that there are no choices. We can postpone discussion of this counterintuitive view for a while, because there is nothing to suggest that either Confucius or Mencius was a determinist; also, I will suggest an alternative reading of "possible."

Another disturbing loose end is the word "decided." Must decision involve an articulation of alternatives along with some process of weighing relevant factors or reasons for action? Or does it count as decision if an agent merely sees two possible paths to follow and immediately follows one? Those of us who are not wedded to an extremely intellectualized image of moral life will surely want to answer "Yes" to this latter question. The matter becomes less easy if we suppose that one of the two possible paths does not even occur to the agent, who immediately goes along the other, especially if there is no hesitation or break in his or her motion. But, then, has the agent in any sense decided or chosen anything? Those who are heavily influenced by the vision of human life found in such works as Sartre's *Being and Nothingness* may still want to answer "Yes"; the alternative is to concede that in many cases vital parts of people's lives are not decided upon or chosen by them, and it may be held to follow from this concession that people are not responsible for those parts of their lives. If it is true that important alternatives often do not register in people's thinking, we are left with a number of unattractive accounts from which to choose. Either we deny that people are responsible for that about which they have been totally thoughtless; or we say that they are responsible even though they have not decided that for which they are responsible; or we say that they have made decisions that they were (in any normal sense) unaware of having made.

We can now return to the word "possible." Let me suggest that the sense appropriate to what we call "choice" is as follows: Y is possible for X in situation S if and only if a reasonable judge, knowing X's character, X's perception of S, and all other knowable antecedent conditions, would not find it astounding if X did Y. This definition of "possible" is deliberately loose ("astounding" is hardly a precise term), and it fudges on determinism. But it does capture the sense in which it is not possible that various prominent scholars of Asian philosophy will run naked through a session of the next American Philosophical Association meeting, and in which their appearing clothed would not be taken to be the result of choice; one takes the disreputable alternative not to be "possible," whether or not one accepts determinism, and even if one mutters that, in the abstract, "anything is possible." It also captures the sense in which, even if determinism is true, it is possible that Z will wear a blue tie at the meeting and also possible that he will wear a red one instead.

The point here is related to a phrase Fingarette uses more than once: "genuine option/alternative." (In William James's [1947] pioneering discussion, the phrases are "live hypothesis"/"living option": a living option is one between two hypotheses, both of which are live.) I shall use the phrase "live option" for anything that is a possibility in the sense just defined. As James's discussion suggests, even though a person might in some sense have any one of an indefinite number of religious beliefs, in practice it is usually the case that the live options are restricted to two: the belief the person was brought up with and disbelief. Along similar lines, we might say that people's live options in moral matters are often rather restricted. How restricted they are is an interesting empirical question.

One of the goals of the elementary moral education to which people are exposed at a very young age is to render certain kinds of behavior impossible. In this, moral education may build on natural sentiments. Whatever the respective contributions of natural sentiment and education may have been, it probably is impossible for any of us to torture a child to death, whatever the circumstances; one can say this without having to take a stand on the issues of determinism versus free will. Beyond this very minimal decency, a great many other things may be impossible for a well-brought-up person. The question may naturally arise: is anything possible, apart from the life the person actually leads or one roughly like it? It should be emphasized again that this question is not the same as the metaphysical question of determinism, and that an anti-determinist can hold that, in matters of consequence, our live options are drastically restricted, while a determinist can hold that we often do (in the sense defined) have more than one live option. There is one further point that will be explored in what follows: It may be that the range of live options varies significantly from person to person, depending on the tightness of integration of different people's lives. It may be, that is, that some people have many live options apart from what they actually do or are, and that other people have essentially none.

With this thought, let us turn to the *Analects*. As I have argued elsewhere (see chapter 2), it is possible to view Confucius as an advocate of a higher naturalness, in which a person's own mind becomes a controlled work of art, and art becomes nature. The life of such a person would be very highly integrated indeed. The scope of the integration is suggested by a passage in the Confucian *Doctrine of the Mean* (124) that claims that "the superior man is watchful over himself, when he is alone." The degree of integration aimed for is suggested by the passage from the Songs, endorsed by the Master,

> As thing cut, as thing filed,
> As thing chiseled, as thing polished,

and by the autobiographical report that only at the age of seventy could Confucius "follow the dictates of my own heart" without worrying about overstepping the boundaries of right (*Analects* c, I.15, 87; II.4, 88). Plainly, the process of integration should continue throughout a lifetime. The rewards in terms of inner satisfaction are considerable and to a great extent render one invulnerable to luck or chance. Thus "[a] true gentleman is calm and at ease; the Small Man is fretful and ill at ease. He "that is really Good can never be unhappy." "The Gentleman" has nothing to fear (VII.36, 131; IX.28, 144; XII.4, 163).

Confucius's picture of the sage fits Fingarette's remarks very well. Such a man would seem to have no live options other than that of the Way (that is, of a sagelike existence), and perhaps, occasionally, when old desires flicker, that of abandoning the Way. The ideal of human life might therefore seem to be, at the extreme, a person who has no genuine choices.

Yet to present this as Confucius' picture of what human life is like would be to overstate the case in two respects. First, the person who has no genuine choices represents an ideal; furthermore, there are many people who are not especially sagelike and who are far from this ideal. The *Analects* laid very heavy emphasis on the presentation of the ideal, as well as on descriptions of Confucius himself, who certainly came very close. But virtually no one has reached the ideal, for a number of reasons, one of them suggested by Confucius's remark that "I have never yet seen anyone whose desire to build up his moral power was as strong as sexual desire" (IX.17, 142). And, in any case, Confucius not only does not deny that there are other forms of human life besides that which is close to the ideal, but also talks about them. I will return to this point shortly.

Second, even someone who is committed to following the Way, and whose psyche is chiseled and polished, can have moments when she or he does not know what is the best thing to do. It is in the light of this potential for uncertainty that we can understand the frequent references in the *Analects* to Confucius's desire to learn and to his sense of his own fallibility. One of his merits is that he is "never obstinate, never egotistic." "If you have made a mistake," he says, ". . . do not be afraid of admitting the fact and amending your ways" (IX.4, 138; IX.24, 143). In reading these passages, one must bear in mind Confucius's repeated acknowledgment of the factor of skill in politics and morality. The advice (XIII.9, 173) to first enrich and then instruct the people is presumably meant for someone who, even with all the good will in the world, might not be clear about the priorities. Similarly, such matters as "using the labor of the peasantry only at the proper times of year" (i.e., when it does not involve a major hardship for them [I.5, 84]) are important in government, and it is imaginable that a decent but poorly informed person could go wrong about this.

At the very least, then, someone who is committed to following the Way might have to choose between doing X or Y because he or she does not know at this point which of them represents the Way. This, however, is a somewhat shallow rendering of what decisions of the kind under discussion amount to. Someone committed to following the Way, who must decide between X and Y without knowing which truly represents the Way, may well to some degree also be choosing her or his character; moreover, one of the alternatives may not be entirely virtuous. As Confucius saw it, part of the problem is that virtues can degenerate into vices; indeed, he probably would have agreed with La Rochefoucauld's contention that "[o]ur virtues contain an element of vice, as medicaments are in part compounded of poisons. Prudence selects and tempers these ingredients" (La Rochefoucauld 1957, maxim 182, 66–67). A Confucian version of this maxim would, however, substitute the word "learning" for "prudence" (see *Analects* XVII.8).

The problems that we have been discussing occur at a fairly high level, one that is not enormously far from the ideal. Many people who have some virtue are not entirely committed to following the Way, or may claim that they lack the necessary strength. Jan Ch'iu, to whom Confucius directed the advice "enrich, then instruct," was one such person. At one point, he said to

Confucius, "It is not that your Way does not commend itself to me, but that it demands powers I do not possess." Confucius's reply (VI.10, 118) was, "He whose strength gives out collapses during the course of the journey (the Way); but you deliberately draw the line." Jan Ch'iu's ultimate moral failure occurred when the head of the Chi family entrusted him with collecting revenues; rather than showing concern for the people, Jan Ch'iu extorted more money. It was on this occasion that Confucius said, "He is no follower of mine. . . . You may beat the drum and set upon him." (XI.16, 156–57).

My first comment is that Confucius's language here sounds like the language of responsibility: there is at least a suggestion that Jan Ch'iu made a choice, a bad one, and should be held responsible. Furthermore, there is nothing in the story of this unworthy disciple to suggest that he had only two options: the Way or depravity. As Confucius's reply to his excuse about lack of strength makes clear, even if Jan Ch'iu ultimately was not going to follow the Way, he could have tried harder and come closer.

By and large the world of the *Analects* is polarized. At one extreme are Confucius, the ancient sage-kings, and most of the disciples: either they follow the Way or come close by trying hard. At the other extreme are various contemporary miscreants, along with the great mass of the common people: they do not know the Way but can be helped toward a life that is in many respects good. Viewing these two groups, one may easily see the alternatives as following the Way or not following the Way. Jan Ch'iu, however, offers us the case of a man in the middle, whose alternatives have to be seen as considerably more complicated.

Let me gather together the threads of the discussion thus far. We have been exploring a conception of choice in which someone has a choice if and only if she or he has more than one live option. Mental cultivation can diminish one's live options by rendering certain forms of conduct highly repugnant or unthinkable. What Fingarette has to say about Confucius is correct in this sense: Confucius thinks that people should not have any live option other than following the Way. The way represents an ideal to which Confucius himself only approximates; but, beyond its biographical function, the *Analects* is dedicated to developing this ideal.

When we move from Confucius to Mencius, the focus changes. Mencius also has something to say about the ideal, and much of this (as in his remarks about ch'i as a source of energy) goes well beyond what is in the *Analects*. But the major difference in relation to our present discussion is this: the *Analects* is largely devoid of what might be termed "existential moments," or points at which a choice is made that will determine not only matters of substance but also a person's character for the rest of his or her life. The closest to this kind of point that we come in the *Analects* is in relation to such behavior as Jan Ch'iu's in extorting money; and even here, it is suggested that what takes place is not a change of character but rather a continuation or working out of past unfortunate tendencies. In any case, we come on the scene not at the moment of choice but afterward, in time to see a response. Mencius, in contrast, does give us existential moments. He suggests that a character can change drastically, that the potential for change is already present and that, with the right prodding from a great philosopher, someone can become a different person.

The best-known existential moment in Mencius concerns the king who spared the sacrificial ox, which shows the king's innate benevolence. Mencius suggests that this benevolence could be extended to the people: the king might also ensure that the people have enough to eat, and that education is provided in village schools (b, book I, A. 7, 54–59). This famous passage really centers on two existential moments. First, there was the moment at which the king (seeing the animal's frightened appearance) spared the ox, without fully understanding why; this points toward a second existential moment, which may or may not be realized, in which the king, having been aided in bringing his benevolence to clear self-consciousness, decides to extend this benevolence to his people systematically. He has the choice.

None of this denies Confucius's view that the perfect sage has no choices. Nor does it represent the simple optimism about unalloyed human goodness that Mencius is sometimes, simplistically, represented as avowing. Instead we are led to realize that ordinary men and women who are not sages have within them a mixture of forces, including benevolence and selfishness, which give them the potential for a variety of types of action, both virtuous and blameworthy. This image of divided selves that can be led to create their own unity by means of an appropriate focus anticipates Pascal and the modern existentialists. The king can focus on his own innate benevolence and thereby become a different, and more successful, person.

Mencius's argumentative strategy is repeatedly to get people to become aware of the benevolent element within themselves. Sometimes the manifestations of benevolence are slight and easily missed: for example, someone who is fond of music, whether sophisticated or popular, will want to share the experience with others (b, book I, B. 1, 60). One may have to set up an extreme and abstractly presented case as a thought experiment—for example, the case of the child about to fall into the well (book II, A. 6)—in order to make clear that there is some degree of benevolence in everyone.

It is as important to avoid a romanticist reading of Mencius as it is to avoid reading him as a simpleminded optimist. Mencius's view is not that, if we become clear about our benevolence and exercise it constantly, we will thereby be guaranteed to behave well on all occasions. Like Confucius, he believes that proper awareness of the details of a situation is important in deciding what is appropriate to it; thus when he praises Confucius's flexibility (book II, A. 2), he is also proclaiming his own. Also like Confucius, he believes that benevolence needs to be complemented by technique; "Goodness alone is not sufficient for government" (b, book IV, A. 1, 117). What is essential, in the end, is acting out of benevolence; you "go into what you have learned in detail so that in the end you can return to the essential," but the details do matter (b, book IV, B. 15, 130). Because details matter, even someone who is entirely dominated by benevolence will have genuine choices to make. Again like Confucius, Mencius leaves room for two kinds of situation in which one might have more than one live option. One is the case in which an entirely benevolent person has to work out what the benevolent course of action is when there are two or more plausible alternatives. The second kind is the case in which someone who has not been entirely benevolent has a chance to behave benevolently. Mencius differs from Confucius in stressing the importance of this latter kind of case, and in arguing for the ongoing live possibility of benevolent behavior for any of us.

As any commentator must be wary of possible misinterpretation or over-interpretation, a note of caution should be sounded here. Mencius never says in so many words that someone who has not been thoroughly good can change his or her character drastically. On the other hand, he urges people who fit that description, such as the king who spared the ox, to begin to behave in a thoroughly benevolent way. And this certainly does suggest that Mencius believed a drastic change of character is possible. Even so, however, we might wonder how quickly Mencius believed someone could change his or her character. Could a drastic change be sudden, or must it occur in stages?

Hume, as previously noted, suggests a very cautious response to this last question. The dominant view, in the *Treatise of Human Nature* and elsewhere, is that character does not (normally) change drastically, and that whatever changes are possible must occur gradually. Hume's view on these matters is so far removed from what people who have read only a little of his work tend to ascribe to him, that the background of his account of character change must be outlined.

First, as Annette Baier (1979) has pointed out, Hume develops a much more positive account of self in books II and III of the Treatise than in book I. At the root of this difference may be Hume's distinction "betwixt" personal identity, as regards our thought and imagination, and as it regards our passions or the concern we take in ourselves (Hume 1739/1978, 253). "The true idea of the human mind," Hume goes on to say, "is to consider it as a system of different perceptions or different existences, which are linked together by the relation of cause and effect." Memory does not so much produce as discover personal identity, and it does so by showing us the relation of cause and effect among our different perceptions (ibid., 261–62). The self, in the account that Hume begins to develop, is a "connected succession of perceptions," which is the object of both pride and humility (ibid., 277). The nature of a person's self is stable enough so that we can speak of her or his character, and this is the object of moral judgment; indeed, Hume says that people are not to be blamed for acts not caused by their characters or dispositions (ibid., 411). "If any *action* be either virtuous or vicious," according to Hume,

> 'tis only as a sign of some quality or character. It must depend upon durable principles of the mind, which extend over the whole conduct, and enter into the personal character. Actions themselves, not proceeding from any constant principle . . . are never consider'd in morality. (ibid., 575, Hume's emphasis)

Normally when we blame someone, it is for something that we consider to be under his or her control. Thus, if Hume is right, if judgments of blame ultimately focus on character, it would seem to follow that character can be controlled, that someone can change his or her character if he or she wants to. But Hume denies this implication by denying a close connection between praise and blame, on the one hand, and possible control of what is praised or blamed, on the other. First, as Hume sees it, there is no sharp distinction between natural abilities and moral virtues; we praise and disparage the former as well as the latter. If it is said that natural abilities are involuntary and therefore have no merit, Hume's response is that many of the moral virtues "are equally involuntary and necessary . . . [i]t being almost impossible for the mind to change its character in any considerable article" (ibid., 608).

The word "almost" in the last passage admits qualifications. These emerge in Hume's essay "The Sceptic." This remarkable work centers on two topics: the objectivity of various kinds of knowledge, and also what nowadays would be termed "philosophy of life." In discussion Hume pays his debts to Cicero and the stoics, while developing an account of the neo-stoic virtue of gaiety. Hume suggests that one cannot change one's character by means of edicts addressed to oneself: "Mankind are almost entirely guided by constitution and temper, and . . . general maxims have little influence" (Hume 1985, 169). Indirect methods such as the formation of ideals can, however, have an effect:

> The prodigious effects of education may convince us, that the mind is not altogether stubborn and inflexible, but will admit of many alterations from its original make and structure. Let a man propose to himself the model of a character, which he approves: Let him be well acquainted with those particulars, in which his own character deviates from this model . . . and I doubt not but, in time, he will find, in his temper, an alteration for the better. (ibid., 170)

Habit is, Hume suggests, "another powerful means of . . . implanting . . . good dispositions and inclinations" (ibid., 171–72). For if one can impose appropriate habits upon oneself, changes of character will gradually follow.

This perspective on character development adds up to a view in which one may have genuine choices in the long run that one does not have in the short run. Existential moments are as much missing from the moral universe that Hume presents as they are from the world of the *Analects*. Instead we are presented with the idea that a well-chosen regimen can gradually lead to a change of character. The concept of responsibility, though, remains in Hume's world, because in this world the connection with genuine choice that it is often assigned has been severed.

The answers that Confucius, Mencius, and Hume provide to the question, "How much choice does a person genuinely have?" (or that can be inferred from what they say) are all univocal but carefully qualified, and, because of the subtlety of the qualifications, difficult to grasp. In contrast, Kant at first appears to be bold and straightforward. My view is that this seeming straightforwardness is deceptive, and that there is more ambiguity and confusion in Kant's view than in those of the philosophers thus far considered. We can see this if we begin with a summary of the standard account of Kant's view of choice, and then go on to raise some questions about this account.

What every properly trained philosophy graduate student knows about Kant's view of freedom is that he gives two answers to our question: (1) that a person never has any genuine choice, and (2) that, at least in moral matters, a person always has a genuine choice. Answer 1 holds if our purview is restricted to the phenomenal world, but consideration of the noumenal world leads us to answer 2. The reason for answer 1 is that one of the categories we impose on experience is that of cause and effect; and, indeed, if the world were a blooming, buzzing confusion of phenomena not governed by causal laws, experience and human intelligence would be impossible. Hence, it is a synthetic a priori truth that every event has a cause. Thus, determinism is true of every event in the phenomenal world, even of actions that would seem to involve moral choices. "If we could exhaustively investigate all the appearances of men's wills, there would not be found a single human action which we could not predict with certainty" (Kant 1781/1985, A 550, B 578, 474).

Why, one might wonder, should "X causes Y" be taken to imply "Given X, Y is predictable with certainty"? Kant never gives a satisfactory explanation of this, but plunges ahead with determinism. Determinism, however, cannot be the last word about actions that we take to involve moral choice; the very existence of morality implies that there are at least some moral choices that are genuine ("ought" implies "can"), and hence there are genuine alternatives to some of the things that people do. Thus (as Kant sees it) we must look outside of the phenomenal world for a source of human freedom. That source is noumenal reason, which we are entitled to posit as the best and only explanation of the freedom that the morality of which we are aware presupposes. Hence we can tell two stories about actions that seem to involve moral choice: (1) the determinism story is good psychology, and is true; but (2) the freedom-grounded-in-noumenal-reason story is also true and represents a deeper (more ultimate) truth.

This is a received interpretation of Kant, and it is also widely accepted that there are great difficulties in Kant's introduction of the noumenal world to account for the freedom that he thinks he must posit. First, we should mention a resolution of the problem of freedom that Kant entertains but does not accept: that a cause in the field of appearance of someone's behavior is not "so determining that it excludes a causality of our will—a causality which, independently of those natural causes, and *even contrary to their force and influence*," can produce empirically determinable behavior (ibid., A 534, B 562, 465, emphasis added). To resolve the problem thus would involve reason's "venturing beyond the limits of possible experience" and coming into conflict with itself, which would work only if appearances were things in themselves (ibid., A 535, B 563, 465–66). The correct resolution requires that we see freedom and determinism not as in conflict, but rather as true in different ways. Freedom applies to the intelligible character of a person, and determinism to the empirical character. Kant says this clearly, but he also says some things that sound different, remarking that how much of the moral character of a person's actions "is ascribable to the pure effect of freedom, how much to mere nature . . . can never be determined"; on his own account this is to ask how two very different modes of explanation can be combined and weighed together (ibid., A 551, B 579, 475n).

The intelligible character is outside of time: as intelligible, one is "free from all influence of sensibility and from all determination through appearances." But, inasmuch as this intelligible character is noumenon, "nothing *happens* in it; there can be no change" (ibid., A 541, B 569, 469, Kant's emphasis). Where in the realm of freedom, one might wonder, is the possibility of moral improvement, or the sheer fact of moral decision? The absence of any developed account of moral education from Kant's work is hardly an accident.

Freedom, in Kant's view, requires actions that are in some sense determined by reason. Now reason has a phenomenal aspect: there are, after all, recognizable phenomena of people thinking and behaving rationally, and a person's rational activity can play as causal a role in her or his actions as any sensuous impulse. Our freedom, though, points beyond phenomenal rationality to what Kant calls reason "in its intelligible character." "The causality of pure reason, he tells us, is outside of time" (ibid., A 551, B 579, 475). Here a possible serious difficulty arises: many commentators have pointed out that cause and effect is a category and hence cannot be applicable to the noumenal world. Indeed, how can there be causality as we know it if there is no temporal order that can separate cause and effect? An alternative version of this line of criticism is that the word "cause" is ambiguous in the Kantian context: whatever it means in relation to phenomena it cannot mean in relation to noumena. Kant was sensitive to this ambiguity, and returned to the point in the second Critique, arguing that, even though he had deduced the objective reality of the category of causality "only with regard to *objects of possible experience*," the seat of the concept was fixed in the pure understanding, "and it can be used even of noumena" (Kant 1788/1898, 171–72, p. 144, Kant's emphasis). Kant, however, must go on to concede that this is so, "without our being able in the least to define the concept theoretically so as to produce knowledge" (ibid.). Thus, he remains vulnerable to the charge that he is, in his own terms, in no position to know what he means when he speaks of the causality of intelligible reason.

One other passage in the *Critique of Practical Reason* deserves mention here. Kant occasionally descends to discussion of how matters appear to common sense. He gives an example of someone who claims to be governed by uncontrollable lust: we ask him, if a gallows were erected and he were to be hanged immediately after the gratification of his lust, could he not indeed control it? The answer, Kant assures us, will surely be "Yes." We can also ask the same person,

> If his sovereign ordered him, on pain of the same immediate execution, to bear false witness against an honourable man, whom the prince might wish to destroy under a plausible pretext, would he consider it possible in that case to overcome his love of life, however great it may be. He would perhaps not venture to affirm whether he would do so or not, but he must unhesitatingly admit that it is possible to do so. (Ibid., 141, pp. 118–19)

I would like to suggest that this example rings true, although in my view it is for very different reasons from those Kant was prepared to supply. Much as the religious live options of most people include the religion in which they were brought up, along with unbelief, so it is arguable that, for virtually everyone, even people who might be considered depraved, a virtuous choice in a case like the one Kant describes will always be a live option. (The smallness of this claim should be noted: a single virtuous choice might be a live option for someone for whom a sustained virtuous way of life might not be possible.) If this is true, then it may be that one of Kant's starting points is the apprehension of a down-to-earth fact about the possibilities of human choice, which fact he then gilds and decorates with the heights of philosophical sophistication and confusion.

What distinguishes Kant, indeed, from Confucius and Hume is that Kant's starting point lies not in a thoughtful awareness of how a person's possibilities are almost always more limited than they might seem to be, but rather in an ideal of scientific rigor that anticipates Laplace's determinism. I have already suggested that the presuppositions of coherent experience do not, as Kant supposes, require determinism: if every event has a cause in the weak sense of there being a set of antecedent conditions that, when grasped, would make it seem to a reasonable person much more likely and less surprising that the event would occur, this is more than enough to give us the sense of a minimally orderly world. To realize that causation in a weak sense would suffice is to see determinism as like science fiction (like it in the sense of affirming something of which we have no reason to be confident on the basis of current scientific knowledge, but which might seem plausible on the basis of an imaginable science more advanced than what we have). Therefore, there is no present reason to prefer a determinist model of what is possible or not possible to the common sense model Kant invokes in reporting the case of the man threatened with the gallows. Nor is there any reason to assume that the question "What is possible for a person in the direction of her or his life?" must take some highly general form that is rooted in metaphysical doctrine. Underlying the subtle differences among what Confucius, Mencius, and Hume have to offer in relation to this issue is the shared assumption that individual character matters to the answer, that the range of what is possible depends on what a woman or man has become.

Reason

To turn from the topic of choice to reason is to look at much the same textual data in a new way. We look again for situations in which a philosopher seems to think that people have a genuine choice to make. This time, though, we go on to look for recommended ways of arriving at a choice, or at what are held to be relevant considerations.

This may seem to some to be a naive approach to our four philosophers. If one thinks of reason along the lines of what is operative in mathematics or in formal logic, it may seem that Confucius and Mencius have nothing to say about it, that Hume is in some respects dismissive of it, and that only Kant upholds the honor of rationality. Many philosophers nowadays would see things in this way, but this is surely a superficial view.

For one thing, the account that Kant builds up of the role of reason in moral decision making concerns something that cannot readily be assimilated to deductive or inductive inference. Unfortunately, Hume's view also turns out to be more complicated than many people would like to believe. It is true that he says, "Tis not contrary to reason to prefer the destruction of the whole world to the scratching of my finger"; but he also says what is "vulgarly call'd . . . reason" is the calmer passions (Hume 1739/1978, 416, 419). "By reason," Hume says, we mean affections that are like passions, but such as operate more calmly, and cause no disorder in the temper"; and it is clear that there is more than one important role in his ethics for something that he would be willing to call reason (ibid., 437). Once we abandon a rigid notion of what is to count as reason, we can see also that there is a role for reason in the ethical philosophies of Confucius and Mencius. I will suggest one similarity between Hume's and Mencius's views of rational sympathy.

In my judgment, the comparisons that follow are useful, and help to shed light on Confucius and Mencius. But it should be emphasized now, especially, that these comparisons represent something like forced interrogation, in that the questions are by and large ones that Confucius and Mencius do not themselves ask. If one gets to know a person fairly well, one can imagine what she or he would be likely to say or do in some unfamiliar situation; and in much the same way, we can use things that Confucius and Mencius did say to reconstruct plausibly what they would have said, if our questions about reason were somehow translated not too inadequately for them. But it is important to remember that the thrust of inquiry was different for them from what it was for, say, Kant. For that matter, it would be wrong to see Hume and Kant as asking exactly the same questions. Among the many differences between them, there is one that stands out: Kant's approach to moral judgment is generally prospective, so that he wants to know how we can decide what we ought to do, while Hume's approach to the same question is generally retrospective, so that his questions center on how people have arrived at a shared vision of what they ought to do.

In Kant's view, it is the form rather than the matter of maxims that is morally crucial: "It is the legislative form, then contained in the maxim, which can alone constitute a principle of determination of the [free] will" (Kant 1788/1898, 140, p. 117). The bare form of the law can only be conceived by reason" (ibid., 139, p. 116). What is grasped here by reason is not a pattern of deductive or inductive inference. It is, rather, the form that is required by a certain kind of thought. Just as aesthetic judgment, as Kant argues in the third Critique, requires disinterestedness, so also moral judgment carries with it certain special requirements, such as a kind of universalizability, respect for persons and the suitability to an ideal world of what is willed. Someone whose thought fails to meet any of these requirements (a failure that Kant seems to suggest entails a failure to meet all of them) has failed to think morally.

In short, the rationality that Kant sees as essential to moral reflection is the ability to enter into specifically moral forms of thought. This view of rationality connects with other elements in Kant's philosophy: the first Critique, after all, centers on an examination of the forms of thought that coherent experience in general demands of us. Nor is Kant's view of morality entirely unprecedented. Robert Paul Wolff (1966) has pointed out that the synthetic a priori truths at the core of how we must think are prefigured in Hume as propensities of human thought as it moves from idea to idea. Similarly, the a priori truths generated by entry into a specifically moral mode of thought are prefigured in Hume by the concept of the moral point of view.

To use moral language, according to Hume (1751/1975, 228–29; 274n.), is to pass from merely personal appeals to others' sympathy or support to more general appeals, grounded in the way human beings ought to respond (can be expected to respond) to the case at hand. One might be reminded also of Confucius's remark (*Analects* II.14, 91) that "[a] gentleman can see a question from all sides without bias." Of course, neither Hume nor Confucius is talking about a source of a priori truths, nor is either attempting to design a universal test of purportedly moral injunctions: this remained to be patented by Kant. But what Confucius and Hume (and, arguably, Mencius as well) share with Kant is the insight that there is a special impersonality that is, or should be, involved when one speaks or thinks of what is right or on the whole best. Hume is perhaps most sharply different from Kant in that he does not directly suggest that some feature of what is involved in entering this distinctive mode of thought and speech can be used in arriving at a judgment of what is right or best in a case at hand, although such a suggestion does not run counter to anything Hume says and I will argue that it is, in some sense, implicit in his view. Confucius's remark about the (presumably superior) gentleman's point of view does seem to me to make such a suggestion, and there is no reason to think that Mencius would not have endorsed it. Confucius's unbiased perception is an arrow that points in the same direction as that in which the machinery of Kant's categorical imperative moves; but this is a similarity in the midst of vast differences. What Confucius provides is in no sense moral machinery, dependent as it is on the character and temperament of the person who takes up Confucius's suggestion; and there is no hint of synthetic a priori truths.

Nevertheless, there is something like "reason" operative in Confucius's ethics, if we are willing to construe the word "reason" so broadly that it is implicated in any positive answer to the question "Is there a good way to decide such matters as whether to increase taxes?" Certainly Confucius does not believe that an acceptable policy about taxation will come to a man if he merely closes his eyes and waits for an answer to pop into his head; nor does he believe that it will come in a surge of emotion. Everything in the *Analects* points to something like this: one should gather and weigh facts about the effects of taxation, and all of this should take place in the general context of a sympathy for the needs of the people. Someone influenced by the ethical philosophy of, say, Charles Stevenson might want to analyze Confucius's approach into (1) a basic attitude (sympathy for the needs of the people), and (2) the formation of beliefs about such things as the effects of taxation. But it is far from clear that the text of the *Analects* can sustain this separation, in that its attitude toward the suffering of the people is shaped and given substance by awareness of the facts, and in that a properly sympathetic attitude counts as what we would call a "reasonable" one.

The process of cognitive transformation of an attitude is outlined with especial clarity by Mencius: each of us has a basic attitude of sympathy, which is extended occasionally (to the ox about to be slaughtered, the child about to fall into the well). The process of becoming a good person does not require that we have a different attitude; rather, it requires that the basic attitude be applied in a systematic and intelligent way. In many cases we fail to behave sympathetically, either because the basic attitude is blocked or overridden (say, by selfishness, or because we are preoccupied with special goals), or because we fail to realize a need for sympathy (perhaps because of insensitivity). Part of the process of becoming thoroughly virtuous is to generalize and free the sympathy that is already in us. But we must also be intelligent in the way we express this sympathy: we should be sure that helpful actions really do help those they are intended to benefit, and we should not be overeager, like the man (book II, A. 2, 78) who pulled up his plants to help them grow. Something like what is sometimes called "reason" is involved both in the ability to generalize sympathy and in the ability to apply it intelligently.

As many commentators have noted, Hume does assign reason a role in his ethics. First of all, there is a role for the milder emotions, which (in a passage already quoted) he equates with what is commonly called "reason." Without these milder emotions we would be like the savage Scythians, whose ethical views can be dismissed because they have lost the sentiments of humanity (Hume 1751/1975, 255).

Second, according to Hume, reason (in the sense of capacities involved in gathering, establishing relations among, and assessing facts) does all of the preliminary work of ethical judgment. Even if we are inclined to approve of what is generally useful, a careful survey of the case may be required for us to know exactly what this is (Hume 1739/1978, 589–90). If the nature of moral discourse requires us to frame an appeal that will be valid from everyone's point of view, then it would seem to follow that everyone's well-being should be given equal weight. Thus, although Hume does not suggest a heuristic role for impartiality in moral thought, it is implicit in the conditions he outlines for acceptable moral judgments.

A simplified modern view of reason and choice is as follows: each of us encounters many situations in which there are two or more alternative things that we perfectly well could do. Reason—more or less the same intellectual processes that we use in inference or calculation—tells us which alternative is best. But none of our four thinkers fits this model. Kant comes closest, in that he provides an elaborate argument for saying that we often have genuine moral choices, although he also provides an argument for the opposite, along with enough ambiguity and obscurity to leave the issue permanently unclear. In any case, Kant does not have a view of reason in morality that matches that of the model. Neither Hume, Confucius, nor Mencius would accept this view of reason's perception of choice, and I have tried to indicate the degrees of their difference from the model and the reasons for their difference. We can attribute to Confucius, Mencius, and Hume views of what might be translated as "reason" and "choice"; but Hume is careful to point out the ambiguity of the word "reason," and in the case of these three thinkers the translation or interpretation is inexact and the differences interesting.

11

REASON AND CHOICE

Afterword

Much of the interest of this topic comes from the fact that we can imagine our lives different. There may be a sense of regret at paths not taken or of fascination with alternative versions of ourselves that would have developed. Our culture encourages a sense that, whatever path we do take, it should represent in some sense a rational decision.

"Rational" here becomes a praise word, which can be applied to a variety of processes. Sometimes it means merely that one is not swayed by the kinds of emotions that frequently lead to mistakes or at least to actions that will be regretted. Sometimes it has to do with a conscious sorting out of alternatives, perhaps with a review of reasons for or against each of them. Such a conscious sorting out can represent the clearest case of what we think of as a decision. But immediately turning one's back on something, or running away, can be a decision of sorts, even if there is nothing remotely resembling a conscious weighing of alternatives. There are cases when quick response is clearly the best form of decision. But it often happens that matters that arguably call for a considered and deliberate response are handled in much the same way.

We may like to think that people, in an intuitive or deliberative way, generally follow their own self-interest, except perhaps in cases in which benevolent tendencies intervene. It is simple and appealing also to represent this pattern in terms of an ongoing calculation (which can be quick and not articulated as such) or weighing of expected results. All of this has much to do with the popularity of game theory, which sometimes masquerades as a priori psychology and in this form appeals to philosophers who prefer to limit their study of reality.

Philosophers who are willing to venture further into the real world need to investigate the conditions in which imaginable courses of behavior are—

or are not—live options for someone, bearing in mind that liveness or genuineness of option may turn out to be a matter of degree. Empirical psychology can supplement or replace abstract models in this, and there certainly is room for investigations of what comes to people's minds as possibilities, and also of the varieties of discomfort and distancing that people can feel in the face of various possibilities. Philosophers (like Confucius, Mencius, Hume, and even Kant) whose philosophy includes an element of moral psychology can offer useful guidance in thinking about all of this, even if their suggestions are open to testing and they cannot provide the last word.

PART IV

The Scope of Ethics

12

THE COMPARTMENTALIZATION
OF WESTERN ETHICS

Many nowadays are uneasy with postmodernism, with its juggling of multiple frames of reference and liking for polystylism and pastiche. But it may be that the diametrical opposite—a unified world of thought—lies far behind us, if it is not simply mythical. Both of the essays in this section make a case that a divided approach to life, as manifested in ethical philosophy, in the West predates the twentieth century and that we can gain perspective on this by contrasting at least one or two classic Asian models of thought about life with modern Western philosophy.

Three oversimplifications need to be avoided. One is that of creating overly stark contrasts between East and West. Arguably, divided approaches to life are not unique to the West. Fung Yu-lan (1948) has emphasized that after a while there was a frequent tendency for Chinese thinkers to combine Confucianism and Daoism both in life and in philosophy.

A second oversimplification is that of generalizing broadly, over either Asian or Western thought. Clearly the kind of "altruism" to be found in Confucianism, for example, is very different from anything in Daoism and contrasts in a different way with early Buddhist philosophy. Much the same point can be made about the presence of ethical recommendations of especial urgency, different in Buddhism from Confucianism; and arguably the tone of urgency as well as the subject matter differs. (In Daoism it is hard to say that there is any tone of urgency in the presentation of central claims.) Further than this, it would be wrong to suggest that all Confucians, or all Daoists, or all early Buddhist philosophers are entirely alike; although in early Buddhist philosophy there certainly is considerable convergence on a strong form of altruism.

Major Western figures such as Kant and Mill offer very different models of divided lives. In Kant's case, the division is between decisions in which the categorical imperative should play a crucial testing role, on one hand, and those in which it would not normally be necessary to refer to the categorical imperative so that hypothetical (nonmoral) imperatives will suffice, on the other. Examples of the latter are the choice in a restaurant of which dessert to order or in a carpentry project of which tool to use. Kant never gives any clear indication of how frequently he thinks explicit moral considerations need enter most people's lives. The imperfect duties of reasonable degrees of self-cultivation and of helping others suggest an answer of "very frequently," as does the thought that, say, being late for appointments violates the categorical imperative. But it certainly would be possible to hold a broadly Kantian view of morality and also to believe that relatively few of most people's decisions call out for testing by the categorical imperative. These moral decisions, though, would be thought of as the most important in people's lives.

For John Stuart Mill the division, as has been noted, is between decisions in which poor choices should be subject to punishment (in the broad sense of appeals to a sense of guilt or to social pressure, as well perhaps as legal penalties), on one hand, and decisions in which poor choices should be the objects at worst of distaste (for the onlooker) or of regret on the part of the agent, on the other hand. Here is a way of getting an intuitive sense of this. Contrast bad behavior (e.g., cruelty) that, when we hear of it, inspires something like anger, with bad (e.g., slovenly, tacky, boorish, or simply foolish) behavior that inspires thoughts like "We would not want to spend time with people like that." Both Mill's first class of behavior and the group of decisions that a Kantian would hold call out for employment of the categorical imperative approximate the realm of the moral; although perhaps they are not "moral" in exactly the same way.

A natural question is, "How do we know when we have a moral problem (or actions that should be subject to moral judgment)?" Mill, in my reading, says more than Kant about the answer to this question, in part because *On Liberty* centers on a revisionist proposal for exempting large areas of behavior (that might be distasteful to some) from moral judgment and the risks of the "tyranny of the majority." The assumption appears to have been that being thought tasteless or foolish generally involves less pressure than being thought immoral does. Mill's view, in any case, was that only actions that directly harm others should be subject to substantial social pressure. The rest of life can be approached, both by agents and onlookers, in a different way.

All of this suggests that neither Kant nor Mill advocates a unified approach to all of life's decisions. Rather, each has a split screen including the moral and the nonmoral. (This description should be even more clear for Mill if one reflects that he recommends that in moral decisions we often rely on rules that distill the experience of the past, and that he also upholds rights whose recognition preempts case by case consideration of whether the consequences of respecting them on *this* occasion will be good.) However, there do seem to be some utilitarians who uphold a unified ethics, even if Mill is not one of them. It is imaginable also that some Kantians might wish to reject the division within life that I claim is implicit in Kant's ethics. This reemphasizes that generalizations, within Western or Eastern philosophy, have to be approached with caution. Sweeping claims and cross-cultural contrasts can be useful and eye-opening, but we must be mindful that there will have to be qualifications and exceptions.

A third oversimplification we need to avoid is (in comparing ways of thinking about life and our choices) the tendency to assume that all of the advantages will be on one side or the other of two contrasting approaches. Philosophies, whether that of early Buddhism or of, say, Kierkegaard, that verge on a unified approach to life have the appeal of manifest integrity. They also seem less vulnerable to abuse: mistakes in shifting gears become most unlikely when there are no gears to shift. On the other hand, there may be advantages in lives that clearly and conspicuously have more than one mode of choice.

Let me suggest that the modern Western amplification of a sphere of privacy, in which we are, so to speak, off duty, has a great deal to be said for it. It makes possible a sense of freedom in most of life that is wonderful and that we would greatly miss if it were taken away. Part of the seriousness of threats to political freedom, indeed, is that indirectly they are also threats to the liberty of private life, which usually is more secure in politically free societies.

The modern Western amplification of a sphere of public life governed by morality and by stable institutions of law is also a great invention. Its contributions to prosperity and to a widespread sense of security are unmistakable. No doubt a thorough Buddhist or a Kierkegaardian who found herself or himself in a society that amplified these two contrasting spheres of life could practice altruistic compassion or committed faithfulness in both spheres, in a unified way. I do not want to suggest that either would have to tear down or reject structures of private or of public life. Nevertheless, these structures could not have been created by people with an entirely unified approach to life. And their usefulness owes a great deal to the fact that most people expect to approach the spheres of public and of private life in different ways.

To criticize what we in the West now have, including the philosophical elements that underwrite it, is not then to declare that it is valueless or that we should return to the past. (Nor is it to suggest that some classic Asian approaches solve all problems.) It usually is the case that the early models of something very useful can be improved. Some separation of the two spheres of life, and of two or more ways of approaching life's' problems, can be developed that is interestingly different from what we now have. Cross-cultural influences can contribute to this process.

Need the amplification of a sphere of private life entail a fading away of the sense that there are standards even in this sphere? Can there be guides to satisfying and humane private life that are very different from the moral apparatus of public life? Can there be a sense of responsibility in personal relations that is different from, and less pressurized than, the sense of moral duty? Is compassion incompatible with, or superfluous to, stable structures of public life? The thrust of the two essays to follow is not in the direction of an either/or choice between modern Western and classic Asian philosophical approaches. It rather is toward eclectic borrowing, beginning with the sense that (generally speaking) any philosophical tradition can help any other with its problems.

Buddhist Ethics

The second of the two essays to follow uses Buddhist altruism as one of two terms of comparison, and some readers may find advance discussion of Buddhist philosophy helpful. One dimension of philosophy here is a way of living. It would be wrong, of course, to assume that all Buddhists, or even all Buddhist nuns or monks, entirely practice a characteristic altruism, just as we need not assume that all Christians turn the other cheek and feel extraordinary responsibilities to the poor. Nevertheless, in both cases, it is reasonable to expect an influence on people's lives, which will be more manifest in some cases than in others.

Part of the influence that Buddhism was thought of as having in its early development in India was against the conventions of caste, and toward compassion (both toward human beings and toward animals). These elements can be appreciated by a contrast with a classic Hindu philosophical text that postdates the introduction of Buddhism, the *Bhagavad Gita*. The *Gita* centers on two ethical questions: one that we would be inclined to view as moral and one that clearly lies in a different region of ethics. As part of the epic *Mahabharata*, it focuses initially on the dilemma of the warrior Arjona, on the eve of a battle in which he believes that he will kill cousins and other family members in the opposing army. Should he fight? His charioteer, who is the god Krishna, advises him on this question, which we should regard as a moral one, and then goes on (at much greater length) to advise him on the possibilities of an enlightened life that both will be deeply satisfying and will lead to personal salvation. This latter kind of guidance we would not normally classify as moral. There is nothing morally wrong per se about leading an unsatisfying life that is banal or dreary.

Krishna's moral advice appeals to the metaphysics of the *Upanishads* and also to traditional beliefs about reincarnation. Intuitively Arjona may feel that killing cousins will make a difference. But they will be reincarnated, so in that respect there is no real difference. Further, in the most deeply acceptable account of reality, everything and everyone (including Krishna and the cousins) is identical to Brahman. Whatever Arjona does, Brahman will be Brahman. Thus, on any level what he does will make no real difference. This assertion supports a recommendation that he fight in the battle. It may be that a crucial assumption here is that, if nothing makes any real difference, either tradition or the responsibilities associated with a caste (Arjona is in the warrior caste) will become the default position.

The larger part of the *Bhagavad Gita* goes beyond the *Upanishads* in exploring a variety of approaches to life that can be highly successful, not least in the quality of lived experience that they promote. The *Upanishads*, in effect, had recommended one, which centered on knowledge (of the identity of the core of self with Brahman) that was both metaphysical and mystical. This approach encouraged a passive and meditative way of life, which in some cases might be pursued only as a final phase after various responsibilities of normal active life had been discharged. The *Bhagavad Gita* takes the pragmatic view that, while a passive and meditative path of knowledge may lead to a highly successful life, other paths that some may find more congenial can work equally well. A warrior like Arjona, in particular, can create a distinctive mode of tranquillity in action. This process requires detachment, especially lack of concern about the outcome of what one is doing, so that one loses oneself in activity. Western analogues to this line of thought are the idea that sometimes "the dancer becomes the dance," and also the "zone" that athletes speak of in which someone is entirely lost in the flow of the game.

The idea, put very broadly, is that there are many possible strategies for loss of self. The *Bhagavad Gita* is naturally read as a manual of purification. But, in the ways in which it insists that this can be accomplished in the midst of life, it also can be read as a brilliant exploration of sources of energy.

Let us return to the idea that believing in reincarnation changes decisions of life and death. There is a certain plausibility, indeed, to the thought that to step on a bug is really to do it a favor, if the bug might be reincarnated in some more favorable form. The kinds of issues that this raises are not unique to Indian thought. Any system of belief that includes entire certainty that there is a heaven, for example, must wrestle with the suggestion that sometimes it would be a distinct benefit for someone to die: if that person's chances for heaven were about as good as they ever would be. Traditions such as allowing someone who is about to die some time in which to say his or her prayers can be understood in this light, as can the appeal of martyrdom in a really good cause.

The bug, however—like the vast majority of human beings—simply does not want to die. An important element in Buddhist ethics starts out from this fact. Many early Buddhist texts are, given the complex Buddhist account of the self (discussed at the beginning of part II), guarded in what they say about reincarnation. However, even if we believe that the bug can be said in some sense to be reincarnated after being stepped on, we need to consider the suffering of fearing—and of experiencing—death. Just what this suffering amounts to in the case of a bug may be debatable, but there is something; and it clearly is a factor in most human lives. This is one of the starting points of Buddhist compassion.

The topic of suffering turns out to be more complex than many might think. Pain and suffering are often closely connected, but the concepts are different in important ways. There is a temporal aspect to suffering: at least in human cases we speak of it most often when whatever has gone wrong is liable to be prolonged, or at least there is no end in sight. Suffering also, as the etymology suggests, typically implies that something (that has negative aspects) is happening over which one has little or no control. Pain often is inescapable, but the idea that it is possible to experience pain without suffering is important to Buddhism. (It also is at the root of the childbirth training now given to expectant mothers. In both cases a degree of taking control makes a difference.) Because of all of this, one can associate suffering with someone's take on an experience that is, or might be thought of as being, painful. Something like this might be part of the view of suffering developed by Nagarjuna, seven hundred years after Buddha, that it is a conventional projection that exists only as it is imputed (Garfield 1995, 202–6).

Another starting point of Buddhist ethics is this. To the extent that early Buddhist philosophy is willing to acknowledge a self, it is thought of as a bundle of thought processes, experiences, and so forth. It is a metaphysical mistake, Buddha held, to suppose that there is any core. (The Hindu *atman* is denied in the doctrine of *anatman*.) The metaphysical image that we are left with, then, is something like a floating array of life-elements. There are ways of drawing boundaries around groups of these, separating them into separate persons; but these are seen as conventional and arbitrary. The nearest contemporary counterpart to this metaphysics is that of Derek Parfit's *Reasons and Persons.*

If this is what the world really is like, then egoism—however natural it is for the vast majority of us—rests on a mistake. It is a costly mistake, because the illusion of something like a substantial self makes possible desires (for various things to be gained or avoided by that self). Desires, in the Buddhist view, entail suffering.

The logic of this connection relies on two highly plausible assumptions. One is that desiring, per se, is addictive. When someone gets what she or he wants, there may be a period of satisfaction, of something that feels like happiness. But, as in any addiction, a new cycle begins, and soon the sufferer begins to feel bored and restless, this leading to the frustrated feeling that attends the growth of new desire. It is a truism that the things that we desire most intensely cannot be immediately accessible or easy to get; and, conversely, even something as simple as a glass of water can be deliciously pleasant if only we first do not have anything to drink for days. Pleasures, in a view like this, are all paid for: beforehand, in the frustration that gives them significance, and then afterward when we enter the post-satisfaction phase of boredom. Sometimes, of course, we pay in frustration and don't even get what we want.

The second highly plausible assumption is that inevitably we sometimes do lose. This is most evident when we consider the facts of sickness, old age, and death. But even apart from all of these, it does look as if people who get everything they want inevitably then want more, so that in the end desire will outstrip satisfaction. When we do not get what we desire, or when it is taken away, suffering ensues.

The cure in personal terms is a life of mild inclinations, which do not have the element of "attachment" and vulnerability characteristic of desire. Desires that involve the well-being of others (such as friends and family) have to be dampened down into mild inclinations, just as much as desires of a more selfish kind. Buddhist ethics is evenhanded in its rejection of self-regarding and other-regarding desires. Nevertheless, because usually the great majority of someone's keen desires are egoistic, the thrust of Buddhist ethics is most strongly against egoism, discounting the initially intuitive difference between other people's well-being and our own. The mild inclinations we will be left with, once our desires are eliminated, will include those characteristic of compassion for others.

It should be added that, although Buddhist ethics at first can sound rather dour in its surrender of pleasure and excitement, it does promise what is variously translated as "joy" and "bliss." This is different from pleasure in its lack of intentionality and dependence on external stimuli. Presumably it is far more durable. Despite this bright promise, it remains true that Buddhist altruism emphasizes the noninfliction and avoidance of suffering at a more basic level than it does positive goals. Buddhists would support John Stuart Mill's hope of eliminating "the grand sources of suffering" (although not necessarily all of the steps that would promote this end), but they—unlike Mill—would insist that the most fundamental cause of suffering is within the psychology of the person who suffers.

The transformation in life that early Buddhist philosophy recommends is to a large degree one in the emotions. Traditionally emotions have been thought of as feelings, of which the person who has them normally can be aware. However, recent philosophy has brought out the dimension of inten- tionality, that is, of direction toward an object or objects that the emotion is in some sense "about" (cf. Solomon 1976; Armon-Jones 1991). Love, for ex- ample, is love of someone or something. Love also normally involves moti- vations in relation to what is loved (such as a motivation to see what is loved flourish or be happy or respond lovingly); this motivational dimension would seem to be a feature of emotions in general. Arguably each of these three elements (feeling, intentionality, and motivation) is typical of emotion but not essential in every case; there is the possibility of the package, so to speak, becoming unglued, so that one or two of the elements are present without the other or others (see Kupperman 1995b, 1997). What Buddhist ethics recommends is less extreme than this, but does involve some dwindling of the force of feelings, which is presented as compatible with persistent motivations.

13

TRADITION AND MORAL PROGRESS

This chapter will examine only a few aspects of a very large subject. In the first section I will explain what a moral tradition is
and what functions it fulfills. In the second I will explain what I mean by
moral progress. Clearly the most interesting philosophical questions concern
the relations, if any, between moral tradition and moral progress. This is a
subject that I have taken up elsewhere (Kupperman 1988), focusing on how
criticism within a tradition makes progress possible. In the third section I will
look at a different set of issues, concerning how exposure to alternative
traditions can be conducive to moral progress. This section can be taken not
only as ethical analysis but also as a defense of pluralism and of the usefulness
of comparative philosophy.

Moral Tradition

The simplest view of what a moral tradition is consists of equating it with a set
of general moral recommendations or prohibitions. Thus, the moral tradition
of the Old Testament might be held to consist of the Ten Commandments plus
perhaps a supplementary list of commands having to do with such matters as
diet and ritual. One difficulty with this view as a general account of moral tradition is that it works less well for an ethics, such as that of Aristotle or Confucius, that is not as strongly rule centered as is the Old Testament. It would be exceedingly peculiar to attempt to grasp the recommendations made by Confucius
and Aristotle in terms of a set of "Thou shalt" 's and "Thou shalt not" 's. Some
elements of the teaching, such as Aristotle on adultery and Confucius on filial
impiety, might lend themselves to this treatment without too great a distortion;
but other elements would not.

A deeper difficulty with equating a moral tradition with a set of general recommendations is that the practice of moral life, within any tradition, has more stages than such a view suggests. Some might be attracted to a two-stage view as follows. Stage one is that situation S occurs and Bloggs knows about it. Stage two is that Bloggs applies his moral tradition to S and determines that what he is about to do is either morally required, morally prohibited, or (the most usual alternative) morally neutral. The real world is more complicated than this process suggests in at least three respects. One is that awareness has degrees. We can be dimly aware of all sorts of things that we neither reflect on nor treat as problematical. As an extreme example, take a driver's awareness of the road during a typical drive in the country. Some elements in our experience, in contrast, become salient. They really register on us; we really notice them. We may, as a result, treat them as problematic and reflect on them, although people who dislike reflection may not.

Second, even when a situation does register on us, it is not, as it were, transparent. There is not a full, equal light on all details of the situation, as each comes forward to announce itself. Even within a situation that really registers on us, some details will be much more salient than others. Furthermore, just what the details are may be a matter either of conscious interpretation or of what might be termed unconscious interpretation—the way the immediate presentation of a situation is structured by the bent of mind or expectations of the perceiver.

Third, it is of course not true that we judge all situations, or even all situations that really register on us, in relation to our morality. Not even Immanuel Kant lived like that. Not even J. J. C. Smart, who is often taken (and has taken himself) to be an act utilitarian, committed to a standard that applies to every human action, has lived like that. Smart (1977) uses the example of himself enthusiastically playing field hockey; his decisions on the field, he says, do not involve direct reference to the greatest good of the greatest number. As he points out, it is better that they do not. What is involved here is not merely the importance of leaving room for spontaneity. One factor is that much of life would lose its flavor if every step were accompanied by reflective demand for justification. But another is that it is simply impossible to treat everything one does as requiring a separate judgment that it is morally acceptable. Anyone who attempted to live in such a way would come close to paralysis. Highly moral and moralistic people take a large number of, but not all, elements of life as calling out for moral justification, or at least moral clearance. Most of us examine morally a rather smaller number of elements. No one subjects every particular action in her or his life to moral examination.

In sum, a moral tradition, whether or not it centers on rules of conduct, also includes the following. It provides training in moral significance, so that certain situations and actions register on anyone steeped in the tradition and can readily be seen as calling for reflection or moral judgment. It also will provide an interpretative scheme so that certain features of these situations and actions will seem salient, and will be perceived within the categories of the tradition.

One other complication in what moral traditions provide also should be mentioned. A tradition typically not only enables adherents to perceive when judgments of what ought to be done are called for, and guides them in making these judgments, but also provides a set of distinctions—or differentiations in weight and feel—within judgments of what ought to be done. One such distinction is that within the Western tradition between moral and other kinds of evaluative judgments, including ordinary practical judgments, aesthetic judgments, and judgments related to etiquette. Henry Rosemont (1978) has pointed out that this distinction does not occur within classical Chinese philosophy. Neither does it occur within classical Greek philosophy. Let me concede this point. I will want, nevertheless, to continue to speak of the "moral" traditions associated with Confucian and Aristotelian ethics. The argument in support of this terminology is that, even if there was not a category of the "moral" within these philosophies, our category of the moral fits fairly well the judgments Aristotle makes about certain kinds of actions, such as adultery, that he says are categorically wrong, and Confucian judgments about children who neglect or harm their parents.

Part of the point here is that a tradition may not assign equal weight to all transgressions. Eating with your fingers while smacking your lips is simply not on a par with murder. In our scheme we tend to treat as moral the issues that surround transgressions that we regard as serious. If another tradition regards certain actions both as categorically wrong and as serious transgressions, and subjects them to especially forceful blame, that will sound to us like morality, whether or not the culture marks something like our distinction with a classification term that we can translate as "morality."

It has come to seem to me that the picture is still more complicated than this. Consider Western moral traditions. Not only have there been distinctions between venal and venial sins, and between deadly and nondeadly sins, but also there have been more subtle differences between kinds of immorality that are treated as serious in different ways. Consider the case of someone who cheats investors out of their money and that of a parent who entirely neglects and refuses to help his or her children. Both are serious transgressions, which elicit highly negative judgments. But the *kind* of immorality and also our sense of what is lacking differ between the two cases. We readily say that the dishonest financier has failed in a socially important way to play the game by the rules and is immoral. I think that our abhorrence of the totally neglectful parent is in some sense moral; it certainly is as serious as our condemnation of the financier. But "immoral" is not the word we reach for, and the inadequacies of the two people seem very different.

Consider also a Confucian pair of cases. The reader may remember the case of Jan Ch'iu, who chose not to live up to the education Confucius had given him, and whom Confucius held responsible. "He is no follower of mine," Confucius said. ". . . You may beat the drum and set upon him" (*Analects* c, XI.16, 156–7; see also VI.10, 118). My suggestion is that Confucius treats the case of Jan Ch'iu differently from the way he would that of someone who has no education or sense and whose very bad conduct is only to be expected. Both are to be condemned, but not in the same spirit.

A moral tradition need not be either unified or static. Some writers, such as Alasdair MacIntyre (1988), have spoken of a number of competing Western traditions. My sense is that these have some resemblances and are not entirely discrete. Also most people who are not philosophers are not, I suspect, so neatly divisible into schools, which suggests that it may not be so easy to individuate traditions within a culture. All the same, MacIntyre is right in pointing out disunity related to competing schools. There also is disunity related to competing models of what ethics principally concerns. If one thinks of ethics primarily as telling us about commands made either by God or by ideal moral legislators, then the subject of ethics would seem to be our duties. If the model is, rather, a contractarian one, then rightness will seem to be modeled on fairness. A model that has not been highly developed in recent Western philosophy but that nevertheless has some influence on ordinary people assimilates virtue to being fully human. Any one of us may reach on different occasions for different models. The parent who entirely neglects his or her children may seem lacking in humanity, whereas the person who cheats investors out of their money may be taken as unfair to those who were cheated or to have neglected his or her duty.

Duty does not loom as large in moral discussions as it appears to have done a hundred years ago, or in Kant's time. This shift is an illustration of how moral traditions can change. In this instance the change appears to be, as it were, from the bottom up. That is, the decline of duty does not seem to be the result primarily of philosophical argument or of any intellectual movement. The form, as well as the content, of moral tradition responds to changes in the structure of society.

It should be clear from the brief account thus far that moral traditions are enormously complicated, more like forms of life than like bits of problem-solving software. Moral traditions carry with them both forms of attention and areas of inattentiveness; they also involve interpretative approaches to reality, so that two competing moral traditions can be like two groups of people who insist, respectively, on seeing the duck-rabbit as a duck or as a rabbit. Moral traditions differ not only in how they notice and see what they condemn, and in what they condemn, but also in how they condemn it. It would be tempting to speak of every moral tradition as having its own voice, but the discussion of current Western attitudes to different forms of transgression suggests that a moral tradition can have more than one voice.

Moral Progress

The idea of moral progress has suffered from the general opprobrium that has affected nineteenth-century ideas of progress (apart from technological progress). It is hard anyway to think of moral progress in a century in which Hitler and Pol Pot have flourished. Let me say first what I do not mean by moral progress, before developing the case that there is such a thing.

I do not mean, first, an improvement in actual behavior. People fall short of their ideals and moralities, or of the moralities available to them, in all sorts of ways; and I would not want to suggest that these phenomena have been becoming less pronounced. At the other extreme I do not mean that the available peaks of human perfection have become higher. It would be foolish to suggest that humanity now can do better than Confucius and Socrates; indeed it probably would be foolish to suggest that it now can do as well.

Let me instead focus on the stock of ways that are readily available to cultivated people for thinking about moral issues. There is some analogy with the set of scientific theories available to university students of the sciences. These will not, on the one hand, represent the heights of ongoing scientific creativity. They are, rather, received knowledge distilled, at least in part, from past creativity. This set of scientific theories will not necessarily correspond, on the other hand, to everyone's thinking about the world, or even to the thinking of every scientist. One might think of contemporary Western creationists, some of whom turn out to have Ph.D.'s in geology, who reject important areas of established scientific knowledge. We can speak of something in the sciences as established knowledge if it has reached the point at which, we might say, the quality and the widespread awareness of the evidence or basis for it are such that there no longer is room for reasonable people to disagree about it. Estimates of the age of the planet earth arguably have reached this point. This does not mean that something like a formal deductive proof is available, and it certainly does not mean that there will be in fact no disagreement.

The idea of scientific progress includes the claim that more things can come to be known in such a way that there is no room for reasonable people to disagree about them. This idea is compatible with the possibility of future theoretical shifts so that what is known today may be known in a different form a hundred years from now. I propose that we view moral progress analogously. Here are three examples of moral knowledge that either has become established in the last 150 years in the manner described or that is in the process of becoming established: (1) Slavery is wrong; (2) Discrimination on the basis of race or religion is wrong; (3) Discrimination on the basis of gender is wrong.

These examples are compatible, in the way I have suggested, with the continued existence of virtual slavery in some parts of the world, with persistent warfare between different tribal groups, and with gross instances of racism and sexism. Nor would the wrongness of discrimination on the basis of religion be likely to win plebiscites in every single country in the world. The moral progress in these cases consists in the fact that not only do cultivated people, in various parts of the world, think that behavior of the indicated sorts is wrong but that the justifications are so familiar that they can take it for granted. It has become received knowledge, not a polemical position. In the seventeenth century Sir Thomas Browne, in *Religio Medici*, argued against religious discrimination. There is a large step from this creative awareness to a situation in which educated people can be generally presumed to understand that religious discrimination is intolerable.

That there has been moral progress in the sense just characterized does not mean that there must continue to be moral progress, or that any shift in moral opinion must count as progress. Regress is always possible, probably more easily in morality than in scientific knowledge. It would be out of place here to rehearse the kinds of evidence and argument that can elevate something, such as the claim that slavery is wrong, from the status of moral opinion to that of moral knowledge. This is a large topic (see Kupperman 1970, 1983). The process by which something becomes not only knowledge but established knowledge, presumed to be shared generally by appropriately educated people, calls for an analysis that is more sociological than philosophical. Let me merely suggest some parts of this analysis.

One facet of the process is a social closing of minds to possibilities. I will dwell on this point, because it might be very counterintuitive. We all associate acquisition of knowledge with the opening of minds, and closed minds with ignorance. But it is arguable that personal perfectibility very often involves the closing off of possibilities, in that certain things (such as brutal or unjust actions) become unthinkable. At the extreme, a Confucian sage, say, would have no choices to make, in that a wide variety of unworthy actions would have ceased to be live options. As Mencius (b, book IV, B. 8, 129) points out, "Only when a man will not do some things is he capable of doing great things." Similarly, when something needs to be explained, a scientifically trained person usually can eliminate many of the alternatives that someone who is untrained might consider. She or he might refuse to consider magic as a possible explanation and might also say something such as "Things do not simply vanish into thin air." Both moral and scientific educations involve narrowing of possibilities, although arguably someone who is a creative thinker in the sciences or in respect to moral matters might on occasions reverse the process and consider possibilities that the ordinary educated person would rule out of hand.

What accomplishes the social closing of minds to unacceptable possibilities? Consider a very recent bit of moral progress, the developed sense among cultivated people in many countries that discrimination on the basis of race or religion is totally unacceptable. For a long time some people have known this, but in a country such as America the process by which it became established knowledge was so quick that it is possible to get a clear view of how it took place. Part of the process was training in sensitivity. In a variety of media, including books, films, and television programs, people were encouraged to see life through the eyes of people of other races. This approach expanded awareness, but it was accompanied by what might be described as brainwashing in a very good cause. Very young children in schools, and the population generally via the media, were indoctrinated with the idea that racism was outside the range of what was tolerable. The word "brainwashing" here should not be taken as derogatory. It refers to a process that, within limits and with proper objects, is highly necessary. One would not want to live in a society in which the great majority of people were not brainwashed at an early age to regard murder, torture, and random brutality as unthinkable.

Americans are so used to thinking of indoctrination programs as centrally directed, perhaps by a totalitarian government, that they may have difficulty in recognizing highly successful and pervasive programs that are not centrally directed. The anti-racism campaign of the last twenty five years is one example. An earlier example concerns law and order, the importance of deferring to law even when it does not seem to work very well, so that one does not "take the law into one's own hands." This issue is the central plot device of many a Western movie. I will return to this point in the final section of this essay. Another, less attractive example is the systematic inculcation of habits and attitudes of deference in the "lower orders" of societies that have pronounced systems of social class. It will be taken as axiomatic that someone of a higher social rank is owed more in various kinds of cases, and respect for one's "betters" will be inculcated at a very early age.

A few remarks about racial and religious distinctions are in order. Even if there are stable and long-term differences between groups—itself a highly debatable proposition—discrimination is wrong, in part because it is wrong to prejudge an individual on the basis of membership in a group. Furthermore, to the extent that group identification remains important to many people, and good morale may require conspicuous successes within a group, there is a strong case for affirmative action (see Kupperman 1989). Also, there is no reason to suppose that differences, if any, between racial or religious groups will persist unchanged through time. Increased opportunities or successes can bring about a change. It is arguable also that, often, when the cultural mainstream broadens, so that a group which has been outside is brought inside, there is an explosion of energy. This might help to account for the fact that most of the greatest English literature of the last hundred years has been written by Irish and Americans rather than by British authors, for the remarkable accomplishments of Jewish intellectuals during the same period, and for the increasing accomplishments now of women artists and scholars. One might mention also the contributions of African-American writers to American literature during the last sixty years, including *The Invisible Man*, in my opinion the best American novel of the period. The point is that accomplishments of various groups have responded, and will respond, to dynamics of social change.

The moral progress under discussion is not the result primarily of considerations such as these. Rather, it reflects considerable friendly persuasion within a culture that certain thoughts are unthinkable and perhaps also that related topics are to be avoided. Many kinds of comparison between racial or religious groups fall under this heading. There is some analogy with the extreme reluctance among many people, including many philosophers, to take up questions such as whether it imaginably ever could be justified to kill or torture an innocent person. Such issues have dogged discussions of utilitarianism, in that it looks very much as if many forms of utilitarianism yield answers of "Yes," so that utilitarians are in the position of advocating (in hypothetical cases) the unthinkable. Exceptionally sophisticated utilitarians, such as R. M. Hare (1981), have devoted some effort to analyzing why what is in question is, and should be, unthinkable. It is indeed very useful that we all regard murder and torture as unthinkable; even if it is true that there are imaginable cases in which they might have some justification, these cases never in fact come up. If we were to start to look for them (or if we relaxed our rigid opposition to the thought of them), the results might be disastrous. The best way to avoid slippery slopes is never to move, or even to look, in that direction.

We readily can imagine cases in which what is regarded within a culture as obvious is morally wrong and what is regarded as unthinkable would be an advance. The classic recent discussion of this issue is Jonathan Bennett's (1974). Bennett suggests the operation of human sympathy as a corrective to moral prejudice, and this is a suggestion that Confucians would find congenial. My own view is that sympathy works well in cases of impairment of happiness and less reliably well in those in which what is at stake is primarily dignity or fulfillment of potential; ethical theories that include a Kantian component can be most helpful in the latter. The point remains that moral traditions inevitably involve selective vision and sensitivity; and, despite the great advantages of these characteristics as compared to utter barbarism or unaligned mindlessness, we should worry about the possibility that we do not see or are insensitive to something that is important.

A deeper one-sidedness is involved if our categories of ethical judgment lead us to reflect in more or less satisfactory ways about some kinds of problems while largely or entirely ignoring others. Let me illustrate this point by examining two sides to moral judgment, either of which could be emphasized within some moral traditions to the virtual exclusion of others. In pursuing this point I do not mean to suggest that morality has only two sides. Indeed, it might be useful to keep in mind the title and theme of a book by Dorothy Emmet, *The Prism of Morality*, throughout the discussion. Nor do I mean to suggest that the distinction I make, which neatly separates two sides, is the only one with which we might possibly approach the subject.

One side is associated with an impersonal conception of justice or of considerations that resemble justice. It yields judgments of rights, protections, and entitlements, which one should recognize others to have regardless of one's relations to them or of what one thinks of them. The other is associated with the quality of one's particular involvement with other people or, perhaps, animals. It yields judgments that are not impersonal, in the sense that they may specify responsibilities or desiderata for one person that would not apply to others. To give an animal-oriented example of the two sides: Smith and Jones both have a responsibility, as a matter of something like justice, not to mistreat Smith's cat, but Smith has responsibilities to the cat that go beyond that and Jones does not.

Now in fact the word "justice" has an ordinary meaning that is much too narrow to do the job that I would like to have done here, or that many philosophers want it to do. If someone, with no provocation, beats you up, that is very wrong but it is not unjust, unless the person beating you up is a representative of a governmental body. The concept of fairness is even narrower. If a policeman beats you up, while this is unjust it is not unfair, unless you had won a contest in which the prize was not to be beaten up, or it was not your turn among the prisoners to be beaten up. Words such as "justice" and "fairness" ordinarily are used within a narrow part of what morality is concerned with. What I want is a word with a much broader use, which I shortly will characterize. Because such a word is not available, I will appropriate the word "justice" for the purposes of this essay, using it in a specified technical (but broad) sense rather than in its ordinary meaning.

Let me suggest that it is highly useful that a society develop a repertoire of rights, protection, and entitlements that apply "irrespective of persons" and that typically have overriding force wherever they apply. I will use the word "justice" in relation to all of these. These may extend even to animals. Our obligation not to maltreat a dog has nothing to do with whether it is a nice dog or not, or whether we have been on friendly terms with it or not, although it should be added that maltreatment is even more shocking if it comes in the context of a history of friendly relations. There is no need to rehearse the range of rights, protection, and entitlements due to human beings; these are very often discussed. It should be emphasized that these not only apply irrespective of persons, but also that they typically fall out of very general formulations. One knows that, say, every human being is entitled to life, liberty, and the pursuit of happiness. Judgments of justice, in the extended sense in which I now am using the word, are distinctive both in the abilities required to make them and in the abilities that are not required. They require an ability to approach moral problems at a fairly high level of abstraction. They require also great steadfastness in applying principles or general rules despite temptations or distractions. They do not require, on the other hand, any unusual sensitivity to the special qualities of persons, because they apply irrespective of persons. Nor do they, insofar as they tend to use broad and familiar categories, require much sensitivity to special features of situations.

In some respects the development of this abstract, impersonal approach to justice is comparable to the development of modern physical science. Both are driven by a passion for generality and an image of an impersonal, objective knower. In both cases, a crucial element is the ruthless exclusion from notice of elements that do not fit the scheme. The moral theory that most closely parallels this is Kant's, in which rigorous insistence on the importance of those features in an action that correspond to what must be included in or excluded by universal law, or that fulfill or violate the requirement to treat other rational beings as ends and not merely as means, is accompanied by indifference (as regards morality) to all other features.

A moral tradition that centers on justice in this extended sense can be contrasted with one that centers on the importance of creating and maintaining a fulfilling and fully human network of relationships. This kind of tradition does not center on rights, protection, and entitlements; rather, it centers on the concern we feel for our family and friends, and for people to whom we are sympathetic. Such a tradition will not be impersonal, in that the stage of human development of a person will always be a crucial factor in determining the options available to her or him, and in that it also will be the case that emphasis on personal relationships will lead to a strong sense of social place. Unlike a justice-centered moral tradition, this tradition, which I will call connectedness-centered, will not encourage reliance on abstractions or highly general procedures in order to decide what should be done. It will instead rely heavily on sensitivity to the projects, hopes, and suffering of others.

What I have just sketched are ideal types, and I do not mean to suggest either that Western traditions, even the one in which John Rawls is a major figure, are exactly like what has been characterized as a justice-centered tradition or that the Confucian tradition is simply connectedness-centered. Confucian ethics has some very good things to say about justice. One might think of the "single thread" that runs through Confucius's thought (*Analects*, IV. 15; see also Fingarette 1979). It is impossible to read Mencius without a strong awareness of his very practical and down-to-earth concern with justice. Conversely, Western moral traditions do seem to have some room for factors related to personal connectedness, although there is more room in consequentialist systems than in Kantian systems.

In the case of the West the picture is complicated by recent suggestions of gender differences in modes of ethical thought (see Gilligan 1982; Kittay and Meyers 1987, especially the essay by Virginia Held, which anticipates much of my present theme; and Held 1984). The depth of the differences is difficult to assess, partly because, as I am going to suggest, different modes of ethical thought are appropriate to different kinds of cases. If women engage in connectedness-centered thinking about cases of kind A, and men engage in justice-centered thinking about cases of kind B, it may be that both are adopting appropriate modes of thought; and it may be also that, as more women find themselves practically engaged with problems of kind B, and more men allow themselves to be engaged with problems of kind A, both kinds of thinking will be equally important to women and men. In suggesting this, I am pursuing a line of thought associated with, among others, Kenneth Gergen, namely, that social generalizations often are time bound (see Gergen 1982; Nicholson 1983).

Let us return to the ideal types. To the extent that a tradition approaches the model of being connectedness-centered, one can expect certain strengths and weaknesses of it. One can expect a rich account of factors contributing to satisfying personal relationships, especially among friends and within a family. Political thought will avoid impersonality by construing both the state and the society along the lines of an extended family, so that personal relationships still matter and people are not supposed to be treated like numbers. These are important strengths. One weakness is that, in a society dominated by such a tradition, someone who in fact does not have the right sort of personal relationships can expect very little. There also will be some difficulty in knowing how to deal with strangers and outsiders (see Hall and Ames 1987, 308–10; Bodde 1967, 33–34). One strategy might be to treat them as if they were within the network of personal relationships, but the pretense might be difficult to sustain.

The strengths and weaknesses to be expected of an entirely justice-centered tradition are very different. Such a tradition will be good in dealing with strangers and outsiders; after all, it will be said, they are just like anyone else, and fair is fair. A country governed by this attitude can be truly a land of opportunity. Not only will there be some degree of fairness to strangers, but, to the extent that the society approximates its ideals, there will be dependable, impersonal administration of justice, thus making possible a high degree of stability and security. If people are governed by respect for the abstract ideals of law and order, rather than by a sense of the worthiness of people with whom they deal or by any other kind of sensitivity, then everyone can know where she or he stands and business can be conducted in a rational way. Such a society might well be more prosperous than most and less subject to cataclysms of various kinds.

The major weakness of a justice-centered tradition will be the mirror image of that of the connectedness-centered tradition. Each will try to approach all situations in terms of its dominant model. One will interpret social justice in relation to the image of society as a giant family. Such an approach may work better in villages than among large urban populations. It may turn out to be difficult over a long period of time, also, to sustain the image of rivals, transients, and far-off peasants as really like members of one's family. The other will view personal relations in terms of duties and obligations of an impersonal sort that follow from abstract general rules, or from an attempt to assimilate all forms of personal commitment to promises. This view is represented by the apocryphal Victorian who, nursing his or her sick spouse, murmurs, "I am only doing my duty." Such an ethics will have little or no room for what is done out of love; it is concerned with what one owes.

As the reader may gather, I doubt that either strategy can be successful for a long period of time. In any event, there is an alternative approach (alternative, that is, to assimilating all major matters of life within its rubric) available to a justice-centered tradition. It can draw a sharp distinction between the part of life that is governed by morality, on the one hand, and the rest of life, on the other, and suggest that we treat these two parts of life very differently. An example is the distinction suggested by Kant's contrast between the categorical and hypothetical imperatives, or the one (already noted) between morality and "expediency" outlined in paragraph 14 of chapter 5 of Mill's *Utilitarianism* and then redrawn more concretely in *On Liberty*. It is natural that the division between morality and other kinds of evaluative distinctions be a product of justice-centered traditions. We may refer loosely to what is on the other side of the distinction as private life. The distinction between the realm of morality, on the one hand, and private life, on the other, has great advantages and disadvantages. It makes possible, as Mill argues it should, a great sense of freedom in most of one's activities. Thus, it is arguable that such a justice-centered society will be likely not only to be more prosperous, stable, and secure, but also to have more personal liberty. The great disadvantage is that, once the distinction is made between the realm of morality and private life, it is not clear that ethics will have much to say about private life or that, if it does, anyone will listen. What results may approach an anarchy of private life. Paul Feyerabend has been quoted as remarking on the extraordinary contrast to be found in some scientists between, on the one hand, the meticulous insistence on standards in professional work and, on the other hand, the virtual absence of standards in personal relationships. A society in which there is an anarchy of private life will be one in which friendships and family relationships often do not go well. It suggests an image of a great many prosperous and free people, many of whom are also disconnected and lonely.

To return to the real world: it should be clear that I have been trying to suggest some faint resemblance between Confucian and Western moral traditions and the two ideal types under discussion, although the realities are much more complicated than the ideal types. What degree of resemblance there is suggests the following. Each tradition could learn a good deal from the other. Western moral traditions would gain enormously from the sophisticated and intricate insights developed in the Confucian analysis of personal relations. Confucians could gain from Western analyses of justice.

Part of the suggestion is that it might be possible for a moral tradition, if it is sufficiently flexible and tolerant of complexity, to have it both ways: to provide adequate and clear emphasis both on impersonal systems of justice and on the importance and peculiar requirements of personal relationships. This might seem a recommendation of double vision. But, if the reader will forgive the optical metaphor, what I am recommending is bifocal ethics.

It is possible to distinguish between cases that best are approached within a justice tradition and those best approached from the standpoint of personal connectedness. This distinction can be made in a number of ways. A Kantian might very well begin with Kant's distinction between cases determinable by use of the categorical imperative and cases that instead call merely for hypothetical imperatives. There is nothing drastically unusable about this distinction; where Kant is chiefly to be faulted is in his bland and jejune assumption that the latter could be lumped together under the pursuit of happiness and particular ends, and (because not matters of principle) are not the concern of ethics. This assumption blinded him to the significance of things that we really ought to do that are matters of love or friendship rather than matters of principle; his attempts, in a discussion of imperfect duties, to assimilate these to the side of life governed by the categorical imperative are in my view not entirely successful. (For more sympathetic discussions, see Hill 1971; Herman 1985; and Baron 1987. But see also Langton 1992.) It is, however, possible for a Kantian to begin with something like Kant's distinction, and then to develop something like a Confucian account of how we ought to conduct ourselves in our relationships with others.

Something similar is possible for a consequentialist. It is often not realized that an insistence on making the world as good as is possible as an ethical standard can function as a way of justifying habits and systems of thought as well as individual actions, and that when it is used to justify habits and systems of thought it normally will be taken as an inappropriate standard for individual actions that are governed by the habits or systems of thought. Thus, Mill, in *On Liberty*, argues that systems of rights are highly useful in a certain stage of social development, and that it is highly useful that we never calculate in individual cases the advantages and disadvantages of respecting rights. In much this way, a consequentialist could argue that it is highly useful to be governed by something like a Confucian view of personal relationships, and that to be governed entirely by such a view is never so much as to entertain the thought of opportunistic violations of standards for the sake of momentary advantages. Consequentialists also could adjudicate the boundary between the realm of impersonal justice and the private world in terms of the competing social utilities of alternative placements. Shifts of the boundary, as when nepotism came to be thought of as unacceptable, can be explained retrospectively in these terms.

This exploration of Kantian and consequentialist responses to justice and connectedness is all sketchy, but then discussions of the future of whole systems of thought are bound to be sketchy. The point remains that it is possible to combine a Western-style justice tradition with a very different kind of tradition, and that the best approach may be one in which different areas of life are guided by different traditions. I do not mean to suggest that there would be no difficulties or complications in this process. In some areas the deliverances of justice-centered morality may have to be tempered by a connectedness-centered perspective, or vice versa. The activities of politics, with requirements of personal negotiation and compromise, may in some respects straddle any reasonable division between two realms of life. But there seems no reason to suppose that what I have called a bifocal ethics would be less equipped to deal with politics than any ethics we already have.

My recommendations have been addressed with the improvement of Western traditions chiefly in mind, although the argument has been that both Confucian and Western traditions could learn from one another. The need to learn, though, may be more crucial for the West. This is because the assumption often made that the private world and the realm of justice are not only separate from but also sealed from one another may turn out not to be entirely true. If we ask where people, as it were, really live, the answer for virtually everyone is in the private world. Perhaps it is possible to maintain indefinitely a societal double life, in which sophisticated and demanding requirements of justice are usually met but in which, also, people often have impoverished and lonely private lives, sometimes marked by sloppiness and downright lack of standards in personal relationships. But it is hard to believe that impoverishment and sloppiness in one realm will not seep into the other. If people lack integrity in the most basic transactions of their lives, can we expect them to maintain it in the public realm? I do not mean to suggest that such questions can be answered a priori; it may be that for many the answer in fact is "Yes," that ethical compartmentalization works for them. But the questions suggest the possibility that development of bifocal systems of ethics may have more than theoretical or personal importance and may in fact counteract forces leading to the erosion of Western traditions of justice.

14

THE EMOTIONS OF ALTRUISM,
EAST AND WEST

In colloquial English, *altruism* means concern for other people, especially concern that is expressed in helpful behavior. Some philosophical studies mirror this usage. Thomas Nagel (1970, 16, n1), for example,
means by *altruism* "any behavior motivated merely by the belief that someone
else will benefit or avoid harm by it." One sense of the word, in its ordinary
usage, equates altruism with giving more weight to the preferences of others
than to our own (Hare 1981, 129). In this essay, I will use *altruism* in a
somewhat different (and technical) sense, to stand for the policy of giving
equal weight to the well-being of all sentient beings, including oneself as
counting for one. Altruism in this sense is a feature of a good deal of utilitarian philosophy, including recent work by R. M. Hare and Derek Parfit.
Something like it is a feature of Buddhism. This chapter will be concerned
with understanding altruism as part of the structure of the life of the altruist,
especially in relation to such a person's emotions.

Altruism

Ernest Albee, in his classic study of utilitarians and of early figures (such as
Hume and Hutcheson) who (without being utilitarians) had some affinity to
utilitarianism, notes a shift between Hume's grounding of morality in his
Treatise of Human Nature (1739) and its grounding in his *Enquiry Concerning
the Principles of Morals* (1751). The springs of action in the *Treatise*, Albee
says, are egoism, altruism (limited largely in its objects to those close to us),
and "sympathy" (in which our idea of another's emotion may become so vivid
as to give rise to the same emotion in ourselves). In the *Enquiry*, Albee suggests, "sympathy" comes to mean "nothing essentially different from the gen-

eral benevolent tendency" (Albee 1957, 95–96). Francis Hutcheson, meanwhile, had arrived at a very similar view; in his *System of Moral Philosophy*, published posthumously in 1755, he speaks of "the notion of the greatest possible system of sensitive beings" and a "calm, stable, universal good-will to all, or the most extensive benevolence" (Hutcheson 1968, 50, 69). This universal benevolence is not, as Hutcheson acknowledges, an element of "the ordinary condition of mankind . . . but of the condition our nature can be raised to by due culture." Doubtless, he says, "some good men have exercised in life only the particular kind affections, and found a constant approbation of them, without either the most extensive views of the whole system or the most universal benevolence" (Hutcheson 1968, 77–78). It is important that we be clearly aware of the difference between "particular kind affections" and "the most extensive benevolence," the latter of which is an aspect of altruism in the sense of this essay. The great majority of human beings experience particular kind affections, and are able to feel sympathy for some human beings (especially those close to them or those who are like them) and for some animals (especially household pets). It might seem at first that there is a scale here that admits of degrees, in that some people are more affectionate and have wider sympathies than others, and that "the most extensive benevolence" simply represents the top of the scale. I wish to argue the opposite, that what Hutcheson describes is a very different kind of thing from particular affections and sympathies, that it is (as he suggests) fairly uncommon, and that when it occurs it is very likely (as he also suggests) the result of a shaping and refining of attitudes that is a peculiar form of cultural enrichment.

The last part of this argument will appear in the final section of this essay. We may turn our attention now, though, to the differences between altruism ("the most extensive benevolence") and particular affections and sympathies. A clear view of the differences will show also how uncommon a thing is altruism (in the sense under discussion).

Familiar examples of particular affections include those of romantic love and those directed toward one's parents or one's children. We care about these people, and, indeed, whether we really do care would come into question if we did not feel satisfaction at their well-being and apprehension at dangers to them. Such "significant others" are thus, in the words of Shakespeare's *Macbeth*, "hostages to fortune": they represent areas of vulnerability in our lives. They are, if we are fortunate in our connections, sources of positive experiences, such as joy, delight, various pleasures, and even happiness. Because nothing in life is certain, they are also potential sources of uneasiness, fear, grief, distress, and suffering. In short, particular affections are sources of emotional agitation. The more people, animals, and the like we care about in this way, the more hostages to fortune we have and the more agitated our emotional life is likely to be. Could someone sleep at night who cared about every member of the human race the way we care about our loved ones? If the emotions of particular affections and sympathies were spread as widely as possible, the result (given the limitations of human psychology) would be psychic overload, benevolence burnout.

It might be objected that this is too quick and simple. If the emotions of particular affections and sympathies were spread as widely as possible, why can we not assume that their intensity would be dimmed proportionately? We can imagine two forms this might take. One is that some affections (e.g., for spouses, parents, children) would retain some moderately high intensity, whereas others would be of suitably low intensity. The other is that all affections would be of suitably low intensity. We may dismiss the first possibility immediately, for the purposes of this essay, simply in that it does not amount to altruism in the sense under discussion (or the sense in which altruism is implicit in Buddhist and utilitarian philosophy). The second possibility, though, points toward a plausible reconstruction of altruism, and corresponds to the respects in which the Buddhist perfect way "refuses to make preferences" and is "freed from love and hate" (Seng Ts'an, "On Believing in Mind," trans. D. T. Suzuki, in Conze 1959, 171). Indeed, this possibility amounts to altruism if the intensity (which would have to be very low indeed) of affection for all sentient beings were equal. But would this extremely low-intensity affection qualify as what we normally call "affection"? Differences in degree can amount to differences in kind; and I suggest that, if one divided all concern for others among the trillions of sentient beings, one's spouse and children would judge that one no longer cared for them.

The second model of altruism, of concern for others divided equally among a very large number of objects, is a useful way of beginning to think about what altruism is. But this model can be criticized as being too hydraulic, treating concern as if it were a quantifiable and divisible liquid. Indeed, if the number of those whose well-being matters is in the trillions, the concern per being (on this model) is infinitesimal and looks very much like indifference. The truth is that the altruist, unless she or he has some administrative or political role, is usually not confronted with the needs and problems of very large numbers of beings at any one time. Hence, a significant degree of warmth and compassion will be possible. But the realization that there are others whose needs and problems are equally important—especially if it is coupled with a belief that it is part of the order of things that those who are not enlightened will often suffer—should prevent grasping onto the welfare and absence of suffering of any particular being or beings as a requirement of life. The popular saying "You win some and lose some" will apply and will shape the attitudes of the altruist. There will be (at least in theory) significant concern without attachment; the concern will be genuinely felt but also will be guarded and limited in intensity, as it were with strings connecting it to the realities of disappointment and suffering.

Thus, another way to look at the difference between particular affections (unguarded and, in some cases, unlimited in their intensity) and altruism as a state of mind is to contrast the emotional ups and downs and disturbances of the person who has particular affections with the evenness and lack of emotional disturbance of the genuine altruist. This eveness implies a transformation of both social and psychological conditions. The two are illustrated well in the Buddhist poem "The Rhinoceros." The enlightened person "fares lonely as a rhinoceros," with "mind that festers not, nor burns" (Conze 1959, 79–82). This calm loneliness is a natural consequence of the Buddhist recommendation of "a boundless good will towards the entire world" (Conze 1959, 186). Whether it is equally a consequence of utilitarian altruism will be examined in the final section of this essay.

Emotional Lives

First, though, we need to look at what emotions are. A skeptical reader might ask whether altruists, as I have been describing them, have emotions. Possibly the title of this essay reflects a confusion. Perhaps it should have been "The Non-emotions of Altruism, East and West"?

Plainly much depends on what we count as an emotion. Motivational force would seem to be linked to the idea of emotion, and there is a traditional argument (a classic formulation of which is found in Hume) to the effect that human action presupposes a motivational element. Reason, Hume says, "being cool and disengaged," is no motive to action, and "directs only the impulse received from appetite or inclination" (Hume 1751/1975, 294). Hence, "taste" is "the *first* spring or impulse to desire and volition."

Hume took care with language, and we should take him seriously when he speaks of the impulse "received from appetite or inclination." We may take it that "appetite" and "inclination" here represent alternatives; otherwise, he would have used one word instead of two. What is the difference between an impulse received from appetite and one received from inclination?

The ordinary meaning of "appetite" is close to that of "felt want." Can someone be hungry or thirsty without *feeling* hungry or thirsty or without (at least) having such feelings close to the surface? If someone says, "I had no idea that I was hungry at all until I sat down and began eating," it is tempting to interpret this statement as meaning that he or she began to feel hungry while eating, and that this was a matter of feelings of hunger surfacing that had been latent all along. Other appetites, such as for sex, power, or love, may be less closely tied to feeling than are hunger and thirst. Even so, the central, paradigmatic cases of appetite for sex, power, or love are ones in which the subject, if induced to be candid, could report feelings that are expressive or indicative of the appetite. Appetites that are not felt will be considered appetites, in large part, because they function, both in patterns of behavior and in associated thoughts and utterances, very much like the familiar cases of appetites that are felt.

There are cases, on the other hand, in which someone stands ready to choose one thing over another without any felt or latent craving for what is (or will be) preferred, without any noticeable feeling at all, and without any of the behavior, thought, or utterances that normally would be associated with felt cravings. Bloggs simply picks X over Y, and perhaps remarks in a calm, dispassionate way that X is better than Y. It may be that Hume used the word "inclination" with reference to cases like this. In Hume's terms such an inclination could qualify as a "mild passion"; he does speak (1739/1978, 165) in another context of our having an impression of a determination of the mind to pass from one object to another.

There does not appear to be any logical or psychological reason that someone could not, as a bare fact, be inclined toward one thing rather than toward another without having the stirrings of appetite for what is preferred and without exhibiting behavior or reporting thought that we would associate with appetite. We need not look at Buddhists and utilitarians in order to find such cases. Many everyday situations in which a person says, "If it's all the same to you, I think I'd rather have X than Y," serve quite well.

We thus can draw from Hume's language the suggestion, I think, that motivational force in some cases is generated by feelings and in some does not require feelings. (In what follows, I will use *motivation* as a technical term that straddles both these possibilities.) One has to be cautious here, in that our introspective reports are generally not precise; and while sometimes we are able to say readily enough whether we have strong feelings or not, the boundaries within territory that includes hardly any feelings at all about X, no noticeable feelings about X, and no feelings about X are somewhat blurred. It may be that the stoic ideal of *apatheia* was meant to encourage an emotional life within that territory, allowing for very slight feelings, or ones of negligible intensity, about this or that. We can similarly interpret the ideal proposed by the seventeenth-century poet Henry Vaughan when he says, "Incite and use thyself to a gallant apathy." Vaughan was praising the courage and effort required to make one's feelings very slight.

An ambiguity in phrases such as "no feelings" also needs to be noted. It can mean no feelings whatsoever, period, or it can mean none of the sort that involve intentionality (i.e., that implicitly refer to and require objects). If we interpret stoics and Buddhists as recommending that we have no feelings, it has to be in the second sense. Otherwise, it will be hard to understand Philip Hallie's linking the ideal of *apatheia* with "spiritual peace and well-being"; it also will be hard to follow Buddhist discussions of "the joy of quietness" (Hallie 1967; *Dhammapadaa*, no. 205, 64). The distinction is apparent in ordinary English: someone who truthfully says, "I have no feelings in the matter," may be feeling very relaxed.

There is a parallel ambiguity involved when someone is spoken of as "unemotional" or as "having no emotions" (which is not entirely the same thing). Someone may be spoken of as having no emotions who is possessed of a calm, quiet inner joy, as can someone who feels no joy and indeed feels nothing (qualifying as "affectless"). Either could be spoken of as "unemotional," although I judge that the term also could be applied to someone who has discernible but mild emotions of the sort that involve intentionality, as long as these emotions were not disturbing.

To return to feelings: there is a tradition in recent analytic philosophy of equating feelings with disturbances, which goes back to Gilbert Ryle's *The Concept of Mind* (1949). Some will think of Ryle's famous list: thrills, twinges, pangs, throbs, wrenches, itches, prickings, chills, glows, loads, qualms, hankerings, curdlings, sinkings, tensions, gnawings, and shocks (Ryle 1949, 83–84). With the possible exception of glows, these are all disturbances, and, indeed, Ryle's bias is made explicit later when he claims that "feelings are intrinsically connected with agitations" (Ryle 1949, 104). It is not difficult to see the appeal of this claim. Not only are most feelings (including the most noticeable ones) connected with agitations, but it can be argued that feelings (like perceptions) can be registered only if there is some element of contrast. Just as a uniform perceptual field that lasted an entire lifetime would not allow any perception, a uniform psychic state that lasted an entire lifetime would not allow for the experience of feelings. Agitation is the most obvious way to introduce contrast into someone's psychic states. But it is not the only way, and, indeed, the *absence* of tension and apprehension that one used to suffer from can be felt. It cannot be emphasized too strongly that some feelings are calm and undisturbed, and do not involve appetites.

A similar point can be made about emotions. Hate, fear, and erotic love are emotions, but is there any reason not to include *agape* and compassion also? Jerome Shaffer's influential discussion of emotion takes emotion to be "a complex of physiological processes and sensations caused by certain beliefs and desires" (Shaffer 1983, 161). It is natural to think of Ryle's list in connection with the phrase "physiological processes and sensations." But much of the literature of Buddhism—Zen Buddhism especially—stresses that there are physiological processes and sensations characteristically associated with a calm enlightenment. Are these caused by beliefs and desires? Philosophical beliefs, including metaphysical beliefs about the self, certainly are at work. Buddhists eschew desire, but this does not mean that their lives are utterly devoid of motivational elements: they are not, in every situation, entirely suspended between available alternatives. The word *desire* is used, in the recent philosophical literature on the emotions, in a very broad technical sense rather than with its ordinary meaning (Baier 1986). In this broad, technical use of *desire*, any motivational element (no matter how gentle and no matter how free of appetite) qualifies one as having a desire; and in this sense, even Buddhists have desires. Their beliefs and "desires" cause physiological processes which are such that enlightened Buddhists, as one Zen text puts it, can like thieves recognize each other without any introduction (*Zen Flesh, Zen Bones*, 129).

There is no clear reason, then, to deny that altruism can involve emotions. If someone pursues an altruistic policy because of certain ethical beliefs that are linked with appropriate motivational elements, and if the altruist at the same time feels calm and dispassionate (as well, perhaps, as having other, associated feelings), what is missing? This is not to say, though, that what is present will be the same in all traditions of altruism. In the remaining section, we need to look at some East-West differences.

Forms of Altruism

Up to this point, no distinction has been made between utilitarian and Buddhist altruism. Indeed, there is a remarkable congruence in formulas. Beside the utilitarian assertions that each sentient being should count equally and Hutcheson's "calm, stable, universal good-will to all" we may place Buddhist affirmations of the ideal of "a boundless good will towards the entire world" (Conze 1959, 186).

This does not mean, of course, that altruism functions, or is meant to function, in the same way in the lives of Buddhists and utilitarians. For that matter, not all Buddhists will be alike, nor will all utilitarians be alike, either in doctrine or in personal lives. But there are characteristic Buddhist forms of altruism, nevertheless, and persistent utilitarian patterns—which are quite different from the Buddhist ones—of attempts to integrate altruism into a life. To explore the differences is to glimpse two different sorts of emotional life.

The Buddhist literature is full of examples of people who have taken the altruistic ideal to its logical conclusion, in the sense of leading calm, even lives with no personal attachments. There is no comparable literature of utilitarian saints. I can record that the prominent utilitarians that I have known have seemed, in my experience, extraordinarily considerate people; but that is not quite the same thing. Is it just that the West, since the Reformation, has not gone in much for saintliness? The explanation runs, I think, much deeper, and is, in fact, mirrored in many of the polemics of recent Western ethical philosophy.

Many ongoing debates take this form. An ethical philosophy (it may be utilitarianism, but Kant is also a favorite target) seems to offer no room for special obligations or responsibilities that we have to others, either because they are close to us or because we care about them. (An especially good formulation of the line of thought that there has to be this room is in Sommers 1986.) The philosophy's defenders might take the line that the special obligations or responsibilities that are appealed to either can be subsumed under general impersonal requirements (e.g., those connected to promising), or (implicit in Hare 1976, 1981) are symptomatic of the fact that we are, after all, human and not ideal beings in whose choices they would not (need not) play a role. It is sometimes suggested also that Kant has room for emotional attachments as ancillary to, or merely regulated by, the workings of the categorical imperative. Utilitarians have held that pursuing particular loyalties is conducive to the greatest happiness of the greatest number (cf. Smart 1977, 128; for interesting discussion of the role in ethics of particular loyalties, see Stocker 1976, Herman 1983; Louden 1991; and Pettit 1988).

Do utilitarians in their everyday lives interpret utilitarianism so that they can cheerfully favor their nearest and dearest over others? The short answer that I wish to suggest is that many (perhaps virtually all) do so for some parts of their lives and not for others. Utilitarian altruism (along with its cousin, Kantian ethics, in which the emphasis is on respect as well as concern for well-being, and the domain is limited to rational beings) is alive and well, but only within the context of a compartmentalization of human life. This means that the emotions of the most prominent form of Western altruism will be very different from the emotions of Buddhist altruism.

The major division that allows altruism to be combined with particular affections is between the public and the private. It roughly corresponds to the division between what is subject to moral judgment and what is not. (David Lyons [1973] has interpreted Bentham as espousing a dual standard, one for public matters and another for private ones. Mill's distinction between the moral and the nonmoral has already been commented on.) A number of lines of thought converge on these divisions. If something is a public matter, then standards of fairness apply. We cannot discriminate; equal cases must be treated equally. Poor decisions are subject to the communal pressure that is characteristic of morality, which itself appeals to standards that should be apparent to all (and hence must be independent of any particular point of view).

If something is a private matter, on the other hand, it is not subject to (or should not be subject to) communal pressure (see Mill 1859/1978). It then can be put under the heading of "expediency" (Mill) or viewed as subject merely to hypothetical imperatives (Kant). There is then no reason in morality why the degree of one's concern for, or involvement with, others cannot be relevant to the question of how best one should behave toward them. The cases of those who are strangers or otherwise unconnected thus can be, in these matters, not equal with those of our nearest and dearest, and there is no requirement of equal treatment.

What is generally a private relationship can, of course, become a public matter if there is an abuse serious enough to warrant communal pressure or to rule out what was done as ineligible to be universal practice. Apart from such abuses, though, the division between public and private corresponds to a division between two spheres of one's life. It may be helpful to think of an area of life in which one is "on duty" and an area in which one is "off duty."

One aspect of the public/private division is that we expect people to be impartial in decisions relating to such matters as promise keeping; adherence to agreed-upon conventions that govern property rights; business and educational hiring, firing, and preferment (nepotism is obsolete); judicial actions; and so on. It is all right not to be impartial among the members of one's society in deciding to whom to give Christmas presents but not in one's activities as a judge, employer, banker, or concerned citizen.

What I have been drawing with a broad brush is a cluster of attitudes and habits of mind that are characteristic of modern Western civilization and that influence educated and responsible people generally as well as utilitarians in particular. These attitudes and habits allow utilitarian altruism to be limited in the range of occasions on which it comes into play. I will refer to the result as "limited altruism." In a way that might bewilder someone unfamiliar with modern Western civilization, it is as if the altruism is turned on and off.

The limited altruism under discussion might be held to be connected with a Western philosophical tradition one of whose major constructs is an individualistic self. There is a contrast here with the Confucian view of the person in which social context and connections assume a much more essential role (see Ames and Fingarette in Bockover 1991.) Confucian altruism, though, is a tertium quid, sharply distinct (in taking account of gradations in our connectedness) from Buddhist altruism and (in not relying on a compartmentalization of life) from what I have been characterizing as a widespread modern Western form of altruism. The individualistic Western construct of self does play a part in the contrast I am drawing between Buddhist and Western altruism, but so does Buddha's insistence that the network of special relationships is part of the sickness from which we must escape.

Buddhist altruism, operating in an unlimited range of circumstances, requires an emotional development that is also required for Buddhist enlightenment: David Kalupahana speaks of "pacification (*vupasama*) of craving and desires" (1976, 60). Unpacified desires are disturbing and also lead to partiality of various kinds. A utilitarian who pursues a strategy of limited altruism, on the other hand, need not pacify her or his craving and desires. In certain contexts (by and large, those of private life) their expression is licit, and may, indeed, promote the greatest happiness of the greatest number. Yet in the public decisions that are governed by morality, they must be out of play.

When a culture, or a segment of a culture, develops a unified worldview, one usually can expect that the attitudes and beliefs that form the worldview will be, on the whole, mutually reinforcing. That is, each element of the worldview will be such that if it is accepted many of the others will seem more reasonable than otherwise they might have seemed. The connections normally will not be as tight as logical implication and might be very difficult to analyze in terms of formal logic; but they will be apparent to most students of the culture.

One element of modern Western culture that supports limited altruism is the persistent claim, found in the eighteenth century in Mandeville and in Adam Smith, that private affections and selfishness are (if regulated or limited in appropriate ways) conducive to the public good. (A very interesting recent exploration of this theme is Ci 1991.) It should be noted that the public good is construed, in these arguments, largely in terms of economic prosperity and the freedom to engage in various desire-laden activities. Thus, the arguments would be unlikely to satisfy any strict Buddhist. But they do have the force, if one accepts the value system embedded in them, of dissolving what looks like a contradiction: between, on one hand, the ideal of altruism and, on the other hand, the claim that in many of the elemental transactions of life it is quite all right to favor oneself or one's loved ones. The arguments suggest that *indirectly* this is as good as—indeed, better than—unlimited altruism.

What are the emotions of limited altruism? It may seem that the answer points toward the range of emotions to be found in one's culture, in that it is all right to have such emotions and to express them, although in some cases the expression is to be restricted to a portion of one's life. This answer is largely right, but does not do justice to the emotional adaptation that is required if someone is to function effectively as an altruist in moral, social, and political decision making. It might seem that we could borrow an analogy from current computer technology: thinking of the limited altruist—or, for that matter, anyone who is scrupulously impartial in a limited sphere—as opening a Buddhist "window" on her or his emotional screen. But this analogy does not fit the reality around us. Judges, politicians, educators, and administrators who succeed in pursuing a policy of one of these sorts are not, typically, like Buddhists in their emotions while they are at work. The typical American law court or office, even if it is staffed by the most high-minded people, is not lit up by a host of gentle, compassionate smiles.

Basically, there is a huge difference between denial of self and holding "dear self" (as Kant puts it) in check in part of one's life. The latter requires emotional mechanisms more closely linked to puritanism than to compassion. In one's private life, the part of life in which one most essentially lives, of course one prefers one's own interests and those of loved ones to those of strangers. But in one's public/moral and political capacity one tries to be fair, recognizing that strangers are human beings and that they count equally, and so forth. A utilitarian may remind herself or himself that even rats and cockroaches are sentient and presumably can experience pain, and this will condition life-or-death decisions. The "window" that comes up on the utilitarian's emotional screen, though, will be not compassion but rather a stance of impartiality, an impersonal distancing from emotions that are at the heart of our being.

This is one reason why extremely fair-minded people in our culture often seem cold, even to each other. The distancing from personal emotion that one sees can look very much like an absence of emotion. Indeed, that is a possibility, especially for someone whose work (or whose moral and political activities) is, as we say, his or her life. We also need to confront the possibility that the compartments of the limited altruist's life may not be as sharply separated as in theory they might be. An element of impersonality may seep into private life. A degree of warmth may seep into public life, leading to the occasional smile of gentle compassion.

In the end, of course, it is impossible to arrive at generalizations about what the emotional life of all sincere utilitarian altruists will be like. We can gesture at likely patterns of emotions and think that we can recognize them in some of the people around us (as well, perhaps, as in ourselves). One further general difference between utilitarian altruism and Buddhist altruism should be remarked upon. By and large, Buddhists, especially in the classic period of Buddhist philosophy, have not been drawn to social and political remedies for the problems of the world. It is easy to see why, given the Buddhist value system: the loss of desire (which is paramount) is a matter of individual effort. Utilitarians, on the other hand, have been strongly drawn, almost from the outset, to social and political reform and organizational programs. It is easy to see why this should be, given not only the values of utilitarians but also the complex social, economic, and political networks characteristic of modern "developed" countries. Utilitarians can plausibly believe that the right kind of social, political, and economic activities can bring great benefits to the general population. They also can plausibly believe that technical knowledge and the ability to calculate consequences (especially in the long run) of various policies are required to know what is for the greatest good of the greatest number. Some utilitarian technocrats thus can practice limited altruism much more effectively than the average person could. Inevitably, this fact imports a paternalistic (or maternalistic) tinge into limited altruism. It also is easily mocked, as when the anti-utilitarian Bernard Williams speaks of "Government House utilitarianism" (Williams 1985, 108–10).

Philosophies can be forms of life. As such, they can change and develop even while retaining their link to a core of classic texts. Philosophers typically concentrate on the texts, along with the logical implications of what is in them. But there is room also for inquiries conducted by philosophers, historians, and psychologists into the role of philosophies in structuring and orienting human lives. This essay should be read as a crude, early attempt to move in that direction.

15

VARIETIES OF ETHICAL JUDGMENT

Afterword

Much ethical philosophy has been written with a single scale in mind. At the top end are actions that are obligatory. Below them (in the degree to which they are imperative) are those which would be wonderful or nice but are not required (and therefore count as "supererogatory"). There is a large territory of actions that simply are permissible, and at the bottom are those that we have an obligation not to perform. This is an attractively simple picture of the recommendations that ethics can have to offer. The unit of choice is an action, and there are a small number of possible recommendations, the ones at the top and at the bottom being the urgent ones.

By now it should be evident that this image is drastically oversimple. Ethical philosophies indeed can yield recommendations of actions—if, that is, we supplement them with ways of interpreting and classifying the cases that come up. They also can suggest orientations in life, values that are especially worth pursuing in a sustained way, and modifications of the ways our emotions are organized. At the most fundamental level, Asian philosophies typically have yielded recommendations of the kind of person we should attempt to be.

These assortments of recommendations also should not be thought of as toneless answers of "Yes," "No," "O.K. if you want to," or "It would be nice but you don't have to." There can be enormous variations in the kinds, as well as degrees, of pressure (or lack of pressure) that accompany recommendations. An ethical philosophy sets up a meaning system that determines these. Judgments after the fact can differ enormously also, as can the emotions they express: think of the difference between anger and contempt. Think also of the differences (which are more subtle) between our severe condemnation of someone who harms others as a result of insensitivity and extreme irresponsibility, and of someone who harms others out of overt malice.

Ethical philosophies can influence our answers of "Yes," "No," and so on, to the various problems that life presents. But they also can influence the form in which the questions are considered, the tone of voice of the answers, and the ways in which they are implemented in a social setting. To the extent that there is a dominant mode of ethical question and response in our culture, a philosophy can recommend changes in this mode.

This is not to suggest that philosophies necessarily can expect to have much effect, either immediately or in the long run, on the ways in which people approach life. There are countries, India and China especially, in which a small number of philosophical texts are foundational, not merely to later philosophy but to the entire culture. No Western country is like that, although at moments France has come closer than most. This is not likely to change, and it would be foolish to exaggerate the influence philosophy can have in a country like America. Nevertheless the question remains: if philosophy can analyze and clarify concepts and conceptual maps, can it not also engage in conceptual engineering that might be fruitful? This section has suggested an answer of "Yes," and that cross-cultural comparisons can play a helpful role.

PART V

The Demands of Ethics

16

EXPECTING MORE OF SOME PEOPLE

The starting point of the two essays that follow is that religious ethics makes special demands. What are these special demands? Most people would immediately interpret this question in terms of a stricter morality. Many moral codes are not as strict as they look: they contain not only commands and prohibitions but also (as it were, between the lines) areas of latitude. Perhaps there is no latitude where murder or theft is involved; but it may be understood by adherents of a code that the occasional lie, broken promise, or indiscretion will not be condemned harshly. In societies in which this is true, the ethics associated with a religion can have the function of enjoining more serious and sustained moral efforts. More may be required, and less may be forgiven.

As true as this sometimes is, it is not the object of my interest. The demands associated with some religious ethics that I wish to examine are special not so much in degree or in severity as they are in the parts of life they concern. Religious ethics sometimes requires attention to, and reflection on, matters that most moral systems slight or ignore.

A very familiar example in Western tradition is the dialogue in the New Testament between Jesus and a rich young man, who asks, "What good thing shall I do?" (Matthew 19:16–22). Jesus' first reply consists for the most part of traditional moral requirements. When more is requested, the reply is "If thou wilt be perfect, go and sell that thou hast, and give to the poor, and thou shalt have treasure in heaven; and come and follow me."

On an extreme interpretation Jesus is expressing (in this, and in what sounds like a dim prospect for salvation of the rich in the remarks that follow the young man's refusal) a negative attitude toward wealth. A less extreme interpretation, which seems much more plausible (and which I accept), is that the problem, from Jesus' point of view, is not wealth per se but rather attachment to wealth. The problem is in the rich young man's attitude, and in where, so to speak, his heart lies.

Much more could be said about this passage. It fits an emphasis in the New Testament on the quality of thoughts and feelings as well as of actions. My concern here is primarily with one unusual feature of the passage. The ethical recommendations express a double standard, in which the higher standard governs territory not governed by the lower standard. There is, first of all, what is recommended for the vast majority of people. The higher standard of "if thou wilt be perfect" relates, as the general standard does not, to what a person cares most about.

Why, one might ask, should one strain to reach a higher standard when one already meets (as the rich young man thinks he does) the general standard? Why does he go away sorrowing? The answer surely is that the higher standard is worth meeting. This is not because of any rewards of the most obvious kind. In particular, there is no suggestion that people who merely meet the general standard will not attain salvation. Nevertheless, the higher standard is enticing for a certain kind of person, because meeting it amounts to being a much better person. There are inner psychic rewards, which in the end the rich young man believes that he will miss.

The Bible of course would be classified as straightforwardly a religious and not a philosophical work. Its appeal has been viewed as one to revelation, and there is very little explicit or implicit argument. The texts of early Buddhism, in contrast, are philosophical as well as in some sense religious. (Buddhism from the start behaved like a religion in many ways, including organization, but there is hardly any creed.) On most readings there is no appeal whatsoever to revelation; and there is a fair amount of explicit argument about the connections among sense of self, desires, and suffering. Nevertheless, part of what emerges from this system is similar in form to the message of Jesus to the rich young man. There is a general set of standards for goodness and also a higher standard, which covers a much wider territory, for those who want to be much better people. One difference between the early Buddhist and New Testament models, though, is that salvation in the former (the Buddhist Nirvana, a blissful cessation of the processes of selfness and desire) is available only to those who perfect themselves.

Both of the essays that follow touch on issues of what is, or is not, a religion. The reader should bear in mind that these are not as straightforward, or as cut-and-dried, as one might think. First, a general concept such as "religion" may well turn out to admit of borderline cases. Asking whether Confucianism really is a religion is not exactly like asking whether whales are really mammals: there can be multiple criteria, some of which will test positive and some of which will test negative. Second, the concept of "religion" is contestable to a degree, in that there is room for argument as to which features should count most heavily, and a person's general outlook or personal commitments can affect the answers she or he gives. It is often said that in philosophy conclusions can be less important than what one sees on the way to them. That is especially true in relation to the topic of religious ethics.

17

CONFUCIUS AND THE NATURE OF RELIGIOUS ETHICS

Students of comparative religion often pause over the question, "Is Confucianism a religion?" Confucius tended to be noncommittal when asked about life after death or about the supernatural (see Creel 1949, 113–22). Can such a man be considered a religious thinker?

Such questions inevitably lead to this one: "What is a religion?" This query often is taken as a request for a definition. I will assume that what Wittgenstein (1953) showed of "game" is true equally of "religion": that the word cannot be defined, and the most we can point to is "family resemblances" that link its usages. I will assume also that what is widely called a religion may properly be called one. From this it follows that Confucianism is a religion and that Confucius is a religious thinker. But what "family resemblances" link Confucianism to other religions, and link the thought of Confucius, which is entirely centered on ethics, to other religious thought?

To answer this question we have to develop a view of the place of ethics in religion. We also have to show that the role ethics often assumes in religious thought is similar to the one it has in Confucius' thought. This will demonstrate that there is, indeed, a "family resemblance" between Confucius and other religious thinkers.

My procedure will be as follows. I will discuss two propositions often asserted or implied in religious ethics and not commonly in nonreligious ethics. These propositions will not be found in all religious ethics nor will they be absent from all nonreligious ethics: for them to constitute "family resemblances," it is enough that they be far more characteristic of religious than of nonreligious ethics. At the same time, I will show that Confucius would support these propositions, thus specifying respects in which his ethics partakes of features characteristic of religious ethics.

To most people in our culture, the words "religious ethics" suggest codes said to be dictated by God or by gods, of which the Ten Commandments is a classic example. But this reading is one-sided, and superficial even in relation to the religions that are most familiar to us. On the one hand, there are important religions in which a theistic element is negligible or is entirely missing (e.g., Buddhism and Daoism, as well as Confucianism). On the other hand, the scriptures even of highly theistic religions, such as Christianity, may have an ethical content more interesting and less codelike than what was learned at one's mother's knee.

We may begin by examining the following two propositions characteristic of much of religious ethics: (A) The most important virtues are intimately connected with what someone prizes most or what gives that person most satisfaction. Broadly speaking, one has these virtues if one desires the right things, or avoids desiring the wrong things, or takes satisfaction in the right things, or avoids taking pleasure in the wrong things. (B) Someone's life will be unusually valuable (i.e., worth living), even at moments when he or she is not making or preparing for a moral decision, if, and only if, he or she possesses the most important virtues. A is broadly worded to do justice both to ethics that recommends that one have certain kinds of desires and to ethics that recommends a loss of desires (e.g., Buddha's teaching). A succinct way of stating A would be as follows: (A1) Someone has the most important virtues if, and only if, she or he embraces the right values.

A variety of religious thinkers could agree upon A1 without agreeing upon what counts as the right values. What makes A1 not trivial is the connotation of the word "embraces": embracing values is a matter of passions or appetites, and thus A1 places the most important virtues in a right disposition of passions or appetites. Furthermore, the passions or appetites that must be rightly disposed are not limited to those directly involved in moral choice: they include all of the passions and appetites that may be involved in valuing something or in thinking it valuable. Thus A1 implies that a man lacks the most important virtues, whatever his moral behavior may be, if what he desires most is base or is worthless.

A1 would be rejected by most ethical theorists. Kant, for example, places virtue in the triumph of duty over inclination. Thus, for him it is entirely possible to be consumed by base desires and yet to have the most important virtue, provided only that duty regularly triumphs over inclinations. John Stuart Mill, also, who in many matters commonly is contrasted to Kant, would reject A1. He would consider the most important virtues to consist of dispositions to make optimal moral choices.

A1 probably would be rejected also by most ordinary people. In this respect, common sense is not close to the characteristic view of religious ethics. Take the example of a man who is scrupulous in following the moral dictates learned at his mother's knee and who is also a complete philistine: his most pronounced desires are to complete his stamp collection and to own a larger car. Most people, as long as they thought this man dependably moral, would consider him not to lack any important virtue; that is, the man would be beyond ethical criticism.

We may criticize a man's taste or suggest that the car that he covets is not really a good one. But, in response to the suggestion that the philistine is *ethically* deficient, most people probably would subscribe to the following argument:

> In a democracy, what someone desires is his or her own business, as long as it does not conflict sharply with the welfare of others.
>
> Something may be labeled an important virtue only if it is the business of society, rather than an individual's own business.
>
> If a man's greatest desires are for a completed stamp collection and a larger car, this does not (if we assume that circumstances are normal) conflict sharply with the welfare of others.
>
> Therefore, it is his own business.
>
> Therefore, no important virtue is at stake.

This, of course, is not the characteristic verdict of religious ethics, which causes people to worry about what otherwise might have been regarded as a "free-play" area of life. To take examples almost at random: Kierkegaard would say that the philistine, if his desires make him vulnerable to disappointment, is sunk deeply in a state of "sin," no matter how scrupulous his moral behavior. Jesus would urge him to give away his car and his stamp collection and to follow him; Buddha would point out that to care deeply about cars and stamp collections is to lose all hope of real excellence. In the hands of Zen Buddhists or Daoists, the man would be in for a prolonged spell of therapy.

A1 is implicit in Confucius's ethics. Throughout the *Analects* Confucius stresses the respects in which someone who is enlightened has finely harmonized desires. There is ideally no desire for what is unworthy. In his progress toward this ideal, Confucius could claim that "At seventy I could follow the desires of my heart without transgressing the right" (a. II.4). Conversely, great pleasure is taken in what is truly valuable. "He who knows the truth is not equal to him who loves it, and he who loves it is not equal to him who delights in it" (a. VI.18).

As I argued in chapter 2, naturalness plays a key role in Confucius's thought. The process of education, properly undertaken, is the process of creating a new self, of making what would have been artificial natural. The person of highly accomplished naturalness centers life on a style that she or he has created and has under control. The emotional life is not abolished but is merely harmonized. It is of vital importance to this ideal that the emotions of its exemplar not be excessive or wrongly directed. The Confucian worthy, above all, must embrace the right values. Ultimately what is most valuable is inner and largely within one's own control; only inferior people have very strong desires for what is outer and largely not within one's own control. Thus it is that "The noble man is calm and serene, the inferior man is continually worried and anxious" (a, VII.36).

B would be treated as obvious within most systems of religious ethics. However, it controverts the view implicit in classical utilitarianism and in the thinking of most ordinary people that a man who lacks virtue yet can have very good moments if he is lucky in his pleasures. Most people might agree that crime occasionally may pay, at least within the bounds of this life.

Let us take the example of a man, addicted to cruelty and other vices, who is phenomenally successful. He suffers few defeats or acute frustrations, lives to a healthy old age, is wealthy and even respected. Such a man is the converse of Job. The verdict of mankind on his life will not be that it is unsuccessful; and if parents wish to discourage their children from following the criminal's example, the argument they give usually is either that the successful criminal is rare (i.e., they will appeal to the odds) or that in an afterlife the balance will be righted.

Most religious thinkers, on the other hand, would consider the successful criminal to be extremely unsuccessful. It is characteristic of religious ethics to weigh what is hidden far more heavily than the visible things that most people crave. What is especially worth noting here is this: many religious thinkers would say that the fundamental trouble with the successful criminal is not that he gratifies his base desires but rather that he has them. To lack the most important virtues is tantamount to a lack of spiritual harmony, which damages the entire character of one's life.

In order to recognize the significance of what is characteristically religious ethics, we must perceive clearly the problems that it purports to solve. One is this: most of a person's life normally is entirely neutral with respect to traditional moral codes; that is, moments of moral choice or action normally will comprise very little of its duration. How then do we achieve high value in the moment-to-moment texture of the larger part of our lives? As we have seen, religious ethics characteristically denies that the immoral person may have a life the larger part of which is of high quality. But this does not mean that the solution to the problem may be found within morality. Even the most scrupulous pharisee need not be happy or fulfilled in moments of moral inaction.

This problem is reflected throughout religious literature. It is reflected in injunctions to be as the lilies of the field; it is reflected equally in the famous Zen story of the courtier who wished to learn to give some value even to moments spent in the routines of court ritual (*Zen Flesh, Zen Bones* 32). Solutions to the problem, of course, vary, but they generally involve an emotional disposition to embrace what are claimed or suggested to be the highest values.

Religious ethics characteristically agrees that whatever the solution to this problem is, it is *not* that success in the nonmoral portion of one's life is a matter of practical skill or luck. A view somewhat like this, on the other hand, is implicit in what philosophers such as Kant and Mill say about happiness. Kant, of course, in his discussion of hypothetical imperatives, places emphasis on prudence and skill. Most men, on the other hand, would give a prominent place to luck and would subscribe to the following argument, which admittedly is far cruder than Kant's or Mill's view:

> What is most valuable, apart from moral uprightness, is the satisfaction of desires.
>
> The satisfaction of desires is accomplished by skill or luck, and only by skill or luck.
>
> Therefore, a person's life will be unusually valuable (i.e., worth living) even at moments when not making or preparing for a moral decision if, and only if, she or he possesses skill or is lucky.

The Confucian *Doctrine of the Mean* (vol. 1, 129) remarks that "The superior man is quiet and calm, waiting for the appointments of Heaven, while the mean man walks in dangerous paths, looking for lucky occurrences." Part of the point is again that the superior man, thanks to his inner resources, can afford to be calm; the inferior man, who depends heavily on external goods, cannot. "The enlightened are free from doubt, the virtuous from anxiety, and the brave from fear" (*Analects* a, IX.28).

Some might wish to maintain that the only difference between the inferior man who happens to be lucky and the Confucian "superior man" is that the latter's chances for happiness all along had been better: the happiness that they achieve, it might be said, is of equal value. This argument misses a crucial point. The anxiety of the Confucian inferior man, like the despair of the Kierkegaardian man who lacks the proper relation to God, may be more visible at some moments than at others. But it is always present, and it is of considerable importance. No matter how lucky the Confucian inferior man is or how skillful he is, his states of mind will never be of high value, because he will never have a proper emotional harmony. His restlessness also will keep him from complete contentment. "A man without virtue cannot long abide in adversity, nor can he long abide in happiness" (*Analects* a, IV. 2).

Let me comment on the ground we have traversed. I have advanced A and B as characteristic propositions of religious ethics to which Confucius would subscribe, but from which many philosophers and most ordinary people would dissent. What is at issue here—the difference, one might say—is not so much one of ethical content as of form and focus. Religious thinkers with sharply differing programs for the transformation of the self, or salvation, could agree on A and B; philosophers with sharply differing moralities could agree upon rejecting A and B.

Most of us are familiar with what might be called "big-moment" ethics. In this, the focus is entirely on moments of sharp moral decision: when someone decides whether or not to rob the bank, commit murder, commit adultery, admit responsibility in previous actions, and so on. A "big-moment" ethics almost inevitably will place the highest virtue in dependably making the right moral decision and almost inevitably will treat life apart from moments of moral choice as what I have called a "free-play" zone. This zone usually will be very large, because most people are not incessantly in the process of making moral decisions. Thus, "big-moment" ethics is both comfortable and dramatic. It is comfortable because it enables us not to worry too much about most of our life, and, indeed, usually does not demand too much thoughtfulness. It is dramatic because it typically highlights convulsive, visible, and brief efforts of the will.

It may be that "big-moment" ethics is so ingrained in the thinking of most of us that what I have argued to be characteristic of religious ethics, which implies a very different form, goes against the grain. It should not be surprising that, even among religious people, this should lead to misconceptions about the ethical nature of what religion has to offer. It should not be surprising either that some religious writers should produce ethics to fit a "big-moment" mold, concentrating, for example, on crucial moral choices in a sexual relationship instead of on the ethics of salvation.

It follows also that the thought of someone like Confucius will be easily misunderstood. It is possible to present Confucius merely as the proponent of a moral code quaintly different from our own, in such respects as its stress on filial piety. This presentation of him, however, misses what is most distinctive and interesting in Confucius's philosophy and especially what makes his ethics religious.

Postscript (1998)

This essay is reprinted largely as it first appeared, even though there are one or two things about which I am now uneasy. What it gets right—it still seems to me—is the characteristic concern of religious ethics with both the motivations and the interstices of life. This point is worth emphasizing, especially because some philosophers who ought to know better have placed exclusive emphasis on the Western and Near-Eastern tradition of religious ethics as divine command. Undoubtedly that is an important feature of, say, Christian ethics; but even there it is very far from being the whole story, and it entirely misses the religious quality of, say, Buddhist ethics.

My sense now is that an account more multifaceted than this essay provided is needed for what constitutes a religious ethics. If we look for family resemblances with paradigmatic cases of religious ethics, resemblances (or lack of resemblances) in many features must be considered. Why is Confucianism so often referred to as a religion whereas the philosophies of Plato and Aristotle never are talked of in this way, despite the presence in these philosophies of elements that do have an affinity with what I argued was characteristic of religious ethics? Perhaps part of the answer lies in the institutionalization of Confucianism; although that cannot be a large part of the answer, in that many things are institutionalized that we never would think of as religious. The philosophy of Confucius, with its high degree of attention to such matters as aesthetics and ritual, and its sense of making demands across the breadth of life, might be seen as more totalizing than those of Plato and Aristotle. A more important resemblance that Confucianism has with paradigmatic cases of religious ethics lies in the cultural dominance that it achieved. Not all religions, or systems of religious ethics, do achieve this; but they all can be thought of as candidates for this status, and naturally systems of religious ethics come to mind that have had a crucial role in formulating or shaping the characteristics of a culture or cultures.

The mix of qualities that constitute the natures of religions is a large subject, and one that would require a separate new essay (at least). It is worth reemphasizing, all the same, that the distinctiveness of religious ethics cannot be viewed as in general a matter of the issuance of a special moral code with special authority. Whether Confucianism in the end does count as a religion or not is very much determined by how one uses the word "religion": it may be that Confucianism lies in a gray area. What is important is the affinity between distinctive qualities of Confucian ethics and distinctive qualities of what is commonly thought of as religious ethics.

18

THE SUPRA-MORAL IN RELIGIOUS ETHICS

The Case of Buddhism

In the previous chapter I argued that there is an important characteristic difference between religious ethics and non-religious ethical systems: one that concerns the very structure of ethical theory. Let me refine this suggestion. My thesis is that the supra-moral characteristically is viewed differently in religious ethics than in non-religious ethics. I will explain shortly what is meant by "supra-moral." But first it is important to indicate the implications of the qualifying word "characteristically."

My thesis is not that all religious ethics treats the supra-moral in the way that I shall describe, or that it is never treated in this way within non-religious ethics. It is rather that usually the supra-moral is present within religious ethics in the manner to be described, and that much less frequently is it present in this way outside of religious ethics. I thus have in mind "family resemblances" in the sense developed by Wittgenstein in *Philosophical Investigations*. A cluster of features identify the supra-moral in religious ethics in a way that is not typical of non-religious ethics.

The first step will be to explain what the supra-moral is, and how it fits into ethical theory. This explanation will be followed by an examination of its characteristic presence in religious ethics. Then the thesis will be illustrated by discussion of the case of Buddhism.

As P. F. Strawson (1961) has pointed out, at the core of morality are the rules that make human society possible. Certainly it is difficult to imagine anything that we could call a morality that did not, at least in some limited way, contain injunctions against forms of behavior, such as murder, that if very widespread would render the existence of society impossible. But whereas non-religious ethical theories may contain prescriptions that go beyond this core, religious theories generally do so, as I will illustrate below.

The distinction between what is considered a moral matter and what in ethics lies beyond morality cannot be drawn entirely in terms of the social need for morality. It instead can be explained by extending the analysis of a concept associated with the ethical philosophy of R. M. Hare, that of prescriptivity. Hare (1963) elaborated upon and defended a view of ethics that he calls "universal prescriptivism." In this, part of the meaning of moral judgments is prescriptive in that they typically function as guides to conduct. Not only are they typically guides to the way others ought to act, but also they are guides to our own conduct.

There are demands that people sometimes make on themselves, or that are suggested to them by others, whose prescriptivity functions very differently from that of paradigmatic moral requirements. The injunctions not to commit murder, torture, rape, and so on carry with them a strong appeal to social pressure, along with an incitement to the agent to feel guilty in the event of a transgression. This prescriptive pressure is a mark of the moral. It is normally lacked by injunctions to have purity of heart, lose one's desires, or love one's neighbor. These lack the strong social pressure, and a normal response to failure is regret and a sense of inadequacy rather than guilt. That an injunction lacks a connection to guilt and any appeal to strong social pressure would normally be taken to indicate that it lies outside of morality. Many kinds of injunction, including those of etiquette, aesthetics, and successful carpentry, lie outside of morality. If an injunction lacks the appeal (characteristic of morality) to social pressure and to guilt in the event of failure, but takes the form of an appeal to be a better person, then it is what I call supramoral.

Let us return to the characteristic qualities of religious and of non-religious ethics. Often, although not always, non-religious versions of ethics consist of little besides a morality. They usually proscribe murder, theft, promise breaking, perhaps certain kinds of sexual conduct, and so on: in short, those kinds of conduct that public society takes seriously as objects of pressure and as fitting occasions for guilt. Often there are few or no recommendations for the rest of life. That is, when you are not engaged in deciding whether to murder someone, steal, and so on, the ethical system very likely will leave you alone: you are free to pursue your own happiness. The importance of this fact can be seen when one realizes how infrequent for most people conscious moral decisions of this sort are. Opportunities or temptations to murder or steal do not impinge all that often on most people's consciousness. Indeed, when morality is thus understood, some might report no more than one or two moral decisions in the average week. A version of ethics that dictates to us only these decisions is both dramatic and comfortable. It is dramatic because it highlights convulsive, brief, and visible efforts of the will. It is comfortable because most of the time it enables us not to worry too much about our life, and indeed usually does not demand too much thoughtfulness. It may not be too cynical to say that most people want ethics to leave them alone most of the time.

Religious ethics typically does not leave people alone most of the time. Usually, although not in every case, a religious ethical system involves an associational life and a sense of community that places as much emphasis on the supra-moral as on the moral. It is not enough that one keep various moral commandments. One also should achieve purity of heart, or love God, or be in harmony with the Dao, or achieve Confucian naturalness. Models and instructions (or at least hints) on how this is to be done are an integral part of the religious cultures. It is in part because of this locus in a religious culture that these supra-moral demands do not have the same kind of force as moral demands. The wider society will not normally be hostile if these demands are not met, nor is moral guilt present when one does not meet them. Nevertheless, given the special religious backgrounds, we can understand why great value is attached to meeting the supra-moral demands, in some cases greater value than is involved in being merely morally upright. Ethical systems that feature such demands require of their adherents more continuing attention to the quality of their lives than many people would like to give.

It needs to be emphasized that prescriptivity can vary in form and degree from group to group within a society, and for that matter that individual uses and responses can vary. There can be people who take moral judgments very lightly, and for that matter supra-moral judgments can be taken in a very pressurized way by some people. But if judgments of a certain kind very generally are taken lightly in a society, or were such that failure was connected characteristically with clucking and mild regret, then we would not readily say that these are moral judgments. If judgments of a certain kind very generally were taken seriously within a society, then we would say that they were taken "moralistically"; and if they characteristically appealed to strong social pressure and to feelings of guilt, we would classify them within morality, rather than within the supra-moral.

The supra-moral as defined covers a great deal of ground: it includes all judgments of what ought to be done whose prescriptivity does not appeal to general societal pressure. Within the supra-moral there is a characteristic area of religious concern. This is the area of desires and thoughts. There appears to be no society in the world in which a person's desires or thoughts, in themselves (apart from action), are judged with the heavy, public prescriptivity characteristic of morality. It is easy to see why this is so. Desires and thoughts need not be overt, so that they are almost as difficult to monitor as they are to control. They also do not, in themselves, overtly threaten the society. Thus, since morality is, after all, an instrument of social control, there is no need to make desires and thoughts in themselves objects of moral judgment. Having said this, I should add that it is not uncommon for an agent's desires and thoughts to be taken account of in moral judgments of actions. But this is a separate matter, as it does not imply moral judgment of desires and thoughts that are not acted upon.

Nevertheless, most religions teach their adherents what their desires and thoughts should be like. My contention, to repeat a disclaimer, is not that this is uniformly characteristic of all religions. It is perhaps more deeply woven into the meaning of the New Testament than of the Old Testament (see for example Matthew 5:21–48). The central injunction of the *Upanishads* is to view one's relation to Brahman correctly, which will involve a loss of desires; Daoism, too, enjoins a way of thinking that for some may not come easily or naturally. Also, as the first essay in this book argues, the central recommendations of Confucianism concern the psychological states and attitudes of the Confucian worthy.

The special characteristic of religious ethics can be seen if we take the case of a man who is filled with anger, but who controls his anger and in all crucial matters acts in ways that others would recommend. For Kant, as long as the man's sense of duty regularly triumphed over his hostile inclinations, there would be in ethics sparse room for criticism. For utilitarians, also, if the man's actions regularly were of kinds that had good consequences, and in fact had good consequences, there would be in ethics little room for criticism. But in the ethical theories of most religious traditions there would be considerable criticism of such a person.

If my general thesis is correct, religious ethics contains characteristically a supra-moral element that is at least as important and interesting as any morality that the religion might sanction and convey. Given the distinction between the moral and the supra-moral, one can distinguish analytically these two spheres within most systems of religious ethics. But nowhere can this distinction be drawn more readily and sharply than in the case of Buddhism.

The ideals of Buddhism traditionally have centered on two goals that one can achieve in one's own life and thinking.

One is renunciation. For the Buddhist saint "the fever (of passion) exists not" (*Dhammapada* b, 34). Renunciation is enjoined "to the end that this sorrow may pass away, and that no further sorrow may arise" (*Questions of King Milinda*, 49). A cold logic links desire, and what is normally termed pleasure, to all human suffering. As the legends surrounding Buddha's own enlightenment make clear, the painful frustration of desire is part of the human condition; and to be sensitive to pleasure is to be sensitive to deprivation.

The second ideal is often linked to the first. A clarity in one's vision of oneself and the world makes renunciation possible. An awareness of the true nature of what is normally termed one's self is crucial. Most contemporary philosophers appear unaware of the Buddhist implications of Humean analyses of the self, although Derek Parfit (1971) is an exception. Imageless thought is sometimes recommended in conjunction with the dissolution of the apparent self (*Lankavatara Sutra*, 45). An analysis of this ideal, however, is beyond the scope of this chapter.

Now the most immediately obvious thing about these supra-moral ideals is that they are very difficult to achieve. It is one thing to acquiesce, intellectually, to the fundamental propositions in which they often are stated. It is another thing to so orient one's being and thinking every moment that no cravings occur, and so that no thoughts are tinged with vestiges of the apparent self. The discipline needed itself requires continual watchfulness. Further, it is not entirely clear how purely the ideal can be achieved. There has not been unanimity in the history of Buddhism on this point, and indeed the major schism originated when Mahadeva charged that Arhats (saintly monks) were having lustful thoughts in their dreams (Conze 1957, 119–20).

It also is clear that failure to realize these supra-moral ideals, even approximately, is not something for which a person normally could be severely blamed. The ideals are removed from what would be considered morality in our society. They also are removed from what corresponds to morality (in terms of prescriptive roles) in the societies in which Buddhism has taken hold.

This is not to say that Buddhist morality is entirely identical to the core morality of the Jewish or Christian tradition. There are predictable similarities, in the prohibition of murder, theft, and so on. But, at least at some times, taking of any life, even animal life, has been treated as immoral. This idea is vividly expressed in the Noh play *Ukai*, about the repentance of a damned cormorant fisherman (*Noh Plays*, 164–70). Having observed this, I should add two comments. One is that at no time has the prohibition of an activity within a morality entailed its scarcity. Taking of life, both human and animal, was of course very common in medieval Japan; there also were what might look like inconsistencies, such as vegetarian samurai casually killing peasants. Second, the boundaries of morality fluctuate. In our own moral tradition, frivolous behavior on the Sabbath and general laziness at some times were considered morally wrong; nowadays it is unusual for people who disapprove of frivolous behavior on the Sabbath or of general laziness to consider such behavior immoral. Similarly, it is generally not the case nowadays in Buddhist countries that all taking of life is considered immoral.

If it is true that taking of any life at some times has been considered immoral among Buddhists, why has not failure to reach the highest ideals also been considered immoral? The answer is twofold. Part lies in the relative difficulties of what is required to reach these supra-moral goals. We apply moral censure only when the correct conduct is within the power of most normal people. The cormorant fisherman could have changed his occupation. It is not quite that simple to conform one's whole thinking and being to Buddhist ideals. The other part of the answer lies in the interior nature of the ideals. Morality, relying as it does on societal pressure, generally requires that conduct to be censured be visible and readily recognizable.

Traditionally, the line between the moral and the supra-moral requirements of Buddhism has run very roughly parallel to another: the line between those who are willing and able to make a full time effort to achieve salvation, and those who either are not willing or are not able. The former generally will be members of the Samgha (which comprises monks, nuns, and hermits): the Samgha has been compared in Buddhist literature to an especially fertile field (Horner, in Conze 1954, 34). As Conze (1957, 53) remarks, it "has been a conviction common to all Buddhists at all times" that "the life of a householder is almost incompatible with the higher levels of the spiritual life."

There are clear practical reasons for this. Family and children generate cravings for their welfare. The practical concerns of maintaining a household, or pursuing a career, also will distract one from the fundamental task of revising the nature of one's conscious states.

Thus, Buddhism as a religion traditionally has maintained two sets of requirements. One is for members of the Samgha; the other is for lay followers. The former requirements include not only the subtle matters of spiritual effort; they include also the basic, not subtle, requirements of poverty and celibacy. There is nothing inherently immoral, from the Buddhist point of view, in being neither poor nor celibate; but members of the Samgha should be both. Poverty and celibacy are finally in any case means to an end, and the efforts expected of members of the Samgha are the pursuit of this end.

The ethical significance of these efforts cannot be grasped without a concept comparable to that of the supra-moral. Buddhism clearly contains a morality. But it recognizes a distinct class of people who are expected to attempt to meet requirements that go beyond morality. The supra-moral character of these requirements is marked by the fact that, while meeting them would be desirable for anyone, they do not apply to everybody in the same way. Buddhism, typical features of which have been used to illustrate the thesis of this chapter, therefore recognizes that ethical prescriptives impinge with different force on persons in different social contexts. And this difference in background is of critical importance for interpreting the distinction between the moral and the supra-moral in ethical theory. One might want to argue that attention to the supra-moral by associational groups has a constructive, radiating influence on societal morality. But I shall not take up that matter here.

19

THE ELECTIVE "OUGHT"

Afterword

A running theme of this book is that consideration of classical Asian philosophy can help us to arrive at a more complicated map of the subject matter of ethics. It may be tempting to see ethics as first and foremost concerned with recommendations of how anyone should or should not behave; the conditional recommendation "Behave thus, if thou wilt be perfect" complicates this scheme. So also does the idea that the goal for someone who tries to live up to a more demanding standard is to be a better person, where "better person" cannot be explained in terms of fulfilling general moral requirements better. Part of the idea may be that there is a kind of psychic purity that is its own reward. What is hardest to sort out is that this psychic purity can have what we think of as a moral value, even though we do not think that it is morally required or morally to be recommended to everyone.

My suggestion has been that the elective "ought" can be seen most clearly in some religious ethics, and that a philosophy such as Confucius's in which it is prominent is thereby more likely to be thought of as like a religion (although other factors also are relevant to whether we might be inclined to classify it as a religion or not). This suggestion points simultaneously in two different directions. It can promote a sense that religions are more multifaceted, and more interesting, than many people are at first inclined to think. But it also points to elements that can be found in some ethics that in the end no one would be inclined to categorize as religious. Ethics needs to be seen as multifunctional. One function that some ethical points of view fulfill is that of providing ideals that are like morality, in being linked to the quality of conduct, but that are unlike morality in being elective.

PART VI

Philosophy as Communication

20

PHILOSOPHY AND ENLIGHTENMENT

The essay that follows was invited in the first instance for a symposium on humor in Asian philosophy. Philosophical accounts of humor often center on a search for a key, a single-factor explanation of what makes some things funny. But of course there is no reason to assume that both the phenomena of humor and its causes cannot be diverse. There can be many forms. One involves the juxtaposition of points of view in which what seems normal from one perspective turns out from another to be distinctly odd. This form touches on something of philosophical importance: the way (arguably) in which different perspectives always are available on any set of phenomena that we think we understand. Another, related form involves incongruity: the example, or the bit of mimicry, that is a bit "off." The joke by Wittgenstein in the essay that follows is humor of this sort. Another example might be the alleged fact that Schopenhauer's favorite joke was the following. A straight line approaches a circle. It gets closer and closer. Finally, it touches the circle at one point, and then goes away. If it is true that Schopenhauer thought the funniest thing in the world was a tangent, that itself is funny.

The striking thing about the literature of Daoism, and also the Zen Buddhism that it helped to influence, is that there is so much humor. The existence of this humor can be puzzling, especially in the case of Zen Buddhism if one views it as a religion. Think of the amount of laughing that typically goes on in churches, synagogues, and mosques. In the case of the *Zhuangzi* (*Chuang Tzu*), the persistent humor can seem puzzling for a different reason. Philosophical theses are in play and in some way are being developed. We think of philosophy, like religion, as serious business. Is it that Zhuangzi is such a modest person that he cannot help undercutting the seriousness of what he is doing?

My suggestion is that the humor both in the *Zhuangzi* and in the literature of Zen Buddhism is in its way serious business. The juxtaposition of (sometimes wildly different) points of view helps to underline the metaphysical anti-realism. This and various instances of incongruity function to unsettle the mental sets both of participants in what is described and of readers. This unsettling is a goal because the metaphysical anti-realism is held to imply the ridiculousness of fixed points of view and of habitual reliance on established categories.

We can appreciate this approach if we contrast two models of what the meaning and function of philosophy is. One is that a philosophical position can be viewed as freestanding, as like a set of formulas that has a relation to something real (perhaps structures of thought or of experience) somewhat like that of formulas of physics to physical reality. The other is to take a philosophy as a communication from a writer or speaker to an audience. The function is to modify the thinking or the experience of the audience in some ways, and the meaning can be viewed in terms of the range of responses that, in the context, reasonably could be intended.

It may well be that each of these models works better for some cases than for others. My sense is that most teachers of philosophy in Britain and America will find something like the first model in general more congenial. But then there should be more effort to work out the details. Just what is it that good philosophy captures? And how does it capture it? Also, what kind of weight can the intention of the writer or speaker have in determining what the meaning is? It is widely agreed that one cannot choose to have words mean whatever one wants. Does this preclude cases in which knowledge of the author's intentions might affect our choice between two or more otherwise plausible interpretations?

Zhuangzi clearly is guided by something like the second model. He presumably would agree with the claim in the *Seventh Epistle*, attributed to Plato, that philosophical knowledge is "born in the soul," and that there are special hazards or limitations when a man ventures "to express his deepest thoughts in words, especially in a form that is unchangeable" (*Epistles*, 237, 239). What Zhuangzi would read into this, however, would be very different from Plato's probable construal, given the two philosophers' contrasting approaches to time and change. Zhuangzi's view of internalized knowledge would have a great deal to do with reactive patterns and in general with fluidity of response.

Philosophy in this view has the function of making someone a more enlightened person. "Enlightened" here needs to be read not in terms merely of what one *does* understand but also of what one *will* understand. Understanding itself has to be taken as not rigid and as remaining open to other perspectives.

A small example of how a philosophy might promote a broader understanding is provided by Norman Malcolm's memoir of Wittgenstein (Malcolm

1958, 32–33). Malcolm had remarked in conversation that he found it inconceivable that there could be any truth in a German claim (in the autumn of 1939) that the British government had instigated an assassination attempt on Hitler. It went against his sense of national character. Wittgenstein became angry at this response; he "considered it to be a great stupidity and also an indication that I was not learning anything from the philosophical training that he was trying to give me." Presumably the philosophical training was supposed to undermine stereotypes, fixed expectations, and rigid points of view.

Zhuangzi's philosophical training certainly is intended to do this and a good deal more. Because it is in part training of the emotions (as discussed in a previous essay), it would preclude, among other things, anger at slow learners. (This may be true for Zen training also. There are, however, it should be said, Zen stories of teachers who can treat slow learners rather harshly, even if they are not angry.) Also—because one never has a final truth, or a final "take" on anything, or a final adjustment to the world—Zhuangzi's philosophical training appears designed to encourage the ability to laugh at oneself. The philosophy is not intended to lead to a comfortable 'complacency.

21

NOT IN SO MANY WORDS

Zhuangzi's Strategies of Communication

There are many varieties of philosophical humor, paralleling the variety of purposes of philosophy. One prominent form makes a point by displaying something amusing and preposterous that might seem to flow from an opposed view. A recent example is from Wittgenstein (1953, 33). Someone tells him to show the children a game, and he shows them how to gamble with dice. This kind of game is presumably not what the request intended, but was the exclusion originally in the mind of the person who made it? The story makes two points simultaneously. One concerns the variety of things that can be considered a game; what kind we are talking about will be determined normally by the context. The other is summed up by the current slogan of many philosophers of language: "Meanings are not in the head."

Mencius also uses humor to demolish a point of view in his story of the man from Sung who was so anxious to help his rice plants grow that he pulled at them (b, book II, A.2, 78). When he went home he told his family, "I am worn out today. I have been helping the rice plants to grow." Of course, the plants had been uprooted and were dead.

Here the amusing and preposterous behavior is a metaphor for a certain kind of hard-driving approach to personal development. Mencius's view is that one builds character and a fund of energy gradually and smoothly, not by drastic and abrupt measures. The story of the man from Sung is one of those Confucian passages that remind us that Confucians and Daoists are not thoroughly opposed and, indeed, have more in common than might at first appear.

A third example of the use of the amusing and preposterous to illustrate the bankruptcy of a point of view is the opening story of the *Zhuangzi*. The cicada and the dove discount the exploits of the P'eng because their own experience is so different (*Zhuangzi* a, 43–44). Their absurd response is a metaphor for a blinkered and prosaic view of human potential, which we are intended to reject.

In all of these cases, it is possible to provide a flat-footed and prosaic summary of the philosophical point, as indeed I have done (or have begun to do). The superiority of the philosopher's humor, then, is literary and didactic rather than philosophical. The prosaic summary pretty much captures the point, but the amusing stories are more interesting and one remembers the point better because of them.

In what follows, I wish to suggest that some of the distinctive and amusing stories to be found in the *Zhuangzi* not only have the merits found in the three stories just mentioned but also go further in that much of the point is lost in any prosaic summary, and that the reason for this lies in the complex structure of pulls and counterpulls to be found in the stories. Clearly, there is no room in an article like this for a complete theory of philosophical humor, and indeed rather than look for generalizations I would like to suggest variety. The *Zhuangzi* is a highly distinctive work in a number of ways. Much in it that is amusing and preposterous is not, unlike the three stories with which I began, intended as a simple *reductio* of an opposing point of view. The most distinctive and interesting feature of the *Zhuangzi*, in my view, is the way in which much of it resists translation into straightforward statements of philosophical claims. I will concentrate on two stories.

We may start with the best-known joke in the *Zhuangzi*. It is the story in chapter 2 of the monkey keeper who, handing out nuts to the monkeys, said, "Three every morning and four every evening." The monkeys were all in a rage, whereupon the keeper said, "All right then, four every morning and three every evening" and the monkeys were all delighted (54). This little story illustrates why the *Zhuangzi* the ultimate text of our day, one that is self-deconstructing. The most obvious level of meaning is that the monkey keeper, by an appropriate "That's it which goes by circumstance," puts the pleasure and anger of the monkeys to use. This strategy is comparable to the way in which the sage "stays at the point of rest on the potter's wheel of Heaven" (54).

The behavior of the monkeys is comical because the difference between three in the morning and four in the evening, or four in the morning and three in the evening, seems so insignificant. A natural thought is that many of the things we care deeply about, obscure objects of desire or specters of anxiety, might be viewed as comparably insignificant. To the extent that Daoism considers striving and strong emotion to be unnatural and harmful, this passage neatly conveys this message.

On the other hand, once we have assimilated the message, we can chew it over and then chew it up. What's the big deal about not caring? If nothing is worth intense concern, then surely this must be true of loss of intense concern. Furthermore, who would not prefer four in the morning and three in the evening to three in the morning and four in the evening?

At this point two contrary impulses can be elicited by the text—and are suggested by it. One is that the very distinction involved in noticing the difference between the two schedules of nut delivery ought not to have been noted. The ancient "lighting up of 'That's it, that's not' is the reason why the Way is flawed" (54). This statement echoes poem 18 of the *Tao Te Ching*: the decline from ancient simplicity has been paved with distinctions invested with normative urgency.

A second impulse is to say, "Why not give the monkeys what they want?" As the *Zhuangzi* remarks, "The reason why the Way is flawed is the reason why love becomes complete." And anyway, "Is anything really complete or flawed? Or is nothing really complete or flawed?" If we are not to make normative distinctions, we should begin by not condemning the monkeys. Their protest is a fact of nature and does not call for any attitude on our part.

All of these responses seem to be indicated by the text, which in an exceptionally charming and concise way questions itself and the assumptions on which it is based. Furthermore, the indicated responses are surely not limited to the ones I have just explored; anyone can continue the series, and the series can be continued in a number of ways. This is one reason that a brief prose statement of *the* meaning of the passage would not say nearly all that the passage says. Shades of irony, doubt, and self-mocking are difficult to capture in such a summary; but also the passage is a key to a dialectical series of responses, and it is by no means clear that any formula for the series could be contained in a prosaic summary.

At the end of dialectical reflection, the sage "finds for things lodging places in the usual" (55). This image suggests that Daoist philosophy, as Wittgenstein said of his own, leaves everything as it is. But of course the situation at the end of dialectical reflection is not precisely the situation at the beginning, since the awareness of what has been realized or rejected has taken effect. This difference makes the results of reflection extremely difficult to report in any summary way: one might conclude with exactly the commonplace statements that could have been made at the beginning, even by a peasant or some other non-philosopher, but the meaning of these statements is both the same and not the same.

"To discriminate between alternatives," Zhuangzi suggests, "is to fail to see something" (57). This is one of those statements that, especially when pulled out of context, might strengthen the widespread temptation to regard Asian philosophies as "the same" when they make similar-sounding points. Advaita Vedanta, the very sophisticated school of Hindu philosophy that centered on Samkara (ca. 800 CE), argues for the ultimate nonreality of all distinctions (see Deutsch 1973). Is Zhuangzi's view the same as this? Hardly: the ultimate justification in Advaita Vedanta is the oneness of Brahman, whereas in

Zhuangzi's philosophy it is the fluidity of reality along with the dependence of distinctions on perspectives. The ultimate vision in one case is everything as Brahman. For Zhuangzi it is reality as nonstatic, seen apart from categories. Thus, he does not recommend a total (monistic) absence of discrimination; best is "an unspoken discrimination, an untold way."

The best-known story in chapter 2 of the *Zhuangzi* is less colorful but more directly philosophical:

> Last night Chuang Chou dreamed he was a butterfly, spirits soaring he was a butterfly (is it that in showing what he was he suited his own fancy?), and did not know about Chou. When all of a sudden he awoke, he was Chou with all his wits about him. He does not know whether he is Chou who dreams he is a butterfly or a butterfly who dreams he is Chou. Between Chou and the butterfly there was necessarily a dividing; just this is what is meant by the transformations of things. (61)

To claim entire understanding of this passage would be presumptuous, but it is possible to go a certain distance in explicating its meaning. The first and most obvious point is that the story is not a joke, but it shares some characteristics to be found in many jokes, such as being fanciful and amusing. Like many jokes it is highly specific at points: just as comedians usually slip on banana peels rather than grapefruit rinds, so Chuang Chou dreams that he is a butterfly, and not a sea slug, a turkey, or an unnamed nonhuman X. Why a butterfly? Part of the answer may be that butterflies have more fun; but the ephemeral character of the butterfly state, in a life that visibly incorporates transformations of things, also may have something to do with it.

Chuang Chou's problem, when first looked at, may seem rather Cartesian. How can he know whether he is dreaming or awake? This question is given an amusing twist by mention of the possibility that, if he is dreaming, it might turn out to be a butterfly that is having the dream that his present conscious states are part of. When we look back at Descartes, one of the most striking features of his discussion of dreaming is the unshakable sense of self-identity that lies behind the puzzle. Either Descartes is awake or Descartes is dreaming: these are the two possibilities. This smugness asks to be punctured: thus, two centuries later we have Lewis Carroll's suggestion that Alice might exist as part of someone else's dream, and two millennia before, there was the thought that what one conceived of as one's conscious existence might be the dream of a being of another species.

Descartes is very serious about his problem; it is important to him to find the truth, and even more important to avoid error. A certain lack of seriousness comes through in the *Zhuangzi*. When the text says, "There was necessarily a dividing," it is likely that the reader is being teased. Let me say something about this reader before we proceed further. It is tempting to think of any expository text as containing a series of messages, although I have already suggested that this would be overly simple and misleading in relation to a work like the *Zhuangzi*, which, as in the case of three-in-the-morning, is willing to guy its messages. One might think of an expository text as also having a group of imagined readers, the serious would-be scientists and perhaps the wavering scholastics of Descartes's *Meditations*, for example. One of the imagined audiences for the *Zhuangzi*, it seems to me, is a person who is willing to take Daoist ideas seriously. This is a combination of (1) something hopeful—the openness to the ideas—and (2) something troublesome—the tendency to take them seriously—thus rigidifying the ideas and turning them into non-Daoist parodies of Daoism. The text keeps saying to this person, "Don't be so serious." Many literary works tease their readers, and there are many reasons for this: one is that any work that continues predictably risks being boring. But there is a special reason for the *Zhuangzi* to tease its readers: some of them really need it.

Anyway, there really is a difference between being a human being and being a butterfly. A modern reader who hears the word "mystical" with a peculiar resonance, and who thinks of the *Zhuangzi* as a mystical work, may need reassurance on that point. What we are offered is not a cosmic blur. This still leaves a number of questions, though. Just what is the difference between being human and being a butterfly? Is it important? How can Chuang Chou know which he really is—at the moment? It is part of the teasing quality of the passage that none of these questions is answered.

A hint, however, is thrown out in the reference to the transformations of things. The *Zhuangzi* espouses a view very much like contemporary Western anti-realism. That is, it strongly suggests that any attempt to provide a literal, objectively correct formulation for any aspect of reality will be mistaken and ludicrous. (That is why it views seriousness as ultimately fraudulent.) One reason for this is simply that other points of view always are available and cannot be dismissed. The *Zhuangzi* makes this point repeatedly, beginning with the story already mentioned that begins chapter 1. It is now time to present it more fully. The story within this story concerns a huge fish, the K'un; it changes into a huge bird, the P'eng, and flies to the South Ocean; its flight is accompanied by marvels, giving rise to questions such as "Is the azure of the sky its true color?" (43). A cicada and a turtledove laugh at this story; the main reason is that the accomplishments of the P'eng are far beyond them, but it is also made clear that phenomena as experienced by the P'eng are incomprehensible to them. If we think that we have arrived at a literal rendering of a reality, how do we know that something that is to us as the P'eng is to the turtledove and the cicada might not have a different version? Perhaps "only at the ultimate awakening shall we know that this is the ultimate dream"? (43). Perhaps there is no ultimate awakening.

Another reason for the *Zhuangzi's* brand of anti-realism, though, is that reality is highly fluid. Even if our literal rendering might be adequate as something like a snapshot of a reality, its adequacy would be at best momentary. Indeed, if one believes that the causal antecedents of something are part of what it is, and that its likely future states are also, it would seem that the literal rendering that leaves out past and future cannot achieve even momentary adequacy. This impossibility applies even to ourselves, and to the bizarre futures that lie open to us. It is sometimes said that every time someone opens a water tap, it is likely that one molecule of Julius Caesar's body flows out; had Julius Caesar had a clear sense of this future, it might have changed his life. In this spirit, Master Li comforts the dying Master Lai. He brushes aside a crying wife and children saying, "Don't startle him while he transforms." Then, lolling against Lai's door, he remarks, "Wonderful, the process which fashions and transforms us! What is it going to turn you into, in what direction will it use you to go? Will it make you into a rat's liver? Or a fly's leg?" (88)

Thus, whatever difference there is between being Chuang Chou and being a butterfly is less stark than it might at first appear. Parts of butterflies become parts of people, and vice versa. Whatever the difference is between being a human and being a butterfly is temporary, and perhaps not all that important.

Again, though, there is no suggestion that there is absolutely no difference between being a human and being a butterfly—that would be taking anti-realism rather far—or that whatever the difference is it is unknowable. On the first point: some commentators, whether they are reading T. S. Kuhn or the *Zhuangzi*, confuse anti-realism, which insists that there is no entirely definitive point of view or theory, with relativism, which holds that all points of view or theories are equal. Daoist anti-realism does not mean that Daoism does not offer a superior point of view to its rivals. Indeed, we should remember that there are, on any reasonable view, large areas of human knowledge in which there are standards of objectivity even though no entirely definitive and final account of a subject is possible (see Kupperman 1975). On the second point: it may be, indeed, that Zhuangzi would have conceded that Descartes's way of knowing whether he was dreaming or not had something to it. After all, the flat negation of a rigid position is presumably also a rigid position, so that a blanket anti-Cartesianism has pitfalls comparable to those of Cartesianism.

Let me expand on what philosophers such as Zhuangzi can claim for themselves. Relativistic philosophies are often criticized as being caught in a self-referential paradox: if what they say applies to themselves, then why believe them? But a philosophy that merely denies that there is any ultimate definitive truth, without insisting that all points of view or theories are equal, allows for the possibility that there are some points of view—including its own—to which it is well worth listening. What it cannot claim is that it offers the ultimate, definitive truth; and this limitation might well affect both the spirit of the philosophy and its mode of presentation. It is worth remarking that most philosophical work, down to the humblest journal article, has been presented with the air of "Here is the truth; the inquiry into this topic now may cease, because all alternative views are incorrect." If this were simply an essay about humor, we might explore the comic aspects of this. But the immediate point is that if a philosopher understands that a final, definitive account is impossible, *and* chooses to mirror this fact in his or her manner of presentation, this should change everything. The philosophy then must be tentative and exploratory. It cannot be serious in the way in which most philosophy is serious.

Thus, it is natural that we are not given a definitive account of Chuang Chou's dream. The meaning of the story of the dream, like that of the story of the monkeys, must be found in a series of resonances—natural reflections and delayed responses—that are indefinite in character and do not admit of a precise termination point. Auditors and readers vary, and it would be wrong to suggest that there is a series of reflections and responses that constitutes all appropriate understandings of the text. But neither is it the case that the text is merely a vehicle for free association, or that like the blots used in Rorschach tests it is merely the stimulus for a response that tells vastly more about the responder than about what she or he is responding to. Anyone who reads the story of the monkeys properly will have a nested series of thoughts that include (1) the thought (which one is free to resist) that it certainly makes sense to give the monkeys what they want, since it makes no real difference; (2) the thought that the monkeys are foolish to make such a fuss; and (3) the further thought (which again one is free to resist) that the preceding thought itself is slightly foolish, since the monkeys, after all, are part of nature and to condemn them is to impose distinctions on the world. But the series need not be limited to these thoughts, nor need it (or should it) end there. The weight and form with which thoughts occur also are optional.

Here is an analogy that may help to explain why the stories in the *Zhuangzi* have meanings that cannot be captured by prosaic summaries. Think of the more common kind of story as something like a series of notes (the beginning, middle, and end of the story) that can be captured by musical notation. The stories in the *Zhuangzi*, which call for the almost simultaneous occurrence of thoughts that clash with one another, would then be represented by a series of chords, rather than a sequence of single notes. But even the chords would not be adequate, for this reason: unlike the average story, these stories have meanings that are keyed to second or further thoughts. The time sequence and duration of these elements of meaning cannot be precisely formulated, and hence no precise notation is possible. In music one can roughly indicate time values by marking quarter notes, half notes, and the like, along with some general notation such as "adagio" or "presto"; the latter can be made more precise by means of metronome markings. But achieving precision becomes more difficult if a note is held so that it resonates, and if echoes are an important part of the piece; and if the echoes and resonances are meant to be able to vary considerably, the notation becomes for practical purposes impossible. In much this way, the stories we have been discussing *do* things that cannot be stated in so many words.

22

PHILOSOPHY AS PSYCHIC CHANGE

Afterword

In a well-known passage Kierkegaard contrasts ethical or "ethico-religious" knowledge, in which the self of the knower is essentially involved, with other forms of knowledge, in which it is not (Kierkegaard 1846/ 1941, 176–77). Where in this contrast, one wonders, would philosophical knowledge fit? The question is complicated by the following consideration. Part of what Kierkegaard possibly had in mind was the role that bits or items of knowledge, rather than frameworks or entire disciplines, might or might not have in modifying the nature of someone's self. Coming to know that it is wrong to harm innocent people would certainly change a person's nature. Coming to understand, say, Newton's Laws, might accidentally trigger a change of nature; but such a change is scarcely implied by coming to have the knowledge, and thus the knowledge is not essentially related to the self. Some bits of philosophical knowledge might well be like coming to understand Newton's Laws in lacking any essential connection to selfhood. Philosophical knowledge, on the other hand, that involved an orientation to a large area of experience or of ethical choice might normally be manifested in a change of self.

There is the further complication that mastering the discipline associated with a subject such as philosophy, is distinguishable from acquiring knowledge within the framework represented by the discipline. Arguably any genuine discipline will normally involve a change of self. The teenager interested in science who becomes a scientist typically will become more methodical, more cautious about making claims that are supported by little evidence, and more ready to subject other people's claims of knowledge to critical scrutiny. Even a discipline less exalted than those of the sciences—say, that involved in becoming a professional sportscaster—is likely to make subtle changes in the personality of those who enter it. Professions typically change lives, and above and beyond the specific changes that a given profession represents there is the generic difference between being a professional at something and not being a professional at anything.

The discipline of philosophy has its characteristic changes of self: in the direction of heightened carefulness with nuances of words, increased awareness of relations of implication or contradiction between things one might want to say, and (like that of the sciences) great caution about making unsupported claims. In these respects philosophy, like other disciplines, can and typically will change lives. Some philosophies, in addition, are designed to make drastic changes in the lives of people who take them seriously. Plato's heightened emphasis on awareness of relations of implication or contradiction, and on the ability to define terms, is well known; it is clear also that Plato's philosophy is designed to promote a loyalty to ideals of psychic harmony and a courage (like Socrates') in the face of the more obvious evils of life.

There is an emotional element in all of this. The *Zhuangzi*, which has been the subject of two of the chapters in this book, and all of the other classics of Chinese or Indian philosophy that have been discussed are concerned with modifying emotional states: in the direction of more calm and detachment, or mild compassion, or dedicated commitment to the social good, as the case may be. To the extent that there is any knowledge in any of this philosophy, the emotional element is a large part of it.

More broadly, philosophies such as the ones discussed can be seen as displaying and encouraging a reactive stance. The reactive stance of the *Zhuangzi* is open, spontaneous, impervious to sudden jolts or emotional upsets, and prepared to be amused. The reactive stance of Confucius is open in a somewhat different way, spontaneous in a way limited by tradition and ritual, and resolutely good-hearted and conscientious. Do such reactive stances represent knowledge? One would not normally speak of them in this way. But they can be seen as forms of intelligence that has been shaped by philosophy.

The parting suggestion is that philosophies can be seen as forms of life. What they display and encourage can be at least as important as specific claims and arguments. I think that this is true for all philosophy: even the most austere and depersonalized piece of logical analysis has much to do with an austere and depersonalized compartment of life. The connection between philosophies and forms of life, though, is most evident, and hardest to ignore, in the classic texts of Asian philosophy. One of their virtues is the way in which they force us to consider the connection.

BIBLIOGRAPHY

Albee, Ernest
    1957   *History of English Utilitarianism* (London: Allen and Unwin)
Allinson, Robert
    1989   *Chuang Tzu for Spiritual Transformation* (Albany: State University of New York Press)
Allison, Henry
    1990   *Kant's Theory of Freedom* (Cambridge: Cambridge University Press)
Ames, Roger
    1996   "The Classical Chinese Self and Hypocrisy," in *Self and Deception,* ed. Roger T. Ames and Wimal Dissayanake (Albany: State University of New York Press), 219–40
Arendt, Hannah
    1958   *The Human Condition* (Chicago: University of Chicago Press)
Aristotle
    4th c. BCE/ *Nicomachean Ethics,* in *The Complete Works of Aristotle* vol. 2,
    1984   ed. Jonathan Barnes (Princeton: Princeton University Press)
Armon-Jones, Claire
    1991   *Varieties of Affect* (Toronto: University of Toronto Press)
Baier, Annette
    1979   "Hume on Heaps and Bundles," *American Philosophical Quarterly* 16, 285–95
    1986   "The Ambiguous Limits of Desire," in *The Ways of Desire,* ed. Joel Marks (Chicago: Precedent), 39–61
Baron, Marcia
    1987   "Kantian Ethics and Supererogation," *Journal of Philosophy* 84, 237–62
Bennett, Jonathan
    1974   "The Conscience of Huckleberry Finn," *Philosophy* 49, 123–34

Bhagavad Gita

ca. 1st c.   Trans. Barbara Stoler Miller (New York: Bantam)
CE/1986

Binswanger, Ludwig

1958   "The Case of Ellen West," trans. W. Mandel and J. Lyons, in *Existence: A New Dimension in Psychiatry and Psychology*, ed. Rollo May, Ernest Angel, and Henri Ellenberger (New York: Basic Books), 237–364

Block, Gay, and Malka Drucker

1992   *Rescuers: Portraits of Moral Courage in the Holocaust* (New York: Holmes and Meier)

Bloom, Irene

1997   "Human Nature and Biological Nature in Mencius," *Philosophy East and West* 47, 21–32

Bockover, Mary, ed.

1991   *Rules, Rituals, and Responsibility: Essays Dedicated to Herbert Fingarette* (La Salle, IL: Open Court)

Bodde, Derk

1967   *Peking Diary* (New York: Fawcett Premier)

Camus, Albert

1955   *The Myth of Sisyphus*, trans. Justin O'Brien (New York: Vintage Books)

Chuang Tzu (see Zhuangzi)

Ci, Jiwei

1991   "Freedom and Realms of Living," *Philosophy East and West* 41, 303–26

Confucius

5th c.   *Analects* (collected 4th c. BCE)
BCE   a. Trans. W. E. Soothill (London: Oxford World Classics, 1962)
         b. Trans. James Legge, in *The Chinese Classics* (New York: Hurst and Co., 1870)
         c. Trans. Arthur Waley (New York: Vintage, 1938)
         d. Trans. D. C. Lau (Harmondsworth: Penguin, 1979)

Conze, Edword

1954   ed., *Buddhist Texts* (Oxford: Bruno Cassirer)
1957   *Buddhism: Its Essence and Development* (Oxford: Bruno Cassirer)
1959   ed., *Buddhist Scriptures* (Harmondsworth: Penguin)

Creel, H. G.

1949   *Confucius, The Man and the Myth* (New York: John Day)

Dasgupta, Surendranath

1962   *Indian Idealism* (Cambridge: Cambridge University Press)

Davidson, Donald

1970   "Mental Events," in *Experience and Theory*, ed. L. Foster and J. Swanson (Amherst: University of Massachusetts Press), 79–101

Dennett, Daniel

1984   *Elbow Room* (Cambridge, MA: M.I.T. Press)

Deutsch, Eliot
    1973   *Advaita Vedanta* (Honolulu: University Press of Hawaii)
    1996   "Self Deception: A Comparative Study," in *Self and Deception*, ed. Roger Ames and Wimal Dissayanake (Albany: State University of New York Press), 315–26

Dhammapada
    ca. 1st c.   a. Trans. Juan Mascaro (Harmondsworth: Penguin, 1973)
    CE   b. Trans. Narada Thera (London: John Murray, 1954)

Doctrine of the Mean
    3rd or 2nd in *The Chinese Classics* vol. 1, trans. James Legge (New York: Hurst and Co.)
    c.
    BCE/1870

Eddington, Arthur
    1928   *The Nature of the Physical World* (Cambridge: Cambridge University Press)

Ehrenzweig, Anton
    1967   *The Hidden Order of Art* (Berkeley and Los Angeles: University of California Press)

Erikson, Erik
    1968   *Identity, Youth, and Crisis* (New York: Norton)

Fingarette, Herbert
    1972   *Confucius: The Secular as Sacred* (New York: Harper)
    1979   "Following the 'One Thread' of the *Analects*," *Journal of the American Academy of Religion* 47, 373–406
    1985   "Alcoholism and Self-Deception," in *Self-Deception and Self-Understanding*, ed. Mike W. Martin (Lawrence: University Press of Kansas), 52–67

Frankfurt, Harry
    1988   *The Importance of What We Care About* (Cambridge: Cambridge University Press)

Funder, David
    1983   "The 'Consistency' Controversy and the Accuracy of Personality Judgments," *Journal of Personality* 51, 346–59

Fung, Yu-Lan
    1948   *A Short History of Chinese Philosophy* (New York: Free Press)

Garfield, Jay L.
    1995   *The Fundamental Wisdom of the Middle Way: Nagarjuna's Mulamadhyamakakarika* (New York: Oxford University Press)

Gergen, Kenneth
    1982   *Toward Transformation in Social Knowledge* (New York: Springer Verlag)

Gilligan, Carol
    1982   *In a Different Voice* (Cambridge, MA: Harvard University Press)

Glover, Jonathan
    1983   *Self Creation* (Proceedings of the British Academy 59)
    1988   *I: The Philosophy and Psychology of Personal Identity* (London: Allen Lane)

Goffman, Erving

    1959   *The Presentation of Self in Everyday Life* (New York: Doubleday Anchor)

Graham, A. C.

    1990   "The Background of the Mencian Theory of Human Nature," in *Studies in Chinese Philosophy and Philosophical Literature* (Albany: State University of New York Press), 7–66.

Hall, David, and Roger Ames

    1987   *Thinking Through Confucius* (Albany: State University of New York Press)

Hallie, Philip

    1967   "Stoicism," in *Encyclopedia of Philosophy*, ed. Paul Edwards, 8: 19b–22b. (New York: Free Press)

Haney, Craig, Curtis Banks, and Philip Zimbardo

    1973   "Interpersonal Dynamics in a Simulated Prison," *International Journal of Criminology and Personology* 1, 69–97

Hare, R. M.

    1963   *Freedom and Reason* (Oxford: Clarendon Press)

    1976   "Ethical Theory and Utilitarianism," in *Contemporary British Philosophy* 4th series, ed. H. D. Lewis (London: Allen and Unwin)

    1981   *Moral Thinking* (Oxford: Clarendon Press)

Held, Virginia

    1984   *Rights and Goods: Justifying Social Action* (New York: Free Press, Macmillan)

Herman, Barbara

    1983   "Integrity and Impartiality," *Monist* vol. 66, 233–50

    1985   "The Practice of Moral Judgment," *Journal of Philosophy* 82, 414–36

Hill, Thomas E., Jr.

    1971   "Kant on Imperfect Duty and Supererogation," *Kant-Studien* 62, 55–76

Hume, David

    1739/   *Treatise of Human Nature*, ed. L. A. Selby-Bigge, rev. P. H. Nidditch (Oxford: Clarendon Press)

    1978

    1751/   *An Enqiry Concerning the Principles of Morals*, in *Enquiries*, ed. L. A. Selby-Bigge, rev. P. H. Nidditch (Oxford: Clarendon Press)

    1975

    1985   *Essays*, ed. Eugene Miller (Indianapolis: Liberty Fund)

Hutcheson, Francis

    1755/   *A System of Moral Philosophy* (New York: Augustus M. Kelley)

    1968

Isenberg, Arnold

    1953   "Critical Communication," in *Aesthetics and Language*, ed. William Elton (Oxford: Basil Blackwell)

Ivanhoe, Philip J.

    1993a   "Skepticism, Skill and the Ineffable Tao," *Journal of the American Academy of Religions* 61, 639–54

    1993b   *Confucian Moral Self Cultivation* (New York: Peter Lang)

James, William

    1947   "The Will to Believe," in *Selected Papers on Philosophy* (London: J. M. Dent), 99–124

Kalupahana, David

    1976   *Buddhist Philosophy: A Historical Analysis* (Honolulu: University Press of Hawaii)

Kant, Immanuel

    1781/
    1965   *Critique of Pure Reason*, trans. Norman Kemp Smith (New York: St. Martin's Press)

    1785/
    1981   *Grounding for the Metaphysics of Morals*, trans. James Ellington (Indianapolis: Hackett)

    1788/
    1898   *Critique of Practical Reason*, in *Kant's Critique of Practical Reason and Other Works*, trans. Thomas Kingsmill Abbott (London: Longmans Green and Co.)

Keats, John

    1970   *Letters*, ed. Robert Gittings (London: Oxford University Press)

Kierkegaard, Søren

    1843/
    1959   *Either/Or*, trans. Walter Lowrie, rev. Howard Johnson (New York: Doubleday Anchor)

    1846/
    1941   *Concluding Unscientific Postscript*, trans. Walter Lowrie (Princeton: Princeton University Press)

Kittay, Eva, and Diana Meyers, eds.

    1987   *Women and Moral Theory* (Totowa, NJ: Rowman and Littlefield)

Kovesi, Julius

    1970   *Moral Notions* (London: Routledge and Kegan Paul)

Kuhn, Thomas S.

    1970   "Reflections on My Critics," in *Criticism and the Growth of Knowledge*, ed. Imre Lakatos and Alan Musgrave (Cambridge: Cambridge University Press), 231–78

Kupperman, Joel J.

    1970   *Ethical Knowledge* (London: Geo. Allen and Unwin, Muirhead Library of Philosophy)

    1975   "Precision in History," *Mind* 84, 374–89

    1983   *Foundations of Morality* (London: Geo. Allen and Unwin)

    1984–
    85   "Character and Self-Knowledge," *Proceedings of the Aristotelian Society* 85, 219–38

    1988   "Character and Ethical Theory," *Midwest Studies in Philosophy* 13, 115–25

    1989   "Relations Between the Sexes: Timely vs. Timeless Principles," *San Diego Law Review*

    1991   *Character* (New York: Oxford University Press)

    1995a   "*Atman* and Self-Realization," in *Man, Meaning and Morality*, ed. R. Balasubramanian and R. Misra (New Delhi: Indian Council of Philosophical Research), 185–95

    1995b   "An Anti-Essentialist View of the Emotions," *Philosophical Psychology* 8, 341–51

1997 "The Disunity of Emotion," in *Emotion in Postmodernism*, ed. Alfred Hornung (Heidelberg: C. Winter Universitatsverlag), 363–81

1999 *Value . . . and What Follows* (New York: Oxford University Press)

Langton, Rae

1992 "Duty and Desolation," *Philosophy* 67, 481–505

Lankavatara Sutra

ca. 2nd c. Trans. D. T. Suzuki (London: Routledge and Kegan Paul)
CE/ 1959

La Rochefoucauld, Francois, duc de

1665/ *The Maxims of the Duc de la Rochefoucauld*, trans. Constantine
1957 Fitz Gibbon (London: Allen Wingate)

Louden, Robert B.

1991 *Morality and Moral Theory: A Reappraisal and Reaffirmation* (New York: Oxford University Press)

Lyons, David

1973 *In the Interests of the Governed: A Study of Bentham's Philosophy of Utility and Law* (Oxford: Clarendon Press)

MacIntyre, Alasdair

1978 *After Virtue* (Notre Dame: University of Notre Dame Press)

1988 *Whose Justice? Which Rationality?* (Notre Dame: University of Notre Dame Press)

Malcolm, Norman

1958 *Ludwig Wittgenstein. A Memoir* (London: Oxford University Press)

Mandeville, Bernard

1714/1970 *The Fable of the Bees* (Harmondsworth: Penguin)

McLaughlin, Brian, and Amelie Rorty, eds.

1988 *Perspectives on Self-Deception* (Berkeley and Los Angeles: University of California Press)

Mencius

4th c. a. Trans. James Legge, in *The Chinese Classics* (New York:
BCE Hurst and Co., 1870; rep. Dover Books, 1970)
   b. Trans. D. C. Lau (Harmondsworth: Penguin, 1970)

Meyers, Diana T.

1989 *Self, Society, and Personal Choice* (New York: Columbia University Press)

Milgram, Stanley

1974 *Obedience to Authority* (London: Tavistock)

Mill, John Stuart

1859/ *On Liberty*, ed. Elizabeth Rapaport (Indianapolis: Hackett)
1978

1861/ *Utilitarianism*, ed. George Sher (Indianapolis: Hackett)
1979

Mossner, Ernest

1970 *The Life of David Hume* (Oxford: Oxford University Press)

Nagel, Thomas

1970 *The Possibility of Altruism* (Oxford: Clarendon Press)

Nicholson, Linda

    1983   "Women, Morality, and History," *Social Research* 50, 515–36

Nietzsche, Friedrich

    1883–91/   *Thus Spake Zarathustra*, trans. Walter Kaufmann (New York:
    1978   Penguin)

Noh Plays of Japan

    1954   Trans. Arthur Waley (London: Geo. Allen and Unwin)

Parfit, Derek

    1971   "Personal Identity," *Philosophical Review* 80, 3–27

    1984   *Reasons and Persons* (Oxford: Clarendon Press)

Pettit, Philip

    1988   "The Paradox of Loyalty," *American Philosophical Quarterly* 25,
            163–71

Plato

    4th c.   *Republic*, in *Dialogues of Plato* vol. 1, trans. B. Jowett (New
    BCE/   York: Random House)
    1937

    /1962   *Epistles*, trans. Glenn R. Morrow (Indianapolis: Bobbs Merrill)

Questions of King Milinda

    ca. 2nd c. Trans. T. W. Rhys Davids (New York: Dover)
    CE/1963

Richards, I. A.

    1925   *Principles of Literary Criticism* (London: Kegan Paul, Trench and
            Trubner)

    1932   *Mencius on the Mind* (London: Kegan Paul, Trench and Trubner)

Rosemont, Henry

    1978   "Reply to Professor Fingarette," *Philosophy East and West* 28,
            515–16

Ryle, Gilbert

    1949   *The Concept of Mind* (New York: Barnes and Noble)

Sartre, Jean-Paul

    1943   *Being and Nothingness*, trans. Hazel Barnes (New York: Philo-
            sophical Library, 1956)

    1950   *Baudelaire*, trans. Martin Turnell (New York: New Directions)

    1962   "William Faulkner's *Sartoris*," in *Literary and Philosophical Essays*,
            trans. Annette Michelson (New York: Collier)

Shaffer, Jerome

    1983   "An Assessment of Emotion," *American Philosophical Quarterly*
            20, 161–73.

Shun, Kwong-loi

    1997   *Mencius and Early Chinese Thought* (Stanford: Stanford University
            Press)

Singer, Marcus

    1961   *Generalization in Ethics* (New York-Alfred A. Knopf)

Singer, Peter

    1979   *Practical Ethics* (Cambridge: Cambridge University Press)

Smart, J. J. C.

1977   "Benevolence as an Over-Riding Attitude," *Australasian Journal of Philosophy* 55, 127–35

Smith, Adam

1776   *An Inquiry into the Nature and Causes of the Wealth of Nations*

Solomon, Robert

1976   *The Passions* (New York: Doubleday)

1996   "Self, Deception, and Self-Deception in Philosophy", in *Self* and *Deception*, ed. Roger Ames and Wimal Dissayanake (Albany: State University of New York Press), 91–121

Sommers, Christina Hoff

1986   "Filial Obligation," *Journal of Philosophy* 83, 439–56

Stocker, Michael

1976   "The Schizophrenia of Modern Ethical Theories,"*Journal of Philosophy* 73, 453–66

Stravinsky, Igor

1970   *The Poetics of Music*, trans. A. Knodel and I. Dahl (Cambridge, MA: Harvard University Press)

Strawson, P. F.

1961   "Social Morality and Individual Ideals," *Philosophy* 36, 1–17

Tanner, Michael

1976–77   "Sentimentality," *Proceedings of the Aristotelian Society* 77, 127–47

Tao Te Ching (a.k.a. *Daodejing*)

ca. 3rd c.   a. Trans. James Legge, in*Texts of Taoism* (New York: Dover,
BCE   1970)
      b. *The Way of Life*, trans. R. B. Blakney (New York: Mentor, 1955)
      c. Trans. Victor Mair (New York: Bantam, 1990)

Taylor, Charles

1989   *Sources of the Self* (Cambridge, MA: Harvard University Press)

Tec, Nechama

1986   *When Light Pierced the Darkness: Christians' Rescue of Jews in Nazi-Occupied Poland* (New York: Oxford University Press)

Upanishads

10th–5th c.

BCE/1965   Trans. Juan Mascaro (Harmondsworth: Penguin)

Van Norden, Bryan W.

1996   "Competing Interpretations of the Inner Chapters of the *Zhuangzi*," *Philosophy East and West* 46, 247–68

White, Stephen

1991   *The Unity of Self* (Cambridge, MA: M.I.T. Press)

Williams, Bernard

1985   *Ethics and the Limits of Philosophy* (London: Fontana)

Wittgenstein, Ludwig

1953   *Philosophical Investigations*, trans. G. E. M. Anscombe (New York: Macmillan)

Wolff, Robert Paul

    1966   "Hume's Theory of Mental Activity," in *Hume*, ed. V. C. Chappell (Garden City: Doubleday Anchor)

Wong, David

    1988   "On Flourishing and Finding One's Identity in Community," *Midwest Studies in Philosophy* 13, 324–41

Zen Flesh, Zen Bones

                    Comp. Paul Reps (New York: Doubleday Anchor)

The Zhuangzi

    4th or 3rd   a. *The Seven Inner Chapters and Other Writings from the Book Chuang Tzu*, trans. A. C. Graham (London: Geo. Allen and
    c. BCE   Unwin, 1981)

                    b. *Chuang Tzu, Basic Writings*, trans. Burton Watson (New York: Columbia University Press, 1964)

INDEX

Russell, Bertrand, 12
Ryle, Gilbert, 150

Samkara, 186
Sartre, Jean-Paul, 4, 23, 26, 42, 69, 72–5, 77, 78, 104
Schoenberg, Arnold, 31
Schopenhauer, Arthur, 181
second nature, 18–20, 22, 31, 33
self, 20, 42–51,57–60, 87, 90–1, 109, 127–8, 150, 153–4, 174
　fluidity of, 3–4, 49, 58–94, 192–3
　formation of, 3, 13, 17–53
　loss of, 20, 127
　sense of, 77, 78, 85, 162
　unity of, 48–51, 67, 74–8, 94
Seng Ts'an, 147
Shaffer, Jerome, 150
Shakespeare, William, 146
Shun, Kwong-loi, 100
sincerity, 91
Singer, Marcus, 26
Smart, J. J. C., 132, 152
Smith, Adam, 154
Socrates, 43, 193
Solomon, Robert, 68, 129
Sommers, Christina Hoff, 152
Songs, Book of, 42, 43, 44, 46, 47, 105
Soothill, W. E., 22, 27
Spinoza, Baruch, 9
spontaneity, 29, 31, 61, 64, 84–9, 92–4, 101, 132
Stalin, Joseph, 12
Stanford prison experiment, 38, 68–9, 76
Stevenson, Charles, 68, 116
Stocker, Michael, 152
stoics, 110, 149
Stravinsky, Igor, 31, 51
Strawson, P. F., 83, 171
style, 21, 24, 26, 30, 32–3, 43, 46, 49, 51, 80, 84

suffering, 86, 127–9, 140, 146, 162, 174
supra-moral, 171–7
Suzuki, D. T., 147

Taoism. See Daoism
Tao Te Ching, 61–3, 66, 68–72, 186
Taylor, Charles, 78
Tec, Nechama, 77
temperament, 17, 42
tradition, 20, 22–3, 26, 36, 43–51, 127, 131–5, 140–4
transformations of things, 187–9

unthinkable, the, 138
Upanishads, 18, 20, 58, 126–7, 174
utilitarians, 125, 138, 147–9, 151, 152–5, 167

value, 6, 8–9, 12, 12, 20–2, 34–5, 89, 165, 168
Van Fraasen, Bas, 71
Van Norden, Bryan, 63
Vaughan, Henry, 149

Waley, Arthur, 22, 28, 29, 30, 36, 43
White, Stephen, 67–9
Williams, Bernard, 155
willpower, 91–2
wisdom, 4, 12–13, 80
Wittgenstein, Ludwig, 84, 164, 171, 181–4, 186
Wolff, Robert Paul, 115
Wong, David, 41, 47
Wren, Christopher, 85–6

Xunzi, 101

Zen Buddhism, 64, 88, 150–1, 166, 167, 181–3
Zhuangzi, 11, 29, 58, 61–5, 79–90, 101, 181–91
Zimbardo, Philip, 68